Race Relations in Britain

The arrival of the SS *Empire Windrush* in 1948 inaugurated the process of post-war black migration into Britain. With ethnic minorities now firmly established in Britain it is time to take stock of the state of contemporary ethnic relations. *Race Relations in Britain* brings together leading experts in the field to explore key issues. The book:

- analyses contemporary trends, articulates a vision of multicultural Britain and explores important theoretical controversies;
- identifies the obstacles that stand in the way of a racism-free Britain, looking at current policy in areas such as immigration, employment, education and the criminal justice system, as well as the role of the media;
- compares British race relations legislation and ethnic experience with those of Europe and the United States.

With a concluding essay by Peter Newsam, an influential figure in highlighting and combating racial discrimination, this book assesses the success of the 1976 Race Relations Act and finds that there is still much work to be done to ensure equality for ethnic minorities in Britain.

Tessa Blackstone is Minister of State for Education and Employment in the Lords. **Bhikhu Parekh** is Professor of Political Theory at the University of Hull. **Peter Sanders** is former Chief Executive of the Commission for Racial Equality.

Contents

Figures and tables

FIGURES

TABLES

Contributors

Yasmin Alibhai-Brown is a Research Fellow at the Institute of Public Policy Research working on the influence of Government on public attitudes towards ethnic minorities. She is also a journalist and broadcaster on race and cultural issues. Among her publications are *Colour of Love: Mixed-Race Relationships* (jointly) (1993) and *No Place Like Home* (1995).

Tessa Blackstone is Minister of State for Education and Employment. After lecturing in social administration she became Adviser to the Central Policy Review Staff in the Cabinet Office (1975–78), Professor of Educational Administration at the Institute of Education, University of London (1978–83), and Clerk and Director of Education, Inner London Education Authority (1983–87). She was made a Life Peer in 1987, and in the same year she became Master of Birkbeck College, University of London, a post from which she resigned in 1997 when she became Minister of State. She has been Director of Project Fullemploy, Thames Television and the Royal Opera House. Her publications include *A Fair Start* (1971), *Social Policy and Administration in Britain* (1975), *Disadvantage and Education* (jointly) (1982), *Educational Policy and Educational Inequality* (jointly) (1982), *Response to Adversity* (jointly) (1983), and *Prison and Penal Reform* (1990).

Ann Dummett is an independent consultant on European policies concerning ethnic minorities. In recent years she has worked mainly for the Commission for Racial Equality. She is also the author of several works on immigration and nationality laws, and is a former Director of the Runnymede Trust.

Marian FitzGerald is Principal Research Officer in the Home Office Research and Statistics Directorate where she is responsible for research on racial disadvantage and ethnic minorities and crime (including victimisation, offending and contact with the criminal justice system). She was previously a freelance researcher and her work included publications and broadcasting on ethnic minorities and the political system, local government policies to promote racial equality, and racial harassment. She wrote the report on ethnic minorities and the criminal justice system for the 1993 Royal Commission on Criminal Justice and was a member of the Council of Europe's Commission Against Racism and Xenophobia for nearly two years from its inception in 1994.

Harry Goulbourne is Professor of Political Sociology at Cheltenham and Gloucester CHE. From 1975 to 1980 he was a senior lecturer in political science at the University of Dar es Salaam, Tanzania, and from 1980 to 1985 a senior lecturer in government and politics at the University of the West Indies in Jamaica, where he was also Dean of the Faculty of Social Sciences for two years. For several years he was a principal research fellow at the Centre for Research in Ethnic Relations at the University of Warwick. He has published extensively on Tanzanian and Caribbean politics, British race relations, and nationalism and ethnicity. His books include *Ethnicity and Nationalism in Post-Imperial Britain* (1991); *Teachers, Education and Politics in Jamaica 1892–1972* (1988); and *Politics and State in the Third World* (1979). *The Colour-line at Century's End: British Race Relations in Historical and Sociological Perspective* will be published early in 1988.

Valerie Karn is Professor of Housing Studies at the University of Manchester. She specialises in research in the fields of housing policy, housing management, housing standards and race relations and has carried out extensive comparative research on Britain, the United States and Western Europe. She is a member of the coordinating committee of the European Network for Housing Research. Her books and major articles of relevance to this volume include: 'Race and housing in Britain: the role of the major institutions' in Young and Glazer (eds) *Ethnic Pluralism and Public Policy* (1983); *Race Class and State Housing* (jointly) (1987); *Home-ownership in the Inner City; Salvation or Despair* (jointly) (1986); 'Racial segregation in Britain: patterns, processes and policy approaches' (jointly), in Huttman *et al.* (eds) *Urban Housing Segregation of Minorities in Western Europe and the United States* (1991); *The Settlement of Refugees in Britain* (jointly) (1995); *Home-Owners and Clearance* (jointly) (1995); and *Ethnicity in the 1991 Census: vol. 4. Employment, Education and Housing* (ed) (1997).

Howard Lasus received his PhD in sociology from the University of Denver and worked as a computer specialist at the A.T. and T. Bell Laboratories for a number of years. He is currently an Academic Research Consultant at George Mason University and teaches in the Department of

Sociology and Anthropology. His research interests include residential segregation and computer applications in the social sciences.

Anthony Lester (Lord Lester of Herne Hill QC) is a member of 2 Hare Court Chambers and of the Bars of Northern Ireland and the Irish Republic and is also Honorary Visiting Professor of Public Law at University College London. He was the first person to advocate the incorporation of the European Convention on Human Rights in this country in a Fabian pamphlet published in November 1968; he has introduced two Private Members' Bills to incorporate the Convention; he was founder of Interights (the International Centre for the Legal Protection of Human Rights) and is its President. Between 1974 and 1976 he was Special Adviser to the Home Secretary (Roy Jenkins) with special responsibility for sex and race equality legislation and human rights. He helped to draft the Green Paper on Incorporation of the Convention. He was also Special Adviser to the Standing Advisory Commission on Human Rights in Northern Ireland between 1975 and 1977, and helped to draft their report on incorporation. He is General Editor (with Professor Dawn Oliver) of *Constitutional Law and Human Rights*, published by Butterworths in 1997, and has written extensively on constitutional and human rights subjects. He has argued many of the leading cases on human rights before both European courts and in various courts of the Commonwealth.

Tariq Modood is a Programme Director at the Policy Studies Institute. He was a lecturer in political theory before entering racial equality policy work, including some years at the Commission for Racial Equality. Subsequently he was a research fellow at Nuffield College, Oxford, and at the University of Manchester. His many publications include *Ethnic Minorities in Britain: Diversity and Disadvantage* (jointly) (1997); (ed) *Church, State and Religious Minorities* (1997); and (ed) *The Politics of Multiculturalism in the New Europe* (1997).

Sir Peter Newsam was, from 1989, Director of the University of London's Institute of Education and, from 1992, Deputy Vice-Chancellor of the University until his retirement in 1994. He is presently acting as a consultant on education and inter-ethnic relations. He began his career as a teacher, and then moved on to educational administration, first in the North Riding of Yorkshire and Cumberland, and then in the Inner London Education Authority, where he became Education Officer. He was Chairman of the Commission for Racial Equality from 1982 to 1987, when he became Secretary to the Association of County Councils.

Bhikhu Parekh is Professor of Political Theory at the University of Hull. He has been a visiting professor at McGill University, Harvard University, the Institute of Advanced Studies, Vienna, and the University of Pompeau Fabra in Barcelona. He was Vice-Chancellor of the University of Baroda from 1981 to 1984 and Deputy Chairman of the Commission for Racial Equality from 1985 to 1990. He is the author of six widely acclaimed books on political philosophy. He has edited ten books and published over a hundred articles in academic journals and collections. He has frequently broadcast on the radio and television on race relations in Britain and has been a trustee of the Runnymede Trust and the Institute of Public Policy Research.

Deborah Phillips is a senior lecturer in the School of Geography at the University of Leeds. She has researched widely in the field of 'race' and ethnicity, with particular reference to housing. Her publications include *What Price Equality?* (1987), and *Ethnic Minority Housing: Explanations and Policies* (jointly) (1989). She has recently contributed to two volumes in the ONS series on *Ethnicity and the 1991 Census*) (1996, edited by P. Ratcliffe, and 1997, edited by V. Karn).

Peter Sanders worked from 1972 to 1993 in race relations, first at the Race Relations Board, where he became Deputy Chief Officer, and then at the Commission for Racial Equality, where he became Chief Executive. As well as writing several articles on race relations, he is the author of books on African history and poetry, and is presently engaged in research on African history.

Sarah Spencer is the Director of the Human Rights Programme at the Institute for Public Policy Research where she has been a Research Fellow since 1990. She was formerly the General Secretary of the National Council for Civil Liberties (1985–89). Her publications on immigration include *Strangers and Citizens: A Positive Approach to Migrants and Refugees* (1994); *Immigration as an Economic Asset: The German Experience* (1994); and *Migrants, Refugees and the Boundaries of Citizenship* (1995).

John Stone is a Fellow at the Woodrow Wilson International Center for Scholars in Washington DC and a Professor of Sociology at George Mason University. He has taught sociology and race relations at Columbia University, St Antony's College, Oxford, and Goldsmiths College, University of London. He is the Founder Editor of *Ethnic and Racial Studies* and the author of several books on ethnic conflict and sociological theory.

Introduction

The year 1996 marked the twentieth anniversary of the Race Relations Act, which enacted a fairly powerful anti-discrimination law and created the Commission for Racial Equality; 1997 marks the twenty-fifth anniversary of the arrival of over twenty thousand British passport-holding Ugandan Asians expelled by Idi Amin. The grace with which Britain admitted and resettled them in 1972 was in great contrast to its rather shabby treatment of Kenyan Asians four years earlier. In 1998 we will be celebrating the fiftieth anniversary of the arrival of SS *Empire Windrush*, which brought 492 West Indians and inaugurated the process of post-war black migration into Britain.

The succession of three important anniversaries provides an ideal occasion to reflect on Britain's success in integrating its 3.2 million, that is, just under 6 per cent, black and Asian population. But there is also another reason to undertake this exercise. Many individuals have made important contributions to achieving such progress as Britain has made in this area of national life. Sir Peter Newsam is one of them. As the Chief Officer of the Inner London Education Authority, the Chairman of the Commission for Racial Equality, and the Director of London University's Institute of Education, he played a most commendable role in highlighting and combating racial discrimination and acting as a vital bridge between ethnic minorities and British society at large. This volume is intended to celebrate his contribution and mark his formal retirement from professional life.

This collection is also intended as a kind of audit of Britain's efforts to create a just multi-ethnic society. As such it is four-dimensional in nature. It is historical in that it examines Britain's record of the past fifty years. It is theoretical in the sense that it seeks to explain why the country did or did not pursue a particular direction and did or did not pursue specific policies. It is also comparative in that it examines the British record in the European and American context. Finally, the collection is normative in that it both outlines the vision of an integrated society and suggests policies likely to realise that vision. Different authors adopt one or more of these approaches depending on their subject matter. Between them they cover most, though by no means all, important aspects of race relations. Constraints of space have regrettably meant that such areas as racial attacks, the changing political vocabulary, and new forms of ethnicity do not receive adequate attention in this collection. However, enough literature is already available elsewhere on these and related subjects.

Before introducing the essays, two points of clarification are in order. The reader will notice that different authors use such terms as race, ethnicity, racism and ethnic minorities in somewhat different ways. We have not sought to impose uniform usage, not only because that would have been arbitrary but more importantly because it would have obscured the very different ways in which different writers conceptualise the situation. The variety of usages is itself suggestive of the current state of thinking on the subject, and deserves to be brought out. Second, we have not attempted to provide a general conclusion either in this introduction or at the end. Rather than attempt an overview ourselves, we asked Peter Newsam to reflect on the essays from his unique background and draw out their important implications.

The collection begins with a wide-ranging theoretical essay by Bhikhu Parekh. Arguing that every society must find ways of reconciling the demands of unity and diversity, he distinguishes five of them. He rejects the proceduralist, assimilationist and millet models as both logically incoherent and politically unrealistic. Although he sees the value of the liberal model of integration, he finds that it too suffers from several limitations, and advocates a pluralist model. He applies his analysis to British society and concludes that it represents an uneasy amalgam of the assimilationist, liberal and pluralist models.

The next two chapters discuss the history of British attempts to combat racial discrimination. Anthony Lester sets out the history of race relations legislation, and examines how it has worked in practice. He discusses the subject within the context of immigration policy and human rights legislation generally, and presses the case for major reform. Approaching the subject from the perspective of a practitioner, in chapter 3 Peter Sanders draws on the experiences of the Commission for Racial Equality to examine the nature and extent of racial discrimination and the strategies for eliminating it. While supporting the Commission's case for strengthening the 1976 Race Relations Act, he argues that more can be done within the existing framework.

The following seven chapters deal with different aspects of ethnic minority experiences. Tariq Modood demonstrates, in chapter 4, that, despite the persistence of racial discrimination, the ethnic minorities have begun to reverse the initial downward mobility caused by migration and racial discrimination. Although all ethnic minority groups continue to be grossly under-represented in senior positions, there are significant differences between them. Broadly speaking the Chinese and East African Asians have achieved parity with whites, the Indians and Caribbeans remain relatively disadvantaged, while the Pakistanis and Bangladeshis continue to be severely disadvantaged. Modood explores how the differences could be best explained.

Sarah Spencer looks at the impact of immigration policy on race relations in chapter 5. Noting that the rationale for this policy over the last thirty years has been that firm and fair immigration controls are essential for good race relations, she asks whether in fact this has been the case. Drawing on the recent experience of the 1996 Immigration and Asylum Act, she demonstrates that both the content and the presentation of immigration policy have had a damaging effect on good race relations. She sets out a strategy for reform arguing, among other things, that the positive benefits of immigration should be highlighted and that the government should give a lead in altering the terms of the debate.

In chapter 6 Tessa Blackstone argues that succeeding at school and going on to college or university is of great importance for ethnic minority young people if they are to avoid the double jeopardy of lack of skills and discrimination. Although the educational achievements of such groups vary greatly and generalisation is difficult, some groups are clearly doing noticeably better than the white majority. She is cautiously optimistic about the educational success of ethnic minorities, especially as a much higher proportion of black and Asian young people than before are now entering higher education.

Yasmin Alibhai-Brown looks at the impact on race relations of the media, especially the newspapers, the television and the radio. In chapter 7 she considers the criticism of the media's coverage of race relations in the 1970s and 1980s, and the responses it provoked, such as the employment of more ethnic minority journalists and the training of white journalists. She emphasises the importance of equal opportunity policies, the monitoring of programmes, the need for more dialogue on crucial areas of disagreement, and the value of seminars and training.

In chapter 8 Valerie Karn and Deborah Phillips demonstrate that there has been substantial progress in ethnic minority housing. This is due both to the removal of obvious barriers and to the enhanced capabilities of the ethnic minority groups themselves. However, ethnic minority disadvantage has persisted into the 1990s, and there are still 'ethnic penalties' in the housing market. In their view the ethnic minorities would benefit greatly from policies which are not specific to them such as increased investment in social rented housing, as well as from tackling racial discrimination and racial harassment.

Marion FitzGerald traces the concerns about 'race and crime' in Britain in the post-war period and the factors which have shaped the perception of the ethnic minorities as suspects and offenders. In chapter 9 she describes the main research findings and statistics which currently inform that debate before discussing their implications. She concludes that all three of the main explanations advanced for the ethnic differences are at work, but the interplay of socio-economic factors, discrimination and ethnic-specific factors is more complex and dynamic than has been appreciated. In her view future research and policy development need to be based on more sophistic-ated understanding of the part played by each of these.

In chapter 10 Harry Goulbourne suggests that when examining the political participation of ethnic minorities, we should not restrict ourselves to the more visible areas of voting behaviour, involvement in established political institutions, and participation in local and national elections. We should look at other activities such as joining pressure groups and forms of spontaneous political behaviour. He analyses several major events to show that political involvement of ethnic minority groups has been instrumental in bringing about desired changes. He concludes by arguing that although their political integration is increasing, there is still some way to go before they are fully represented in political parties, Parliament and the government of the day.

In chapters 11 and 12 Britain's record is examined in a comparative context. In chapter 11 Ann Dummett describes the current debate on European legislation to outlaw racial discrimination, a debate in which British experience plays an important part. She provides valuable back-ground information on the European institutions, and briefly indicates the differences between the domestic legislation of Britain and other countries. In her view European law is likely to be of increasing importance in shaping the debate on British race relations.

John Stone and Howard Lasus, in chapter 12, identify some of the important similarities and differences between the British and American experiences of race relations and immigration in the post-war period. While recognising the basic contrast between an immigrant and homeland society, and the longer history and larger size of the minority presence in America, they notice convergence in the patterns of race and ethnic relations. They think this could be attributed to such shared factors as ambivalent political leadership, economic forces generated by the global economy, and tension between the liberal tolerance of diversity and the majoritarian democracy's demand for conformity.

In the concluding chapter, Peter Newsam draws on his own experience at the ILEA and the CRE to spell out the lessons of the past and to point the way forward. He points to the improvements in educational performance and employment prospects of some minority groups, and sees this as a basis for cautious optimism. His optimism is tempered by the fact that the Home Secretaries who succeeded Roy Jenkins showed little commitment, and that the courts have narrowly interpreted and emasculated many of the crucial provisions of the Race Relations Act.

Peter Newsam's remarks aptly sum up the general thrust of this collection of essays. The ethnic minorities have made progress, no doubt some more than others, and Britain is now a more integrated and equal society than before. There is also greater awareness of the disadvantages that ethnic minorities suffer, and the need to tackle them at both local and national levels. In spite of these and other advances, racial prejudice and dis- crimination persist in many areas of life, the incidence of racial attacks is unacceptably high, equal opportunity is denied to many members of ethnic minorities, their presence in positions of power is severely limited, and the vision of a plural Britain accepting and delighting in its multi-ethnic character remains a distant dream. Although not as racially troubled as Germany and even the United States, Britain still has a long way to go before it can claim to have ensured equality and justice for its ethnic minorities and become a society whose citizens are wholly at ease with each other. The theoretical and political agenda that this sets is clear. Legislation needs to be tightened up, but that alone is not enough. We need well-thought-out policies on economic, educational, housing, immigration and other matters and a clear and positive lead by the government in appreciating the great contribution the ethnic minorities have made and will continue to make to British society.

This book has been in preparation over two years and all the articles in it were completed by the end of December 1996. Accordingly they do not take account of the results of the May 1997 general election. However, this does not in any way affect the basic message of the book. We have been concerned to set an agenda for any future British Government and like to hope that the Labour Government will be much more sympathetic to it than any other.

1   Integrating minorities

Bhikhu Parekh

A multicultural society, that is, a society which includes several distinct cultural, ethnic and religious communities, needs to find ways of reconciling two equally legitimate and sometimes conflicting demands. Its minority communities generally cherish and wish to preserve and transmit their ways of life. A society, however, cannot last long without some degree of cohesion and a sense of common belonging. It also has its own way of life which it is equally anxious to preserve. This raises the question as to how it should integrate its minorities and organise its collective life so that it satisfies their legitimate aspirations without losing its unity and continuity. In this chapter I do two things. First, I outline and assess the adequacy of the various models of integration canvassed in the literature on the subject, and second, I use my theoretical analysis of these models to elucidate the manner in which Britain has sought to integrate its ethnic minorities.

I

Broadly speaking a political community can integrate its minorities in one of five ways. Although these modes or models overlap, they are distinct enough to be distinguished for analytical purposes.

First, one might argue that in a culturally diverse society the state should be culturally neutral as otherwise it would end up preferring and enforcing one culture or way of life, thereby both treating other cultures unequally and subjecting them to an unacceptable degree of moral coercion. The state should be a purely formal institution pursuing no substantive goals of its own and requiring no more of its citizens than that they accept the established structure of authority and obey the law. Such a state gives its citizens, including the minorities, the maximum possible freedom to live the way they like and also ensures unity and cohesion. The minorities are free to embrace the majority way of life, or to do so only partially, or to evolve a synthetic way of life, or to lead totally isolated and self-contained lives, provided that they discharge their basic legal obligations to the state. This view was first articulated by Hobbes, and for convenience I shall call it a proceduralist view of the state.

Second, it might be argued that no polity can be stable and cohesive unless all its members share a common national culture, including common values, ideals of excellence, moral beliefs, social practices, and so forth. By sharing a common culture, they develop mutual attachments, affections and loyalties, and build up the necessary bonds of solidarity and a common sense of belonging. The state is a custodian of the society's ways of life, and has both a right and a duty to ensure that its cultural minorities assimilate or merge into the prevailing national culture. The choice before the minorities is simple. If they wish to become part of and be treated like the rest of the community, they should think and live like the latter; if instead they insist on retaining their separate cultures, they should not complain if they are treated differently. For convenience I shall call this an assimilationist model of integration. Rousseau, Herder and nationalist writers are its most eloquent spokesmen.

Assimilation can take several forms. One might argue that minorities should adopt the majority way of life and live, think, speak and behave like the rest. One might go further and demand that they should also intermarry with and become socially and biologically assimilated into the majority community. One might go yet further and insist that they should 'love' and show unconditional 'loyalty' to the community, accept its history as 'their' history, 'identify' with its people, and so forth. This last form of assimilation, which claims the soul of the minorities and seeks their total identification, goes far beyond the ordinary forms of cultural and even biological assimilation and is best called nationalist assimilation.

Third, one might take a half-way position between proceduralism and assimilationism, and advocate partial assimilation. One might argue that proceduralism is too formal and empty to hold a society together, and that assimilationism is unnecessary, undesirable, or both. All that is necessary for the unity of a polity is that its citizens should share a common *political* culture, including a common body of political values, practices and institutions, collective self-understanding and a broad view of national identity. Without such a common political culture and the implied uniformity of political beliefs and practices, public debate is impossible, political disagreements cannot be resolved, and collective action is paralysed. Minorities should therefore accept, and become assimilated into, the political culture of the community and, subject to that, remain free to live the way they like. In this view of integration, the private–public distinction plays a crucial role. The unity of the society is sought and located in the public realm, whereas diversity belongs to the private realm which includes not just the family but also neighbourhood and communal associations. It is difficult to think of an appropriate name for this model. In much of the British, American and even French literature, it is called integration and distinguished from assimilation as sketched earlier. However, this is both linguistically arbitrary and obscures the fact that it involves at least partial assimilation and differs from the latter only in degree. It might be better called a bifurcationist or, since it has found most favour among liberals, a liberal mode of integration. In one form or another it finds support in the writings of John Locke, the founding fathers of the American republic, and John Rawls – especially his *Political Liberalism*. Habermas's 'constitutional patriotism' is another modern version of it.

The fourth model of integration shares several features in common with the third, but it is also quite different. According to it the bifurcationist mode of integration has two basic disadvantages. It places the community's political culture beyond negotiation and revision, and expects minorities to become assimilated into it. Since the political culture does not reflect the presence and values of minorities, they would not be able to identify with it and offer it their whole-hearted support. Furthermore, in a society dominated by a specific culture, minority cultures suffer from obvious structural disadvantages and need more than mere tolerance to flourish or even survive in the private realm.

Advocates of the fourth approach therefore argue that, rather than assimilate minorities into the political culture of the community, the latter should be pluralised to acknowledge their presence and to embody their values and aspirations. The prevailing political values, practices, symbols, myths, ceremonies, collective self-understanding and view of national identity should be suitably revised to reflect its multicultural character. 'We' cannot obviously integrate 'them' so long as 'we' remain 'we'; 'we' must be loosened up to create a new common space in which 'they' can become part of a newly constituted 'we'. So far as the private realm is concerned, the state should not follow a policy of cultural indifference or *laissez-faire* as that would work in favour of the dominant culture. If the otherwise disadvantaged minorities are to survive and flourish, they need public recognition, encouragement and material support not in order to protect them from change but to create conditions in which they enjoy the security, self-confidence and broad equality necessary to make uncoerced choices. For convenience I shall call this a pluralist mode of integration. It is difficult to think of any classical writer who offers a coherent philosophical defence of this view. Among our contemporaries Charles Taylor, Will Kymlicka and Rainer Bauböck have proposed various versions of it.[1]

Finally, one might argue that individuals are above all cultural beings and embedded in specific communities, the ultimate source of what gives meaning to people's lives. All that deeply matters to them – their customs, practices, values, sense of identity and historical continuity, norms of behaviour, patterns of family life, and so forth – are derived from their cultures. The state has no moral status, and its sole *raison d'être* is to uphold and nurture its constituent cultural communities. It is not a community of communities, for that implies that it has an independent moral basis and its own distinct goals, but rather a union of communities, a bare framework within which they should be free to pursue their traditional ways of life and engage in necessary social, political and economic interactions.

Although this model of integration resembles the proceduralist view mentioned earlier in viewing the state as a largely formal institution with no substantive purposes of its own, it differs from it in requiring the state to maintain the existing communities. The state is expected not only to refrain from interfering with their internal affairs but also to recognise and institutionalise their autonomy. It should respect their internal structure of government, enforce their diverse customs and practices, fund their educational and cultural institutions, and so on. So far as the unity of the state is concerned, it is grounded in the willing support of the constituent communities for the common framework that both protects their autonomy and regulates their mutual relations. Members of the state owe their primary loyalty to their respective cultural communities and derivatively and secondarily to the state. It is difficult to think of an appropriate name for this model of integration. For convenience I shall call it the *millet* model of integration because of its obvious historical associations.

Four general points need to be made about the five models of minority integration mentioned above. First, I have sketched only their basic outlines, assumptions and guiding principles, and ignored the diverse forms that each of them can take. As we saw, the assimilationist model can take cultural, biological and nationalist forms, and this is equally true of the others. Second, the five models are neither mutually exclusive, for they overlap in several respects, nor collectively exhaustive for, although they represent major ways of thinking about integration, others are not inconceivable.

Third, the five models are logically distinct in the sense that they conceptualise political unity, diversity, and their relationship in very different ways. The first three privilege unity, and treat diversity as a largely residual, contingent and parasitic category confined to areas in which unity is not a central concern. The fourth model seeks to assign them equal status, while the fifth gives pre-eminence to diversity and assigns unity only an instrumental and derivative value. Again, in the proceduralist model the state transcends society and takes no notice of its cultural composition. In the assimilationist model it is deeply embedded in the culture of the community and acts as its protector. In the bifurcationist model it is partly embedded in society and partly transcends it, actively assimilating the minorities in the political life but otherwise leaving them alone. In the pluralist model the state is dialectically related to society and both shapes and is shaped by the prevailing cultural diversity. In the millet model it is neither embedded in nor transcends its constituent communities, but exists *outside* of them and lacks the independence required to shape them or to follow substantive purposes of its own.

The five models also entail different conceptions of citizenship. In the proceduralist model citizenship is purely formal in nature and consists of the enjoyment of certain rights and obligations. In the assimilationist model it is grounded in the national culture and requires the citizen to share it as a necessary precondition of full membership of the political community. In the bifurcationist model the citizen is committed to sharing the political culture of the community. In the pluralist model citizenship has a plural cultural basis, and citizens bring their diverse cultures to the public realm and enjoy a culturally mediated membership of the political community. The millet model privileges communal membership and has no, or only a highly attenuated, notion of citizenship.

Finally, the five models of integration are not just logical types but have all been tried out in history in one form or another and simply or in combination with others. We can therefore form some idea of how they are likely to work in practice. The proceduralist model characterised the absolute monarchies and some early medieval kingdoms in Europe. The assimilationist model has dominated France since 1789, and the bifurcationist model is favoured in Britain and the United States, though the latter also has some features of the pluralist model. Pluralism has found favour in India, Canada, Australia and other self-consciously multicultural societies, though India has several features of the millet model as well. Different forms of millet model are to be found in the Ottoman Empire, British administration of many of its colonies, traditional Muslim kingdoms, and post-independence Lebanon.[2]

II

In the previous section I sketched five different ways of integrating minorities into a political community. Our choice between them is based on such things as whether their accounts of the nature and basis of political unity are coherent and realistic, what minority aspirations they regard as legitimate and whether they are able to satisfy these aspirations.

The proceduralist model is logically incoherent, for no political community can be culturally neutral and be based on procedural foundations alone. Every political community has at least two basic features: it has a specific structure of authority, and it makes and enforces collectively binding laws. Neither of these can be morally neutral. The structure of authority refers to the community's mode of governance and can be devised in several different ways. It might be secular, theocratic, or a mixture of the two. If secular, it might be based on universal franchise or on one limited by race, class or gender. The universal franchise might be equal or weighted in favour of the intellectual elite as J. S. Mill had argued. The system of elections might be direct or indirect, and might represent individuals as liberals advocate or corporate groups as Hegel, some pluralists and others have urged. The authority of the state might be absolute or limited by a constitutionally prescribed system of rights. The choice between these and other ways of structuring authority is based on such factors as the society's views on how human beings should be treated, the rights they should enjoy, the nature and limits of political power and the proper functions of the law; in short, on its conception of the good life. Since every structure of authority is thus embedded in and shaped by the wider society's moral beliefs, it is biased towards a specific way of life and cannot be morally neutral.

The laws and the policies of the state cannot be morally neutral either. Should it allow slavery, polygamy, polyandry, incest, public hanging, euthanasia, suicide, capital punishment, abortion, violent sports involving animals, coerced marriages, divorce on demand, unconventional sexual practices, lesbian and homosexual marriages, rights of illegitimate children to inherit 'parental' property, inequalities of wealth, acute poverty, racial discrimination, and so on? If it does not legislate on these matters, it indicates that it does not consider them sufficiently important to the moral well-being of the community to require a collective, uniform and compulsory mode of behaviour. If it legislates, it takes a specific stand. In either case it presupposes a specific view of the good life. A morally neutral state, making no moral demands on its citizens and equally hospitable to all cultures, is logically impossible. And since every law coerces those not sharing its underlying values, a morally non-coercive state is a fantasy. Some states can, of course, be morally less partisan and hence less coercive than others, but no state can be wholly free of a moral bias and of the concomitant coercion. Even the most liberal state imposes such values as liberty, free speech and the equality of the sexes and races, and hence coerces those totally opposed to them.

Since the structure and exercise of political authority are informed by a specific conception of the good life, the unity of a political community cannot rest on procedural foundations alone. A political community involves far more than an agreement on procedures, and the latter are never morally neutral either. This means that to ask minorities to accept the prevailing structure of authority is *ipso facto* to require them to accept the underlying conception of the good life. To suggest otherwise, as the proceduralist does, is to be disingenuous.

III

The assimilationist model suffers from the opposite defects. Assimilationism is an incoherent doctrine for it is not clear *what* the minorities are to be assimilated into. Although the moral and cultural structure of a society has some internal coherence, it is never a homogeneous and unified whole. It is an unplanned product of history and made up of diverse and conflicting traditions; it consists of values and practices which can be interpreted and related in several different ways; and so on. The assimilationist has to ignore all this in order to arrive at a homogenised and highly abridged and distorted version of the national culture, and then the minorities are assimilated not into the collective culture in all its richness and complexity but into an ideologue's misguided account of it.

Furthermore, assimilation does not always work in practice. If people are left free to negotiate their relations with each other and have an incentive to do so, they might over time come closer and even perhaps assimilate as happened with the Anglo-Saxons, the Normans and the Danes in Britain. However this is not always the case, and is most unlikely to occur when assimilation is rushed, imposed, or both. The Jews have survived two millennia of Christian oppression; the ethnic and cultural minorities in the ex-Soviet Union have outlived the most brutal repression; and not all the assimilationist economic and cultural pressures of the United States have succeeded in creating a melting pot. What is more, assimilation is rarely able to redeem its promise of full and unqualified acceptance. The demand for it springs from intolerance of differences, and for the intolerant every difference is one too many and a source of intense unease. Even the thoroughly assimilated German Jews fared no better than the unassimilated ones at the hands of the Nazis.

Even if assimilation had a chance of success, it would not be an option available to liberal societies. The liberal society is committed to equal respect for persons. Since human beings are culturally embedded and derive their sense of identity and meaning from their cultures, respect for them implies respect for their cultures. Respecting cultures does not mean that they may not be criticised any more than respect for persons places them above criticism, but rather that they should be understood and appreciated in their own terms, that they should not be resented or suppressed simply for being different, and that our criticisms of them should be based on criteria they can comprehend and in principle share. As we saw assimilation entails coercion and cultural engineering, which sit ill at ease with such basic liberal values as choice and personal autonomy.

IV

Although the bifurcationist model avoids many of the mistakes of the assimilationist and has much to be said in favour of it, it suffers, as we briefly noticed earlier, from two major defects.

First, every political community that has lasted a while develops a widely shared body of values, practices, institutions, myths, conception of its past and future, a mode of public discourse, and so on, all of which constitute its shared political culture or identity. Although the political culture is deeply inscribed in its way of life and is the basis of its unity, it is neither monolithic nor unalterable. Its values and practices might discriminate against or bear unduly heavily on those who are new to it, or whose historical experiences are different, or who have long been marginalised and ignored. These groups might therefore rightly question their content or inner balance, and seek their redefinition. This is what women have done, and there is no reason why cultural minorities should be denied the right to do the same.

What is true of the community's values is also true of its political symbols, images, myths, ceremonies, view of its history and so on. They too reflect and reproduce a specific conception of its identity, and need to be suitably revised when they are shown to misrepresent, distort or ignore the presence, experiences and contributions of marginalised groups, or to be out of step with the changes in the social composition of the community. Old and marginalised as well as newly arrived groups can rightly ask that the political life should grant them suitable public recognition by incorporating their symbols, ceremonies, views, etc. into the collective expressions of national life. Such recognition confers public legitimacy on their presence, recognises them as valued members of the community, and helps integrate them into it. The community's political identity is not a brute and unalterable precipitate of history and settled once and for all, nor a matter of arbitrary collective choice and crude political bargaining, but a historical inheritance to be periodically and judiciously reconstituted in the light of new demands and experiences.

The second defect of the bifurcationist model is that its attempt to combine a monocultural public realm with a multicultural private realm is likely to undermine the latter. In every society the public realm enjoys considerable dignity and prestige, which generally far outweighs those of the private realm. When one culture is not only publicly recognised but also institutionalised, it becomes the official culture of the community, an expression of its collective identity, and enjoys great prestige, power, state patronage, and access to public resources. By contrast the excluded cultures come to be seen as marginal, peripheral, even deviant and inferior, only worth practising outside the public gaze of society and in the privacy of the family and communal associations. Since the public realm prizes uniformity, diversity gets devalued throughout society.

Lacking prestige, power, resources and collective encouragement, minority cultures suffer from often unintended structural disadvantages and can only survive with the greatest of effort. Their members, especially the youth whose roots in their parental cultures are precarious and shallow, tend to feel nervous and take the easy path of assimilation. As the older generation of Jews have pointed out, many of them used to feel deeply embarrassed when their parents spoke in Yiddish in public or could not reply in English. The sad phenomenon is still pervasive as many minority parents and their children testify. A couple of years ago when I was travelling by train from London to Hull, I was sitting opposite an elderly Pakistani couple and next to their adolescent daughter. When the crowded train pulled out of King's Cross station, the parents began to talk in Urdu. The girl felt restless and nervous and began making strange signals to them. As they carried on their conversation for a few more minutes, she angrily leaned over the table and asked them to shut up. When the confused mother asked for an explanation, the girl shot back: 'Just as you do not expose your private parts in public, you do not speak in *that* language in public'. Though no one had presumably taught that to her, she knew that the public realm belonged to whites, that only *their* language and customs were legitimate within it, and that ethnic identities were to be confined to the private realm. In a society dominated by one culture, tolerance alone is not enough to sustain diversity. Without necessarily endorsing all their values and practices, the community collectively needs to affirm, value and cherish its minority cultures, to give them public recognition, and to offer them such moral, cultural and material help as they need and cannot otherwise obtain. Since the bifurcationist model is generally inhospitable to this, and leaves cultural diversity to survive precariously in the overpowering shadow of the dominant culture, it fails to create a climate in which cultural minorities can feel secure and confident enough to experiment with, retain, revise or freely reject their ways of life.

V

The pluralist model which affirms and encourages multiculturalism in both the public and private realms is free from the defects of the bifurcationist model. It cherishes both unity and diversity and privileges neither. It also appreciates their interplay and does not assign them to separate and unrelated realms. The multicultural public realm that it seeks to create publicly recognises and accepts minority cultures as a legitimate and valued part of the community and makes it easier for them to identify with it. In so doing it acquires both the right to demand their loyalty and support and the power to mobilise their moral and emotional energies.

The multiculturally constituted public realm institutionalises and embodies diversity in the very self-conception of the community, making it as normal and valued a part of collective life as unity. By creating a climate conducive to diversity and by giving minority communities such help as they need and merit, the pluralist model minimises assimilationist pressures and enables them freely to negotiate their relations with the dominant culture. Some minorities might wish to assimilate completely; some might do so partially; yet others might prefer to experiment with different forms of intercultural synthesis. Whatever their decision, they arrive at it freely, without duress and coercion, and at their own pace. Since they do not feel nervously protective about their identity, they are likely to enter into a dialogue both with each other and with the majority culture. The dialogue not only prevents them from becoming inward-looking, rigid and static but also requires them publicly to defend their beliefs and practices, thereby encouraging internal debates, making them more open and reflective, and promoting intercultural understanding and exchange. This helps create a rich, shared and multicultural private realm capable of underpinning an equally rich and multicultural public realm.

In the pluralist model unity and diversity are not confined to two separate areas of life but are dialectically related and reinforce each other. When unity and diversity are disjoined, unity remains abstract and devoid of energy, and diversity, lacking a regulative principle, encourages fragmentation and isolation. The pluralist model avoids this mistake. The unity of the community here is not formal and abstract and located in a transcendental public realm; rather it is grounded in a multiculturally constituted public realm which both sustains, and is in turn sustained by, a multiculturally constituted private realm. There is no hiatus, no clash of organising principles, between the two realms. Both cherish diversity and unity, and the spirit of multiculturality effortlessly flows from one to the other within the framework of a shared and plural collective culture.

The pluralist model is based on a vision of society in which its different cultural communities, interacting with each other in a spirit of equality and openness, create a rich, plural and tolerant collective culture affirmed alike in all areas of life, including and especially the political. The vision is not easy to realise and has its own problems. Some cultural communities might not be open and experimental and might jealously guard their inherited identities; for example, the Amish in the United States and some Aboriginal peoples in Canada, Australia and elsewhere. A multicultural society needs to respect their wishes, for they generally cause no harm, do not threaten political unity, and in their own different ways add a valuable dimension to social life. Their values and practices may differ from, and even offend against, those of the majority, but they should be tolerated subject to such collectively agreed minimum principles as respect for human life and dignity.

Since public resources are necessarily limited, decisions about the competing claims of different cultural communities are never easy, and call for a good deal of accommodation. Besides, the minority communities might sometimes be hostile to and penalise the choices of their dissenting members, and then the wider society has to find ways of reconciling the legitimate demands of both. It cannot ignore the dissenters altogether, but nor can it allow their rights always to trump the community's desire to preserve itself. This is a difficult issue, and no plural society has yet found ways of resolving it. Again, pluralism presupposes both the willingness to live with differences and the ability to find one's way around in them, and these qualities are generally not readily available. Some might think that the tolerance of differences has gone too far, and others that it has not gone far enough. Since the conflict between the two is inescapable and cannot be easily resolved, a plural society needs to evolve a broad consensus on the value and limits of diversity, never an easy task.

VI

We may now turn to the millet model, whose defects are too obvious to need elaboration. It rests on the belief that human beings are culturally embedded and find their fulfilment in their membership of specific cultural communities. This is a highly static and impoverished view of human beings for they need access not only to a stable cultural community but also to a variety of cultures in order to appreciate the specificity and correct the inadequacies of their own. That in turn requires a wider and democratic political community accommodating diversity within a framework based on common citizenship, shared values, and so forth. Since the millet model fragments society into neatly isolated communities, reinforces their inherited prejudices and mutual suspicions, and prevents the emergence of a shared collective life, it rules out an interactive democratic community and is inherently unsatisfactory. The Ottoman millet system worked for centuries only because the imperial form of government ruled out a shared public life and treated non-Muslims as second-class citizens. It had great virtues including a remarkable record of religious toleration that put Europe to shame, but it also froze religious communities, rigidified their internal structures, and arrested the growth of common bonds and a shared political life.

The millet model suffers from other defects as well. Individuals belong to several communities, such as the ethnic, the religious and the cultural, which do not necessarily coincide, thereby making it difficult to decide which community to protect. Even when a cultural community can be individuated, its members rarely take a uniform view of its identity, with the result that protecting its autonomy often institutionalises the dominant elite and denies the dissenters redress. Again, the millet model might make some sense in an undeveloped agricultural economy but none in an industrialised society, whose constant mobility and close interactions both break through the communal barriers and necessitate a common body of rules, norms and practices. To grant a measure of self-government to such cohesive communities as the Aboriginal peoples and the Amish is one thing; to make this the organising principle of the entire political community is altogether different.

VII

In the light of our discussion it should be clear that, in my view, the pluralist model better reconciles the legitimate demands of unity and diversity than the others, and is best suited to a multicultural society. The proceduralist view offers an incoherent account of the unity of the state and leaves diversity to the precarious mercy of the dominant culture. The assimilationist model ignores the cultural claims of minorities, takes an impossibly stringent view of integration, and threatens the unity of the state both by locating it in a non-existent uniform national culture and by provoking minority resistance. The bifurcationist model does nothing to relieve the alienation of the cultural minorities from the public realm, is unable to command their enthusiastic support, and cannot provide a stable basis of unity. And since it does nothing to reduce the structural disadvantages of its minority cultures, it not only discourages diversity in the private realm but also runs the risk of encouraging fundamentalism among its nervous minorities. As for the millet model, it clearly offers the least coherent and plausible account of the unity of the state.

Although the pluralist model of integration is better than the rest, it cannot be held up as an ideal model for all societies. A society has to start from where it is and choose a model that best coheres with its history, traditions, self-understanding, moral and cultural resources, level of economic and political development, the nature, number and demands of its cultural minorities, and so forth. If a society consists of long-established and mutually suspicious communities with no tradition of cooperative action, it might be wiser to opt for some version of the proceduralist or millet model, at least in the short run. Or if an otherwise open and plural society includes an economically and culturally self-contained minority that does not wish to integrate with the rest of society as is the case with the Amish in the United States and the Aboriginal peoples in many parts of the world, they should be left free to govern themselves subject to a body of minimum and collectively agreed principles. Again, if an otherwise liberal society were to include an insecure minority, as was the case with Indian Muslims in the aftermath of the country's partition, it makes both moral and political sense to win over its trust by respecting its customs and practices, funding its educational and cultural institutions and, in general, protecting its cultural space. All these are obviously second-best alternatives, and the ultimate hope should be that the various communities would over time feel relaxed and trust each other enough to evolve an appropriate model in which they can retain, revise, enrich or reject their respective cultures as they please within an open, plural and commonly shared collective culture.

VIII

Our discussion so far has been abstract and intended to identify and evaluate the various ways in which a society might integrate its cultural minorities. I will now use these theoretical tools briefly to analyse the way in which Britain has gone about integrating its post-Second World War black and Asian migrants.

After the war Britain badly needed labour to rebuild its economy.[3] Although it would have preferred whites, as the records of contemporary Cabinet discussions show, they were not available and so it turned to its past and present colonies. Initially successive governments thought that the British tradition of tolerance, the economic ambitions of the immigrants, and the booming economy would ensure that the migrants would find an appropriate niche in British economy and society. The widespread resentment and discrimination against them and the riots of 1958 in Nottingham and Notting Hill shattered the illusion. Since Britain was believed to be a tolerant society and since unemployment was virtually nil, the discrimination and the riots needed an explanation, which was found in the fact that the immigrants were 'coloured', something to which the country was hitherto unused. Britain was now judged to have a 'colour' problem and, since colour was taken to signify a distinct racial group, a 'racial' problem. The solution of the problem consisted in creating good 'race relations', which were taken to consist in the peaceful coexistence and mutual acceptance of whites and the 'coloured' immigrants. Since colour or race was thought to be the source of the problem, the two groups were neatly separated and homogenised. The consciousness of colour was imposed on the immigrants by white society for they did not define themselves in terms of it. West Indians stressed their British heritage and defined themselves as British, no doubt black but only incidentally. Asians stressed their national origins and, again, thought colour irrelevant. It was largely because they were defined as blacks that they saw the British as whites. As Gordon Lewis put it, 'the black immigrant comes to feel less like a West Indian in English society and more like a black man in a white society.'[4]

Two interrelated factors were judged to stand in the way of good race relations, namely the number of immigrants and white society's discrimination against them. Although the British were a tolerant people, the presence of too many 'coloured' immigrants 'understandably' provoked their deepest economic, political and cultural anxieties and stretched the limits of their tolerance. This led to resentment and discrimination, which in turn caused frustration and anger among the immigrants. Successive governments therefore decided upon the interrelated and mutually legitimising policies of restricting black and Asian immigration and combating discrimination. There was some disagreement about the best way to achieve the latter, conservatives generally preferring to rely on public education, popular pressure and conciliation, and liberals and others insisting on the additional sanction of the law. It was eventually agreed that a balance of both was the most effective method.

Until the early 1960s there was a broad consensus that creating 'good race relations' was the national objective, and that a combination of restricted black and Asian immigration and anti-discrimination measures was the best means to achieve it. Very little public thought was given to how to integrate the immigrants into British society. Since Britain has neither the strong assimilationist tradition of France nor the American tradition of integrating waves of newcomers into common citizenship, the oversight was understandable. The question, however, could not be ignored once the immigrants began to raise their families and the race riots in the United States started making alarmist headlines in the British press. The mid-1960s marked the beginning of the public debate on the appropriate model of integration. Britain began to appreciate that its immigrants were not just 'black' or 'coloured' but distinct social groups with their own cultural identities, and that it was now a culturally diverse or plural society. Increasingly it came to be described, especially in liberal circles, as multiracial, multi-ethnic, multicultural, in the aftermath of the Rushdie affair as multifaith, or simply as plural. Although the terms were rarely defined and distinguished, the contemporary usage indicated that the first term was preferred when the Afro-Caribbeans were in mind, the second when both they and the Asians were intended, the third when both of them and white subcultures were in mind, the fourth when the reference was to religious groups, and the fifth when all forms of diversity were intended. Since the term 'race' was increasingly seen to be problematic and not to include such groups as Asians, Jews and the Gypsies, and since the term 'culture' was too wide, the term 'multi-ethnic' became most popular. Given the historical specificity of the British liberal tradition, blacks and Asians were generally described as *ethnic minorities* rather than as ethnic *groups*, a term widely preferred in the United States and Canada, or as *minority communities*, a term rarely used in any other Western country.

Conservative and nationalist spokesmen in Britain well knew the power of words, and felt concerned that the emerging vocabulary foisted an identity on the country they strongly disapproved of. To call Britain multicultural or multi-ethnic was to imply that whites were *just* one group among many, that they did not enjoy a historically or politically *privileged* status, that ethnic minorities were *integral* to British identity, that the country was not only multicultural as a matter of historical fact but *should* remain and even relish being one, and that its minorities were not just collections of individuals sharing certain features in common but organised *communities* which demanded to be treated as such. Not surprisingly conservative and nationalist spokesmen rarely used such terms as multicultural, multi-ethnic, ethnic minority, and minority communities. They were convinced that Britain's multiculturality posed a deep threat to its stability and identity, a view of which Enoch Powell's 1968 'rivers of blood' speech was an excellent example. Despite conservative resistance, however, the majority of British society increasingly defined Britain as a 'multicultural' society consisting of 'ethnic minorities'. This was a great symbolic achievement and publicly affirmed a new view of British national identity.

As for the appropriate mode of integrating the minorities, two models were canvassed. Broadly speaking most conservatives preferred the assimilationist, and most liberals the bifurcationist model which they called 'integration'. Until the late 1970s the latter commanded widespread but not uncritical public support; thereafter the assimilationist model prevailed though not completely, for it had to adjust to the intellectual and institutional legacy of its rival.

The assimilationist model had a distinctly nationalist orientation.[5] According to its advocates, Britain was a cohesive nation bound together by a common language and culture, a sense of kinship and common descent, a shared view of history, and a strong sense of national identity. It was basically an extended family whose members shared common attachments, affections and loyalties both to one another and to the nation and approached their past and the inherited institutions with piety and pride. Their sense of nationhood was the source of such characteristic virtues as patriotism, public spirit, solidarity, spirit of sacrifice, and respect for the law.

Since the British cared deeply about the integrity of their nation and regarded it as their highest moral and political value, they 'instinctively' felt protective about it and resisted all attempts to weaken it.

Not surprisingly the ethnic minorities, a term intensely loathed by nationalist assimilationists, were widely perceived by the latter as a deep threat to their nationhood. In the assimilationist view the minorities had only two choices, to get fully assimilated into the British nation or to leave the country. Full assimilation consisted in 'identifying' with Britain, cultivating 'love' for and 'loyalty' to its way of life, taking 'pride' in its history, abandoning their cultures in favour of the British national culture, and so on. The terms 'love' and 'loyalty' made frequent appearances in the assimilationist literature, Norman Tebbit's notorious loyalty test being a clumsy product of this way of thinking. A small number of assimilationists thought that the ethnic minorities would not or could not assimilate, and should therefore either be repatriated or retrospectively demoted to the status of the German guest workers.[6] Most, however, felt confident that they could and, under appropriate pressure, would assimilate. Assimilation was to be brought about by a well-coordinated and vigorously pursued programme of action. It included such things as a nationalist school curriculum, spontaneous or officially induced popular pressure, unofficial loyalty tests, official endorsement of ideologically acceptable black and Asian spokesmen, and an even more restrictive immigration policy including a more or less complete embargo on overseas spouses so as both to encourage interracial marriages and to curtail the flow of cultural influences from countries of parental origin.

Unlike the assimilationist view, the bifurcationist, liberal or integrationist view was hospitable to cultural diversity.[7] As Roy Jenkins, one of its ablest spokesmen, put it in a statement partly directed at nationalist assimilationists, integration was quite different from the 'flattening' process of assimilation which deprived the minorities of their 'national characteristics and culture', and aimed to turn them into 'a series of carbon copies of someone's misplaced vision of the stereotyped Englishman'.[8] Although the integrationists were clear about what they did not want, they were rather vague about what they did want. By and large they proposed the following. First, the ethnic minorities should accept the values, practices and institutions deemed to be central to the British way of life and become assimilated into the British political culture. Unlike the assimilationists who took a holistic and organic view of British nationhood, the bifurcationists took a liberal view of it, stressing loyalty not so much to the nation as to the values and practices deemed to be integral to it. Although the latter went unspecified, they included such things as liberty, free speech, personal autonomy, equality of the sexes, respect for the law, spirit of moderation, parliamentary democracy, and secularism. Mostly the bifurcationists relied on schools, public policy and the power of public opinion to cultivate these values in the minorities.

Second, subject to the constraints of these values, the minorities were free to preserve and transmit their languages, cultures, religions, and so forth, the state observing more or less strict neutrality. Over time liberals came to see the value of multicultural education, partly to alleviate the alleged alienation of minority children from the educational process, partly to build up their self-esteem and cultural self-confidence, and partly to educate majority children into minority cultures hoping thereby to improve inter-cultural understanding. The Swann Report, suggestively entitled 'Education for All' and published in 1984, provided a coherent defence of this view, only to find itself attacked by the conservative press and disowned by the Conservative government.

Although the bifurcationists and the assimilationists differed in important respects, they also shared much in common. The former, too, regarded British political culture as given and expected the ethnic minorities to assimilate into it. Politically there was therefore little significant difference between the two groups. Since liberals relied on education to assimilate the minorities, the political values did not remain confined to the public realm and had wider assimilationist consequences. Even in many liberal schools minority children were discouraged from speaking their languages lest that should impede their acquisition of English; their social and cultural practices, systems of marriage, dress and food were mocked or treated as strange and odd; their religions were judged defective; and their alleged lack of autonomy and sexism were constant targets of attack. Some schools did celebrate minority religious festivals, music, arts, etc., but the latter were often exoticised or treated as a 'bit of fun'. Others went further and included minority languages, history and literature in their curriculum, introduced bilingual education, challenged traditional textbooks, developed innovative multicultural courses and new ways of teaching them, and so on. Although these were commendable experiments and created a fairly strong multi-cultural ethos, even they did little to question the Anglocentric core and the Eurocentric orientation of the prevailing curriculum, and lacked a critical, radical and transformative thrust. Multiculturalists were also anxious not to appear too political, and avoided tackling the racist strand in the dominant culture. Unlike the United States multiculturalism and anti-racism in Britain therefore went their separate ways to the detriment of both, the former increasingly becoming narrowly culturalist and the latter blatantly partisan and dogmatic.

IX

The differences and similarities between the assimilationist and bifurca-tionist models were dramatically highlighted in their reactions to Muslim protests against the publication of *The Satanic Verses*.[9] The assimilationists accused Muslims of 'disloyalty' to and lack of 'love' for Britain, the former because they had shown greater respect for Khomeini than for the British law, the latter because they showed no concern for the good name of Britain and the views and feelings of their fellow-citizens.[10] Many were just as harsh on Rushdie, accusing him of such things as 'bad manners', 'poor judge-ment', 'provocative utterances' that violated British norms of decency, jeopardising the country's vital trade interests, and 'hatred' of Britain.[11] In their view he was just as poorly assimilated into the British national culture and just as alien as his largely illiterate fellow-religionists. For the assimilationists the Rushdie affair showed that the multicultural experiment had failed, that its liberal progenitors had shown poor judgement and done much harm to the country, and that a vigorous assimilationist programme which they had presciently pressed for years was now a national priority.

Like the conservative assimilationists, liberals too were highly critical of Muslims. However they accused them not of disloyalty and lack of love for the country but of violating such basic British values as free speech, respect for the law, tolerance, democracy and secularism. In the liberal view the Muslim violation was trebly disturbing: first, because the values were central to British political identity; second, because they had inspired the very anti-discrimination measures that had done much to improve Muslim lives; and third, because liberals had for years fought the white society's intolerance of its ethnic minorities only to find themselves now confronted with the latter's own intolerance of one of them.

Not surprisingly they heard in British Muslim protests echoes of Iranian fundamentalism, and formulated the central issue not in terms of law and order or intra-ethnic or intra-diasporic conflict but as a battle between free speech and fundamentalism. Like the conservative assimilationists, many liberals attacked not only the protesting Muslims, or even all British Muslims, but all Muslims everywhere and even Islam itself. Roy Jenkins lamented that 'we might have been more cautious about allowing the creation in the 1950s [sic] of a substantial Muslim community here', and even reached the bizarre conclusion that the whole event had strengthened 'my reluctance to have Turkey in the European community'.[12] Fay Weldon, a liberal with a leftist past, became an instant expert on the *Koran* and unfavourably compared the 'loving' God of the Bible with the 'blood thirsty' Allah. While attacking Muslims, liberals, unlike the conservatives, rightly felt protective about Rushdie. And though a few questioned his judgement, most praised him for his courageous exploration of a great theme even at the risk of incurring the wrath of his own community.

Liberals wondered why even after three decades Muslims had not integrated into British political culture, and whether their model of integration needed revision. Some such as Fay Weldon concluded that the model had failed, and switched their loyalty to the assimilationist model.[13] Some others saw nothing wrong with it and decided to press on with renewed vigour. A small minority of liberals thought that although their model had not completely failed, it needed to be revised along pluralist lines.[14] In their view Muslim protests were provoked by, among other things, a deep sense of cultural insecurity and even moral panic generated by years of assimilationist and integrationist pressures. They could not help noticing that the Rushdie affair had broken out during the heyday of the New Right, and at a time when the Thatcher government had passed a law stressing the importance of religious teaching especially Christianity in British schools. Pluralist liberals argued that a greater public appreciation and support of minority cultures than hitherto was therefore necessary to create a climate in which they felt confident and secure enough to take a relaxed view of their identity. In their view the British national identity should emphasise its multicultural character, national symbols and ceremonies should be broadened to include minority inputs, the school curriculum should make a greater space for minority cultures, history and religions, and the country should more willingly accept and cherish its diversity.

Like the race riots of 1958 and 1981 and Powell's speech of 1968, the Rushdie affair represented an important landmark in the history of race relations in Britain, and had several important consequences of which four are relevant to our discussion. First, the public discourse on integration, which had so far centred on the assimilationist and bifurcationist models, was now broadened to include the pluralist model, hinted at before but not taken seriously. Second, hitherto the public debate on integration had largely been conducted among whites, the minorities largely seen as passive objects of integration. The Rushdie affair demonstrated that the minorities had their own ideas on how they wished to integrate, to what degree and in what areas, and that they wanted to be equal partners in the national debate on their future. Furthermore integration, which had hitherto been defined in terms of minority adjustment to British society, was now seen as a two-way process in which the majority culture too had to undergo changes. Third, the Rushdie affair called for a radical reconsideration of the dominant definition of race relations. As we saw, from the late 1950s onwards there was a national consensus that Britain had a racial problem and that it should aim at 'good race relations'. The Rushdie affair showed that Britain had an additional cultural problem, that the two problems overlapped and cut across each other, that the social reality was too complex to be conceptualised in racial terms, and that Britain needed new conceptual tools. Fourth, minorities cannot participate in the national debate on integration without developing a collective view of their own. So long as the traditional form of racism was the issue, they shared a broad consensus of which the Afro-Caribbeans were the most effective spokesmen. Now that religion and culture had entered the public arena, a new consensus was needed. Since it has not yet emerged, the minorities have not been able to develop either the coalition and strategy or the kind of national grassroots movement and leadership that existed until the mid-1970s.

IX

The British public debate on the integration of minorities remains dominated by three related but different models. The assimilationist model still holds sway, but it has lost some of its earlier zeal and self-confidence. The bifurcationist or integrationist model continues to enjoy liberal support, but it too displays self-doubt. The pluralist model has gained some popularity, but it both lacks a coherent and well-worked out philosophy and continues to arouse anxieties about Britain's political unity and social cohesion. It would seem that the undecided country has decided to keep all three models in play. Two examples illustrate the prevailing intellectual confusion. The pluralistically disposed Prince Charles wants the monarch to be the 'defender of faith' rather than of 'the faith' so that all religious minorities can feel publicly and equally affirmed and identify with the monarchy; conservative nationalists want to retain the established Anglican church as an integral part of national identity and expect it to give the country moral leadership; liberals want to disestablish the church altogether. Again, the pluralist body of public opinion wants schools to have multireligious assemblies, conservative nationalists want them to be predominantly Christian, whereas most liberals cannot see the point of them at all and believe that acts of worship should occur in places of worship and not in schools. Current British practices and public policies in many other areas display a similar depth of ambivalence. It is difficult to say whether and when a new national consensus will emerge and in what form.[15]

NOTES

1 For Charles Taylor's *The Politics of Recognition* see Amy Gutmann (ed.)
   Multiculturalism and the 'Politics of Recognition', Princeton University Press,
   1992. See also Will Kymlicka, *Multicultural Citizenship: A Liberal Theory of
   Minority Rights*, Oxford University Press, 1995; David Miller, *On Nationality*,

Oxford University Press, 1995; Rainer Bauböck, *Transnational Citizenship*, London, Edward Elgar, 1994; and Jeff Spinner, *The Boundaries of Citizenship*, Baltimore, Johns Hopkins University Press, 1994.

2 Under the millet system Muslims, Christians, and Jews were self-governing units enjoying the right to impose their religious laws on their members, with the help of the state when necessary. The system lasted for nearly five centuries and was known for its humane toleration of group differences. Some of the Ottoman jurists and political theorists offered fascinating defences of the system and advanced ingenious theories of collective rights.

3 For a useful historical account, see Dilip Hiro, *Black British, White British: A History of Race Relations in Britain*, London, Grafton Books, 1991. See also my *The Experience of Black Minorities in Britain*, Block 3, Unit 10, Milton Keynes, The Open University Press, 1982.

4 'An introduction to the study of race relations in Britain', *Caribbean Studies*, vol. 11, 1971, p. 22.

5 Its spokesmen include Roger Scruton, Enoch Powell, John Casey, Peregrine Worsthorne, Maurice Cowling and, of course, Margaret Thatcher.

6 This was proposed by John Casey, 'One nation: the politics of race', *The Salisbury Review*, autumn 1992.

7 Some of its prominent advocates include the authors of *Colour and Citizenship*, Oxford: Oxford University Press, 1969; the Swann Report called *Education for All*, London: HMSO, 1985; Roy Jenkins, Michael Banton, Roy Hattersley, and others.

8 Although Jenkins was not happy with the term 'integration', it soon gained currency and was contrasted with assimilation in both popular and academic literature. The French and Canadian usages of the two terms are similar, but the American usage is somewhat different.

9 For a detailed account, see my 'The Rushdie affair and the British press: some salutary lessons', in Bhikhu Parekh (ed.) *Free Speech*, London: CRE, 1989.

10 Peregrine Worsthorne thought that a large number of minorities 'don't want to stop hating this country, let alone start loving it'. Cited in John Solomos, *Black Youth, Racism and the State*, Cambridge University Press, 1988, p. 229.

11 Peregrine Worsthorne in the *Sunday Telegraph*, 19 February 1989 and Hugh Trevor-Roper in the *Independent*, 10 June 1989. Trevor-Roper said that he 'would not shed a tear' if someone decided to 'waylay' Rushdie; indeed 'society would benefit and literature would not suffer'.

12 *Independent*, 4 March 1989.

13 Fay Weldon, *Sacred Cows*, Chatto, 1989. As she put it: 'Our attempt at multiculturalism has failed'.

14 See Melanie Phillips, *Guardian*, 3 March 1989 and Gerald Kaufman, *Guardian*, 1 March 1989.

15 I proposed to the Runnymede Trust in 1993 that it should set up a national commission to help develop a coherent national consensus, and prepared both the kinds of questions it should address and the language in which they should be framed. I am glad that after some delay in obtaining the funds, the Commission is now being set up under the able chairmanship of Sir John Burgh. A somewhat different kind of commission was set up in France a few years ago. It took televised evidence from important public figures and decisively influenced the national debate on French identity.

2 From legislation to integration

Twenty years of the Race Relations Act

Anthony Lester

Every democratic society should be concerned with promoting what Roy Jenkins memorably defined thirty years ago as a national goal: 'equal opportunity, accompanied by cultural diversity, in an atmosphere of mutual tolerance.' The twentieth anniversary of the Race Relations Act provides us with an opportunity to reflect upon the original strategy for the Act, and to examine how that strategy has, or has not been, implemented. It is an opportunity to look beyond the legislation itself, celebrating the great cultural and ethnic diversity of modern Britain, acknowledging the important contributions made by those from ethnic minorities to our society, and making some attempt to anticipate the future.

In 1975, a decade after the introduction of the first race relations statute in this country, I attempted to set out coherent principles for new legislation in the White Paper on Racial Discrimination.[1] Our proposals, which eventually formed the basis for the 1976 Act, were expressed to be based:

> On a clear recognition that the overwhelming majority of the coloured population is here to stay, that a substantial and increasing proportion of that population belongs to this country, and that the time has come for a determined effort by Government, by industry and unions, and by ordinary men and women to ensure fair and equal treatment for all our people, regardless of their race, colour or national origins.[2]

Twenty years since the Act entered into force these notions are as valid and pertinent as ever. I would hope that this anniversary will provide the necessary impetus for radical reforms to the Act and to the body of anti-discrimination legislation in the United Kingdom, to save it from falling into disrepute with those whom it was designed to benefit, and to take it forward into the twenty-first century.

According to the 1991 census, which included for the first time a question on ethnic group, the ethnic minority population of the United Kingdom is just over 3 million, or 5.5 per cent of the total population. The Government has consistently taken the view, in Europe and in its reports to the various international human rights monitoring bodies, that for the purposes of tackling racial inequality the 1976 Act is entirely adequate.[3] Yet there is no doubt that racial discrimination persists in the United Kingdom, despite the legislation.

Ethnic minority groups continue to live in substantially poorer housing conditions than the white population.[4] Unemployment among the Black African, Pakistani and Bangladeshi populations is more than three times the national average,[5] and they are over-represented in semi-skilled and unskilled manual work.[6] In education, although the Chinese, Asian and Indian populations tend to be better qualified than British-born whites, they are likely to be employed in inferior positions to British-born whites with similar qualifications.[7]

In the criminal justice system, ethnic minorities are over-represented in the prison population and under-represented in positions of responsibility.[8] There are no High Court judges of ethnic minority origin,[9] eleven Queen's Counsels out of 891[10] and only six MPs out of 651.[11] Ethnic minorities make up 3.9 per cent of civil service executive officers, but only 2.1 per cent of those employed at grades 7 and above.[12] Only 1.4 per cent of the armed forces is black, or Asian,[13] and while ethnic minorities make up 1.7 per cent of the police service, there are no ethnic minority officers above the rank of Chief Superintendent.[14]

Race relations in contemporary Britain are increasingly characterised by feelings of political disenfranchisement and social alienation among ethnic minorities and among the young in particular. There is a lack of confidence in the apparent fairness and impartiality of the justice system.[15] Public references to the 'nation', 'British heritage' and 'tradition' often seem little more than a code for xenophobia and the fires of racism have been stoked on occasion by an unsympathetic mainstream press.[16]

The ethnic minority population of Great Britain has grown rapidly since the end of the Second World War, and since the mid-1950s in particular. By the 1960s Britain had, for the first time, to find solutions to the new problems arising out of its transformation into a multiracial society, and successive Labour governments enacted the first statutory measures to combat race discrimination in this country.

Legislation alone cannot create good relations and change attitudes. But it can set clear standards of acceptable behaviour and provide redress for those who have suffered injustice at the hands of others.[17] If law can play a repressive role by sanctioning racial segregation and discrimination, as it did in Nazi Germany, the American South, Rhodesia and South Africa, it can operate with equal force in the opposite direction by declaring that equality of opportunity, regardless of race or colour, is to be pursued as a major social objective. It is a statement of public policy, by Parliament, intended to influence public opinion.

The unjust exclusion of people, solely on racial grounds, from the opportunities, facilities and services of modern life is at least as substantial an injustice as the breach of a contract, the defamation of someone's reputation, or a damaging act of negligence. It is a waste of their skills and talents. For centuries past this and every other country which has played a part in the mainstream of world events has benefited immensely from its immigrants. Britain's newcomers have rarely failed to make a positive contribution out of proportion to their numbers, in founding and rejuvenating business firms, in contributing to our national welfare and prosperity, and in enriching our universities and cultural centres.

The arrival, in December 1965, of a liberal and receptive Minister, Roy Jenkins, at the Home Office was of decisive importance in the making of the Race Relations Acts. The first Race Relations Act, which had come into force barely a month before, did not deal with the worst problems of racial discrimination, and its conciliation machinery lacked teeth. Despite scant support from his Government, the Labour Party and the trade unions for new legislation so soon after the 1965 Act, Jenkins decided from the outset that further legislation was needed and devised a careful strategy to win over the opposition.

Although the 1968 Act extended the scope of the law, and established a Community Relations Commission to complement the work of the Race Relations Board, it still contained unnecessary exceptions and there were serious deficiencies in its enforcement provisions. So when Labour came to power in 1974 I abandoned my practice at the Bar to help Roy Jenkins secure the enactment of effective legislation tackling race and sex discrimination.

Our aim, as stated in the White Paper, was to fashion a 'coherent and long-term strategy' to deal with the interlocking problems of immigration, cultural differences, racial disadvantage and discrimination. This was to be achieved, first, by strengthening the existing statute law, and second, by instituting a 'wide range of administrative and voluntary measures' to give practical effect to the objectives of the law. Legislation was intended to be but one part of what would eventually become a comprehensive strategy for tackling racial disadvantage.[18]

We adopted many of the novel and radical proposals of the Street Committee, whose report was published in October 1967.[19] On the basis of a survey of United States and Canadian legislation, Street proposed a broad statute, to be administered and enforced by a powerful anti-discrimination Board. The report also recommended that conditions should be inserted in government contracts requiring a wide range of affirmative duties on contractors.

The 1976 Act attempted to broaden the scope of the 1968 Act, removing loopholes and anomalies by redefining many of its provisions, and harmonising it, where possible, with the sex discrimination legislation. The meaning of discrimination was enlarged to include not only 'direct' but 'indirect' discrimination.[20] It made discrimination on grounds of nationality unlawful, overturning the *Ealing* case.[21] It extended the Act to cover acts of the Crown,[22] educational establishments and authorities,[23] trade unions[24] and certain clubs and associations.[25] It also permitted a limited number of 'positive actions' in favour of minority groups.[26]

The Act made one radical departure from the Street Report. Instead of channelling all complaints through the new Commission for Racial Equality as an exclusive enforcement agency, we decided to give individuals a direct right of access to legal redress, and to combine this with the strategic function of the Commission, which would have what we described as a major role in enforcing the law in the public interest.

Unfortunately, for a variety of reasons, our aims and ambitions in the White Paper have never been fully realised, although I continue to believe that they were, and remain, appropriate and attainable. After we left the Government in September 1976, our legislative work was not backed up by the strong administrative measures that we had planned. The new Commission for Racial Equality was under-resourced, and not always keen on using its considerable investigative and enforcement powers to tackle the really important but really different problems of discrimination. Subsequent interpretation of the Act by the courts has occasionally undermined its aims and objectives and has left it ill equipped to perform the role originally envisaged.[27]

The Race Relations Act 1976 established a body of law, which was broad in scope and was, as it still is, unique in Europe. It is, however, drafted too technically,[28] and contains unnecessary exceptions and limitations.[29] Most of the areas left unregulated by the Act occur in the governmental arena, 'precisely where the individual is most vulnerable'.[30]

Although sections 75(1) and (2) of the Act apply to its acts by or on behalf of the Crown and statutory bodies, in *ex parte Amin*[31] the House of Lords effectively neutered these provisions by interpreting them as applying only to acts resembling acts which might be done by a private person. Exclusively 'public' duties, such as the administration of justice,[32] police action in the course of their operational duties,[33] the operation of much of the criminal justice system[34] and immigration procedures[35] are therefore largely excluded from the ambit of the Act.

Section 75(5) of the Act permits the Crown, as employer, to discriminate on the basis of birth, nationality, descent or residence, and has provided scope for wide-ranging limitations on eligibility for the Civil and Diplomatic

Services.[36] The power of ministers to issue certificates on grounds of national security under section 69(2) of the Act has been used, in practice, to block the effective access of individuals complaining of unlawful discrimination in employment to industrial tribunals.[37]

Turning briefly to the enforcement of the Act, the force of our decision to give individuals a direct right of access to legal redress has been largely weakened by the unavailability of legal aid in industrial tribunal cases. The typical length and complexity of discrimination cases means that the under-represented applicant is at a severe disadvantage, increasing the importance of gaining assistance from the CRE.[38] So our aim of freeing individuals from dependence upon the enforcement body has not been achieved.

In relation to the vital strategic role which we had envisaged for the Commission, the Street Report had made telling criticism of the manner in which the North American anti-discrimination Commissions had exercised their powers, and at the time of drafting the 1976 Act, when the decision was taken to merge the Race Relations Board and the Community Relations Commission, I must say I disagreed. The Board was a strong, effective enforcement body, investigating individual cases involving alleged viola-tions of the law, and engaging in preventative work of an educational and advisory kind. The Commission was less focused and on the whole less effective in its role, and I was concerned lest the Board's high enforcement standards be diluted.

Although my worst fears have not been realised, the effectiveness of the Commission has certainly been hampered and its approach to enforcement has never been as strategic as was originally intended in the blueprint for the Race Relations Act. In the words of Lord Denning, then Master of the Rolls, in *Amari*,[39] the Commission 'have been caught up in a spider's web spun by Parliament from which there is little hope of their escaping. . . . The machinery is so elaborate and cumbersome it is grinding to a halt'.

From the beginning the CRE's formal investigations ran into difficulty, because of the complexity of the procedures contained in the Act[40] and the limitations subsequently imposed upon its powers by the courts. The combined effect of the *Prestige*,[41] and the *Hillington*[42] cases was to call into question a substantial number of investigations under way at the time and substantially to derail the Commission's strategy.

In the absence of a right to bring class actions on behalf of groups of victims, the role of formal investigations in the enforcement of the Act is particularly important, and the limitations placed upon their conduct by the judiciary all the more regrettable. Formal investigations, if used con-structively, are a more effective use of legal powers in certain areas than the numerous individual claims, which the Commission assists through tribunals.

The Commission's power to issue codes of practice is limited to the areas of employment and housing, and these codes remain legally unenforceable. It also has the power, following an investigation, to issue non-discrimination notices,[43] but it is unable to use these notices to prescribe appropriate changes in practice.

A key part of the strategy behind the 1976 Act was that an undertaking to comply with the provisions of the Act would be a standard condition of all Government contracts. As we recognised in the White Paper: 'the politics and attitudes of central and local government are of critical importance in themselves and in their potential influence on the country as a whole'. The Department of Employment was to monitor compliance with these clauses by requiring contractors to provide reasonable information about their employment practices and policies.

Yet in sharp contrast to the position it has taken in Northern Ireland,[44] the Government has made no attempt to introduce this type of positive monitoring.[45] Indeed current local government legislation[46] prevents local authorities and many other public authorities from asking for ethnic monitoring data relating to the workforces of proposed contractors.

In 1972 I expressed the hope that 'Parliament would not regard the present [Race Relations] statutes as the end of wisdom in the use of law to combat racial discrimination'. I would echo this sentiment today. I would like to see the law amended to remedy the weaknesses and defects I have just mentioned, in line with the suggestions of the CRE in its two Reviews of the Act. As in 1976, as a first step in fashioning an effective and ongoing strategy to deal with racial discrimination and disadvantage, we need to strengthen the legislation, to remove unnecessary exceptions and loopholes, to restore the powers of the CRE to the extent originally intended by Parliament, and to introduce comprehensive, compulsory contract compliance monitoring.

The 1975 White Paper recognised, however, that for there to be truly effective progress towards equality of opportunity, a wide range of administrative and voluntary measures was necessary to give practical effect to the legislation. Equality of opportunity will remain a pious declaration of hope so long as there is high unemployment, residential concentration in decaying neighbourhoods, gross deprivation in primary and secondary education and inadequate social benefits. Effectively tackling racial disadvantage requires a wider approach than the civil law allows.

Within the next twenty years 40 per cent of London's population will be from ethnic minorities. Within the United Kingdom there is an enormous variety of different communities. There are black, brown and white communities; Scots, Northern Irish and regional communities. There are African, Jamaican, Indian and Pakistani communities and Chinese and

Malaysian communities. There are cultural minority communities, Muslims and Sikhs. Every citizen of the United Kingdom is also a citizen of the European Union. Each of these communities is just one aspect of what it means to be 'British'.

The challenge for the next century will be to rethink the concept of 'Britishness', to find values that each of these communities, and the many I have not mentioned, can share, without losing their cultural, religious and ethnic diversity. William Butler Yeats once described the Irish as 'a community bound together by imaginative possessions'. Every country has its imaginative possessions. Regrettably the current 'imaginative possessions' of the British appear at times to be little more narrow racism and blind anti-European xenophobia. We need to look deeper, at the influences and experiences which have shaped and are currently shaping British culture. Indeed these are some of the issues which the Commission on the Future of a Multi-Ethnic Britain,[47] established by the Runnymede Trust, under the chairmanship of Sir John Burgh, will be examining in the near future.

We need to crack the glass ceiling, and make more use of the positive action sanctioned by the 1976 Act,[48] rather than engaging in positive discrimination; to give individuals the skills they need to succeed, instead of imposing paternalistic solutions upon communities; and to build individuals' confidence in the state, instead of viewing them as an unwelcome drain upon its resources.

The Government has a key role in this task. Political leaders should try to shape public opinion, celebrating the positive contributions of migrants and refugees. Race relations has become an issue dominated by political rhetoric and calculations of electoral advantage. Immigration measures such as the recent Asylum and Immigration Act,[49] and the statements and assertions in Parliament and in the press which marked its passage through Parliament, inevitably impair the endeavours of the Commission for Racial Equality to persuade employers, trade unions, local authorities and commercial undertakings to treat people equally, regardless of colour or race. They encourage profound insecurity and anxiety in minority communities in Britain.

The Government should see international human rights standards as guidelines to good practice, rather than as awkward obstacles which must be circumvented or overcome. Although the United Kingdom has ratified a number of international instruments relating, directly or indirectly, to racial discrimination,[50] in the absence of the domestic incorporation of any of these instruments international human rights standards have not played a critical role either in the detail of the drafting of domestic legislation on race discrimination, or in the subsequent interpretation and implementation of that legislation.

Although Article 26 of the International Covenant on Civil and Political Rights provides an independent and free-standing guarantee of equality, successive British Governments have refused to permit individuals to petition the Human Rights Committee about alleged breaches.[51] They also continue to oppose a right of individual petition to the Committee on the Elimination of All Forms of Racial Discrimination.[52] Neither Committee has the power to compel the United Kingdom to accept its recommendations and change domestic law to bring it into line with its often-damning conclusions.[53] Whereas the European Convention system provides an effective enforcement mechanism, the guarantee of equality without discrimination in Article 14 is narrowly confined to cases involving breaches of other Convention rights and freedoms.[54]

Under the incoherent constitutional arrangements of this country, it is unlawful to discriminate on religious grounds in Northern Ireland, but not in Great Britain;[55] it is unlawful to discriminate on grounds of sex throughout the United Kingdom. None of these acts have priority over other statutes, or acts authorised by other statutes, orders and ministerial authority.[56] This is a profoundly unsatisfactory state of affairs.

In the area of sex discrimination, European Community law has been able to come to the rescue of the scope and the substance of the Sex Discrimination and Equal Pay Acts.[57] Furthermore, following the decision of the European Court of Justice in the second *Marshall*[58] case, in which it held that national remedies must be sufficiently effective to deter employers from discriminating, the Government agreed to remove the upper limit on compensation for victims of race discrimination[59] in addition to victims of sex discrimination. Regrettably the same cross-fertilisation has not occurred in the other areas where the United Kingdom sex discrimination legislation has been found wanting by the European Court.

Community law has been able to come to the rescue of our sex discrimination legislation because the founders of the European Community included in the Rome Treaty the principle of equal pay for equal work without sex discrimination. They also included appropriate safeguards against discrimination on grounds of nationality. However, they were oblivious to the need to forbid discrimination on other invidious grounds, such as colour, race, religion, ethnic origins or sexual orientation. The Commission for Racial Equality has therefore not had the same opportunities as have the two Equal Opportunities Commissions to remedy the defects in the laws that they are charged to administer and enforce.

It is all too apparent from the recent warfare in Bosnia that racial discrimination and ethnic hatred are serious and increasing problems across Europe in the 1990s. It is unjust and socially harmful that, purely for historical reasons, gender discrimination and nationality discrimination should be well protected under Community law, but that, because of a lack of political will, other forms of invidious discrimination should be unprotected by Community law and only weakly protected by European Convention law.

There is a pressing need to introduce effective European legal safeguards and remedies by adding Article 26 of the International Covenant to the European Convention and to the Treaty of Rome. The current Inter-Governmental Conference provides the ideal opportunity for the latter. It is to be hoped that the governments of the member states, and the United Kingdom in particular,[60] will realise that some action must now follow the constant stream of non-binding measures and NGO initiatives on racism.[61]

The twenty-year anniversary of the Race Relations Act is not simply twenty years service for the Act. We stand at a convenient, as well as a very necessary stopping point from which to reflect upon the effectiveness of the body of anti-discrimination legislation in the United Kingdom, and, more widely, upon the most effective ways of protecting the weak in society.

In the other member states the principles of equality of treatment and of equal protection of the law are fundamental constitutional principles applied to all forms of unfairly discriminatory treatment. In this country these principles are inadequately secured by piecemeal and fragmented pieces of legislation, accompanied by pathetically weak remedies. I would like to see a unified Code of rights and freedoms incorporated into our law, providing a general right to equality of treatment.

The Code would be administered by a powerful Human Rights Commission, with many of the powers and responsibilities of the current EOCs, the CRE and the Fair Employment Agency in Northern Ireland, but with stronger powers of enforcement and a more wide-ranging mandate for investigation. It would be more visible and, I believe, would ultimately command greater public support. The Commission could also advise a new Parliamentary Human Rights Committee, which would scrutinise current and future legislation for compliance with the Human Rights Code, and with international human rights standards. It would be an eagle eye on society's behalf, advising, educating and carrying out investigations where violations were suspected.

When I look back on more than thirty years of campaigning for race and gender equality, in voluntary groups such as the Campaign Against Racial Discrimination, in Opposition, in Government, in the Courts, and in Parliament, I recall a lecture given by Oliver Wendell Holmes, over a century ago, on 'The profession of the law'. Holmes observed with 'the sadness of conviction' that in law, as elsewhere, a man 'may wreak himself upon life, may drink the bitter cup of heroism, may wear his heart out after the unattainable'. That is the fate of those of us who labour in this area. We will never attain all that we seek, but it is our privilege and our duty to redouble our efforts now, in preparation for the next century.

NOTES

1 'Racial Discrimination', Cmnd 6234 (1975).

2 Ibid. at para 5.

3 Although the Government responded to the Commission's Second Review of the Race Relations Act, in 1992, none of the Commission's recommendations have been directly implemented. On the few occasions on which the Government has altered the scope of the Act in the past twenty years, it has done so in minor respects and in piecemeal fashion: see, for example, Local Government and Housing Act 1989 (s. 180); Courts and Legal Services Act 1990; Broadcasting Act 1990 (s. 38); Criminal Justice Act 1991 (s. 95).

4 Ibid. p. 21. Twenty per cent of the Bangladeshi population live in overcrowded conditions, compared with 0.4 per cent of the white population.

5 Ethnicity in the 1991 Census, Volume 2, 'The ethnic minority populations of Great Britain', Ceri Peach (ed.) 1996 (London: HMSO), p. 21.

6 Ibid. p. 22.

7 Ibid.

8 According to Home Office provisional figures for 1995, of the total number of British nationals in prison, 9.9 per cent of males were black and 3.2 per cent were Asian; 11.6 per cent of females were black and 2.8 per cent were Asian: *Race and the Criminal Justice System*, Home Office, March 1996, Appendix 2. Yet only 1.7 per cent of the police service, and 2 per cent of prison officers and governors were from ethnic minorities: ibid., Appendix 1.

9 Figures as at 1 December 1995, drawn from Annex 12 to the Lord Chancellor's Department memorandum to the House of Commons Home Affairs Committee on *Judicial Appointments Procedures* (1995–96 Session, HC Paper 52-II, *Minutes of Evidence and Appendices*, p. 161).

10 As at May 1995: *Race and the Criminal Justice System* 1995, Home Office, March 1996, Appendix 1.

11 Of the PPCs for the 1997 election, two of those standing for the Liberal Democrats, and one of those standing for the Conservatives were Afro-Caribbean. Labour had at least four black PPCs in winnable seats.

12 Report of the Advisory Panel on Equal Opportunities in the Senior Civil Service: Cabinet Office, September 1994, at p. 59.

13 Defence Statistics 1995, Fig. 2.16, published July 1995.

14 Fourth Periodic Report by the United Kingdom to the Human Rights Committee, October 1994, at para 451.

15 According to *Politics for All*, a survey by Amin and Richardson for the Runnymede Trust (1992), 75 per cent of black people, 48 per cent of white people and 44 per cent of Asians felt that the police treated people from ethnic minorities worse than they treated white people; 25 per cent of people stopped and searched by police in 1993/94 were from ethnic minorities (ethnic minorities make up 5.5 per cent of the population): Hansard HC Deb, 2 December 1994, col. 1468.

16 See generally Gordon, P. and Rosenberg, D., *The Press and Black People in Britain*, 1989.

17 In their first annual report, published in April 1967, the Race Relations Board summarised the role of legislation as follows:

    I   A law is an unequivocal declaration of public policy.

    II   A law gives support to those who do not wish to discriminate, but feel compelled to do so by social pressure.

    III A law gives protection and redress to minority groups.

    IV A law thus provides for the peaceful and orderly adjustment of grievances and the release of tensions.

    V   A law reduces prejudice by discouraging the behaviour in which prejudice finds expression.

18 '*Racial Discrimination*', Cmnd 6234 (1975), at paras 22–26.

19 H. Street, G. Howe and G. Bindman, Street Report on Anti-Discrimination Legislation (1967).

20 RRA 1976, s. 1(1)b.

21 RRA 1976, s. 3; cp. *Ealing London Borough Council v Race Relations Board* [1972] AC 342 (HL).

22 RRA 1976 ss. 75 and 76.

23 RRA 1976 ss. 17 and 18.

24 RRA 1976, s. 11.

25 RRA 1976, s. 25.

26 RRA 1976 ss. 35, 37 and 38.

27 For example, in *Commission for Racial Equality v Imperial Society of Teachers of Dancing* [1983] ICR 473, the Employment Appeal Tribunal found that a prior course of dealing had to exist between an instructor and an instructee before discriminatory instructions could be challenged.

28 Indirect discrimination was defined by Parliament in the technical language of income tax legislation. It is not therefore entirely the fault of the courts that they have interpreted that language in a technical and restrictive way, requiring nothing less than absolute requirements or conditions (see, for example, *Perera v Civil Service Commission* [1983] IRLR 166, and *Meer v Tower Hamlets London Borough Council* [1988] IRLR 399), and complex statistical comparisons of relevant pools of advantaged and disadvantaged groups, before finding that there is a prima facie case of indirect discrimination to be answered by proof of an objective justification (see, for example, Balcombe LJ in *Hampson v Department of Education* [1989] ICR 179 (CA) at 191). The fault lies more with the makers of the law than with the judges.

29 In the field of employment, for example, employers are not vicariously liable for the discriminatory acts of their employees if they 'take such steps as are reasonably practicable to prevent the employee from doing that act': RRA 1976, s. 32(3). On employers' liability for acts of discrimination committed during the course of employment, see generally *Raymondo Jones v Tower Boot Co Ltd* [1997] 2 All ER 406 and *Rahim and others v Wolverhampton and Dudley Breweries Limited* (unreported).

30 Second Review of the Race Relations Act (CRE: 1992), at para 30. For example, s. 41 exempts discriminatory acts done under statutory authority from the scope of the Act. In *R v Cleveland County Council, ex parte Commission for Racial Equality* (1992) 91 LGR 139; *The Times*, 28 October 1991; the Divisional Court found that a local authority which acted in a discriminatory manner in complying with its duty under s. 6 of the Education Act was protected by s. 41.

31 *R v Entry Clearance Officer, ex parte Amin* [1982] 2 AC 818 at 835 (HL).
32 E.g. the selection of juries: see *R v Ford* [1989] QB 868 (CA). The Runciman Royal Commission on Criminal Justice recently recommended that a right to be tried by multiracial jury be applied in exceptional cases: see Royal Commission on Criminal Justice: Report (London 1993), 133–4, paragraphs 62–64.
33 HL Deb. vol. 374, col. 525, 29 September 1976.
34 The Criminal Justice Act 1991, s. 1995, requires the Home Secretary annually to publish such information 'as he considers expedient for the purpose of . . . facilitating the performance by [persons engaged in the administration of criminal justice] of their duty to avoid discriminating against any persons on the ground of race or sex or any other improper ground' (Publications include *Gender and the Criminal Justice System*, 1992, and *Race and the Criminal Justice System* 1992, 1994 and 1995). The CRE has argued that this vague non-discrimination duty should be made more explicit, and backed by code-making powers together with proper ways of airing grievances: *Second Review of the Race Relations Act*, CRE, 1992, p. 31.
35 *R v Immigration Appeal Tribunal, ex parte Kassam* [1980] 2 All ER 330, *Ex parte Amin*, above.
36 Civil Service Order in Council 1991; Diplomatic Service Order 1991.
37 There is no longer an analogous power in relation to individuals alleging unlawful sex discrimination, as a result of *Johnston v Chief Constable of Royal Ulster Constabulary*, C-222/84 [1986] ECR 1663. Applications 20390/92 *Tinnelly and Others v United Kingdom* and 21322/93, *McElduff and Others v United Kingdom*, which concern a similar power under s. 42 of the Fair Employment Act 1989 in relation to complaints of religious discrimination, have recently been declared admissible by the European Commission of Human Rights.
38 Of the seventy-two cases successful before industrial tribunals in 1995, the Commission represented forty-one (57 per cent): CRE Annual Report 1995. The CRE has suggested that the low success rate of applicants in industrial tribunals is partly attributable to a lack of knowledge and expertise on the part of tribunal members, and has recommended the establishment of specialist tribunals: see its Second Review of the Race Relations Act (1992) p. 22.
39 *CRE v Amari Plastics* [1982] IRLR 252, at 255.
40 For example, 'discriminatory practices' occur where a person applies a requirement or condition that constitutes *indirect* discrimination, but there is no victim. Where the practice constitutes *direct* discrimination, the CRE is not empowered to bring proceedings. So where an employer would refuse to employ a black person, for example, but none apply for the job, he or she is immune from CRE proceedings.
41 *CRE v Prestige Group plc* [1984] 1 WLR 335.
42 *R v CRE, ex parte London Borough of Hillingdon* [1982] AC 779.
43 RRA 1976, s. 58.
44 Where ss. 38 to 43 of the 1989 Fair Employment Act place employers under an obligation to provide religious monitoring data, which has been tied to their eligibility for public contracts. They are also bound to carry out periodic reviews aimed at fair participation and to draw up affirmative action plans. The preface to the Government's White Paper, *Fair Employment in Northern Ireland* (Cm 380, 1988), states proudly that the measures contained therein 'use the Government's economic strength to support good practice'.

45 Despite the recommendations of the CRE: Second Annual Review of the Race Relations Act (1992), p. 41.

46 Local Government Act 1988.

47 The Trust has also established a Commission on Muslim Communities in Britain, under Professor Gordon Conway, to examine the concerns of British Muslims and the nature and the origin of anti-Islamic and anti-Muslim attitudes.

48 Which created a criminal offence of employing an undocumented worker, and removed the duty of local authorities to provide accommodation, housing assistance and child benefit to certain categories of immigrant.

49 Which created a criminal offence of employing an undocumented worker, and removed the duty of local authorities to provide accommodation, housing assistance and child benefit to certain categories of immigrant.

50 These include the European Convention for the Protection of Human Rights and Fundamental Freedoms (1950); the International Convention on the Elimination of All Forms of Racial Discrimination (1965) and the International Covenant on Civil and Political Rights (1966).

51 Under the Optional Protocol to the Covenant.

52 Under Article 14 of the Convention.

53 See, most recently, the HRC's comments on the United Kingdom's Fourth Periodic Report, CCPR/C/79/Add. 55, 27 July 1995;

54 Save where the discrimination is so serious that it can be described as 'degrading treatment' for the purposes of Article 3.

55 Although Gypsies (*Commission for Racial Equality v Dutton* [1989] 1 All ER 306 (CA), Sikhs (*Mandla v Dowell Lee* [1983] 2 AC 548 (HL) and Jews (*Seide v Gillette Industries Limited* [1980] IRLR 427 at 430) have been classified in UK courts as 'racial groups'. Rastafarians have been held not to constitute such a group: *Dawkins v Department of the Environment* [1993] IRLR 284.

56 See, for example, *R v Cleveland CC ex parte CRE* (1992) 91 LGR 139, where the Court of Appeal held that parental choice under the 1986 and 1988 Education Acts could be exercised in a discriminatory manner.

57 For example, the Court has held that the Equal Treatment Directive is directly effective as against public employers, effectively striking down the exception in the Sex Discrimination Act permitting sex discrimination in retirement ages: *Marshall v Southampton and South West Hampshire Area Health Authority (Teaching)* [1986] ECR 723, [1986] 1 CMLR 688. It has insisted upon effective access to justice in discrimination cases and the need to construe exception clauses narrowly: *Johnston v Chief Constable of the Royal Ulster Constabulary*, Case 222/84, [1986] ECR 1651, [1986] 1 CMLR 68. In Case C-127/92, *Enderby v Frenchay Health Authority* [1993] IRLR 591 it breathed new life into the concept of indirect discrimination.

58 *Marshall v Southampton and South West Hampshire Area Health Authority (no. 2)* [1993] 3 CMLR 293.

59 In the Race Relations (Remedies) Act 1994.

60 The Government's recent White Paper on the IGC states: 'As for questions of discrimination, the Government is proud of its national record, and convinced of the adequacy of the legal framework already in place. It believes that the problems of discrimination (particularly on such sensitive questions as race and religion) are best dealt with in this way, through national legislation', Cm 3181 at para. 57.

61 See, for example, the Starting Line initiative (Brussels: Churches' Committee for Migrants in Europe); the Final Report of the Consultative Commission on Racism and Xenophobia (The Khan Commission), 6906/1/95-Raxen 24, 23 May 1995 and the recent Commission Communication on racism, xenophobia, Islamophobia and anti-Semitism, and proposal for a Council decision designating 1997 as European Year against Racism [COM(95) 653 final].

3 Tackling racial discrimination

Peter Sanders

INTRODUCTION

In 1985, when he was still Chair of the Commission for Racial Equality, Peter Newsam called for 'a concerted effort to reduce the level of racial discrimination'. Having set out his programme of what needed to be done – a mixture of voluntary effort, contract compliance and stronger law enforcement – and having acknowledged the valuable progress made by many organisations and individuals, he concluded that 'the task of . . . providing equal opportunities for all citizens is certainly not beyond reach. What remains in question is the strength of society's commitment to bring it about.'[1] His words have even greater force today, when we have ten more years' experience of the workings of equal opportunity policies and anti-discrimination legislation.

Eliminating racial discrimination is a settled matter of public policy and, in this article, drawing mainly on the experience of the Commission for Racial Equality, I consider how best it can be achieved. To concentrate, as I do, on tackling discrimination is not to imply that legal and administrative responses are more important than political, social and economic developments. What is gained through reducing discrimination may sometimes be offset by what is lost through broader policy decisions. Efforts to reduce racial discrimination in rented housing, for example, may be offset by the shift in investment from the public sector, where great efforts have been made to ensure equal opportunity, to the private sector where discrimination is still rife. More generally, the lot of ethnic minorities in this country may be worsened by widening social divides and, as other chapters in this book make clear, anti-discrimination policies can be undermined by hostile rhetoric about welfare scroungers and bogus asylum seekers.

Although there can be endless discussion about the terms to be used in the debate, for the purposes of effective action against discrimination we have to begin with the definitions laid down in the Race Relations Act 1976.

Direct discrimination (though the term is not used as such in the Act) is defined as treating a person less favourably than others on racial grounds, i.e. on the grounds of colour, race, nationality, or ethnic or national origins. Indirect discrimination (though again the term does not appear in the Act) is defined as applying a requirement or condition which is such that the proportion of persons of a particular racial group who can comply with it is considerably smaller than the proportion of persons not of that racial group who can comply with it and which is not justifiable. Neither definition is satisfactory conceptually, if only because the use of the term *race* may be regarded as implying the acceptance of race as a meaningful objective category. More important, as Anthony Lester argues in the preceding chapter, the definition of indirect discrimination is much too 'technical' and has given rise to serious practical difficulties. The CRE has recommended a simpler and wider definition, but the Government has not yet made any substantive response. For the time being, therefore, we have to work with the terms as they stand.[2]

In general the Race Relations Act 1976 makes discrimination in the public domain unlawful but not discrimination in the private domain. It covers most of employment, housing, education and the provision of goods, facilities and services to the public, but not the ways in which individuals conduct their private lives. While private discrimination can be wounding and embittering, it does not strike directly at people's rights as citizens and it has never been seriously argued that it should be made unlawful. For the most part, the arguments for extending the scope of the Act do not relate to the boundary between public and private, but to the removal of certain exemptions within the public domain. The CRE has recommended that the definition of the provision of goods, facilities and services to the public should be extended to cover all areas of governmental and regulatory activity, whether central or local, such as acts in the course of immigration control, the prison and police services, and planning control; and that the Act should take precedence over all earlier legislation unless expressly provided for by statute. In effect the Government has rejected these recommendations, except that planning is now covered. Regardless of this outcome, however, it is obviously important that the administration of regulation and control should be free from racial discrimination. It is just as damaging, if not more so, for a policeman to discriminate when exercising his powers of stop and search or for a judge to discriminate when passing sentence as for an employer to discriminate when selecting an employee for promotion. Such actions may not be subject to law enforcement under the Race Relations Act, but they are a matter of serious public concern.

THE IMPORTANCE OF EQUAL OPPORTUNITY POLICIES

The surest way to reduce discrimination would be for all those in positions of management and control, whether employers, housing managers, principals of educational institutions, chief constables or others, to adopt, implement and monitor comprehensive equal opportunity policies. Such policies vary from one area to another, but certain broad principles apply throughout. There must be a declared statement to which everyone at the top of the organisation is committed. Every effort should be made to ensure that the policy is understood, accepted and supported by the entire workforce in the organisation. Everyone should be aware of his or her responsibilities under the policy, and, where necessary, training should be provided. Above all, wherever possible the implementation of the policy should be monitored, appropriate targets set, and action programmes formulated to achieve them.

Ethnic monitoring consists of far more than ethnic record keeping. It also involves analysing the information gained through these records to find out whether the organisation's targets are being met; if not, whether racial discrimination is occurring, taking into account all other relevant factors; and what action needs to be taken in order to meet the targets in future. In practice there are many degrees of ethnic monitoring. An employer, for example, may monitor recruitment, promotion and dismissal, but not disciplinary action. A housing association may monitor allocations to tenancies but not take account of the varying quality of its housing units. The more comprehensive the ethnic monitoring the better.

Some advance can be made without ethnic monitoring and the setting of targets. In any large organisation there will be people who respond to statements of policy and whose behaviour changes accordingly, and there will be members of ethnic minorities who can surmount the barriers of discrimination and prejudice. As Tessa Blackstone's chapter demonstrates, encouraging progress has been made in education,[3] an area in which ethnic monitoring is particularly difficult. In most areas, however, monitoring and targeting are essential if discrimination is to be either prevented or detected and if real progress is to be made towards equal opportunity. In a recent survey of the employment policies of local authorities, the CRE found that, while there was 'a weak but positive correlation' between equal opportunity practices generally and the participation ratios of ethnic minorities, there was 'a clearer correlation' when policies 'driven by equality targets' were considered.[4]

The arguments for ethnic monitoring and then targeting were first deployed in the context of employment. When, in the mid-1970s, the Race Relations Board began to advocate ethnic monitoring there was strong resistance from both employers and trade unions. It was only in 1983, when the CRE's Code of Practice was approved by Norman Tebbit as Secretary of State for Employment and by Parliament, that monitoring received the backing that it needed.

At that stage the setting of targets was still a bridge too far. It could be argued that it was inherent in the concept of under-representation of a particular ethnic group, which was one of the conditions for positive action, but this was not spelt out in the Code. The CRE began pressing for targeting in 1986 and, like the Race Relations Board before it, it ran into a storm of opposition, mainly because the setting of targets was often confused with the setting of quotas. Eventually it received public endorsement from Michael Howard when he was Employment Secretary in 1991. In the same year the census for the first time included an ethnic question.

In the end the Commission was fortunate. First, it was swimming with the managerial tide. Output measures and performance indicators were now the order of the day. Ethnic monitoring and target setting could be presented as a normal and consistent part of good management practice. In the words of one managing director, 'If you can't measure it you can't manage it'.[5] Second, it was putting forward its ideas at a time when selection procedures and criteria were becoming more formal. Finally, it added to the CRE's persuasiveness that the Code and targeting had been approved by Norman Tebbit and Michael Howard, two ministers who were not normally associated with bold advances in civil rights.

Once ethnic monitoring and target setting were accepted in employment there was no reason in principle why they should not be accepted in other areas as well. Over time they became pivotal in all the guidance issued by the CRE, and there was increasing, though not total, acceptance and approval by the various Government departments concerned. But the pace of change varied from one area to another, with employment and housing leading the way and other services following behind.

The uneven development of ethnic monitoring has been due partly to the comparative importance attached to different areas in the context of equal opportunity, but partly, as well, to questions of practicality. It is much easier to carry it out in employment and housing than, for example, in education, the provision of health services or certain aspects of the criminal justice system.

Broadly speaking, ethnic monitoring and targeting can be fully effective only if two conditions are met. First, there must be certain recorded decisions that can be examined and, in the case of large organisations at least, subjected to statistical analysis. Second, there should be clear criteria on which these decisions are made, so that the effect of any racial discrimination, direct or indirect, can be identified.

Employment lends itself particularly well to ethnic monitoring and target setting. There are recorded decisions such as recruitment, promotion and dismissal which can be examined and subjected to statistical analysis, and increasingly there are well defined criteria laid down on the basis of which these decisions are made.

Rented housing in the public sector, whether by local authorities or housing associations, also lends itself to effective monitoring and target setting. Again there are recorded decisions which can be subjected to statistical analysis, notably the allocation of tenants to property, and again there are clear procedures and well-defined criteria on the basis of which these decisions should be made.

Education, however, is more difficult, mainly because there are so few decisions comparable with selection in employment or the allocation of property in housing. For the most part the kind of discrimination that takes place consists of differences in treatment and expectation in the classroom, and these are impossible to measure in any simple and manageable way. The decisions that can best be monitored are exclusions from schools and various forms of selection – selection for particular schools (which is now being extended and is a potential source of increased discrimination), selection for bands, sets and streams within schools, selection for entry for examinations, and selection for higher and further education. In theory, examination results – the allocation of marks by examiners to candidates – could be treated as decisions of this sort but, in practice, because examiners are often unaware of candidates' names and ethnic origins, and because in some cases the answers to questions are so defined that they leave no scope for discretion in the marking, they are more useful as measures of achievement by the students (however inadequately some may believe they serve this purpose) than as indicators of possible racial discrimination by the examiners.

Some parts of the criminal justice system are also difficult to monitor. In order to establish what is happening each stage in the process needs to be carefully studied, from arrest and prosecution all the way through to conviction, sentencing and the operation of the parole system. Here I concentrate on two types of decision – cautioning and sentencing. In both cases there are recorded decisions which can be examined. In cautioning it is relatively easy to identify the criteria that are used, but in sentencing it is much more difficult.

There is evidence which suggests that Afro-Caribbeans are less likely than whites to be given the benefit of a caution. In deciding whether or not to give a caution the police use three main criteria – the seriousness of the offence, the offender's previous record, and the willingness of the offender to acknowledge that he or she has committed the offence. From the very limited research that has been done so far it seems that the first two criteria fail to explain the different cautioning rates between Afro-Caribbeans and whites, but that the willingness to admit the offence may be a crucial factor. It would clearly be possible to establish a model for ethnic monitoring in which the three 'non-ethnic' criteria were controlled for.[6]

In the most reliable research that has been conducted into custodial sentencing it was found that in the West Midlands Crown Courts during 1989 Afro-Caribbean men were 17 per cent more likely than white men to be given a custodial sentence when convicted. The criteria for custodial sentences were not set out formally like the criteria for selection in employment or for the allocation of public housing, and the research team had to devise a set of fifteen key variables which were most likely to lead to a custodial sentence, such as the use of violence, the number of previous convictions, and the vulnerability of the victim. When these variables were controlled for the gap was narrowed, but Afro-Caribbean men still had a 5–8 per cent greater chance of imprisonment. When the most serious cases and the least serious cases were omitted from the analysis, i.e. the cases in which a custodial sentence was almost inevitable and the cases in which it was extremely unlikely, the differences widened again, so that Afro-Caribbean men had a 13 per cent greater chance of imprisonment.[7]

This was a highly sophisticated research exercise. While it would be a relatively simple matter for the police to introduce the ethnic monitoring of cautioning as a matter of regular management, it would be more difficult for the judiciary to introduce the ethnic monitoring of custodial sentencing. It would, of course, be possible to collect the numbers of persons from different ethnic groups who were convicted and sentenced to prison, but the detailed analysis required to identify any discrimination that might be occurring would be so demanding that it could probably be done only on a selective basis.

The examples given do not exhaust all the variations and problems in ethnic monitoring, but they illustrate at least some of the most significant factors that determine its possibilities and limitations.

All the examples given are of large-scale operations. In one way it is easier for the managers of such operations to detect discrimination since the figures with which they are dealing are more likely to be statistically significant. On the other hand the managers of small organisations can have a much closer knowledge of what is happening, and people like small landlords, one-person accommodation agencies and independent publicans have only their own actions to consider.

In general, therefore, we can agree with Peter Newsam. Those in a position of management and control do have the capacity to reduce discrimination, even if in some areas it is more difficult than others. Yet when we look at the processes involved – at the policies and practices that have been adopted – it is clear that the concerted effort for which he called has not been concerted enough, and when we look at the outcomes of these processes it is clear that discrimination is still widespread and substantial.

THE USE OF EQUAL OPPORTUNITY POLICIES

In employment, where the action that needs to be taken has been clearly known for the longest time, the policies and practices of many employers still fall far short of what is needed to put an end to discrimination. In its 1975 White Paper, *Racial Discrimination*, the Government acknowledged that it had 'a special responsibility as an employer' and spelt out the steps that were needed to achieve equal opportunity in all Government departments. In the event, partly because of trade union reservations, the Government was very slow to introduce ethnic monitoring into the Civil Service, and it was only in 1985 that its practice conformed to the CRE's Code of Practice.

In the armed forces progress has been even slower. In 1987, in defiance of the Code, while agreeing to monitor applicants and recruits, the Ministry of Defence refused to monitor the treatment of serving officers. It was only in 1992, after a series of well-publicised cases of racial bullying and discrimination, that the Ministry agreed to extend monitoring to serving personnel.

Local authorities were among those who were quickest off the mark, partly, in some cases, because of their political commitment, and partly because they had a statutory duty under section 71 of the Act to promote equal opportunity. The GLC in particular set the lead, and in 1984 it could show that since it had introduced its equal opportunity policy three years earlier the number of its ethnic minority employees had risen by 27 per cent. More generally, however, progress was uneven. In 1995 the CRE published its report on a survey of the employment policies of forty-one local authorities. While about one in three had achieved a workforce that reflected the local ethnic minority working population (although this achievement was not reflected at more senior levels), about one in four could not even provide an analysis of their administrative, professional, technical and clerical employees by ethnic origin, and more than one-third were unable to do so by grade.[8]

In 1986, when the CRE carried out research into the reception of its Code of Practice, it found that the public sector had been more responsive than the private sector and that large firms were more likely to have taken action than small companies. In its 1995 report on 168 large companies, however, it found that 63 had either no equal opportunity policy at all or only a statement of policy, while 75 had action programmes and the rest had devolved responsibility to subsidiary companies. Of the 149 subsidiaries examined

122 had no policy or only a statement, and only 20 had action programmes. Although these figures were a great advance on what would have been found ten years before, they still fell a long way short of what was needed.[9]

On rented housing in the public sector there is less information to enable us to judge what progress has been made. While many local authorities have excellent policies and practices, Valerie Karn and Deborah Phillips describe their overall record as 'patchy' and, summarising the findings of a CRE investigation, they conclude that housing associations have done rather better, at least in England, mainly because of the Housing Corporation's regulatory framework.[10]

In education many Local Education Authorities and schools have been enthusiastically committed to equal opportunity policies, but, for the reasons already given, progress in ethnic monitoring has only recently been evident. In 1993, following the Commission's formal investigation into Hertfordshire LEA, which found indirect discrimination in school admissions practices, the Department for Education agreed that school admissions should be monitored, but rejected the recommendation that ethnic monitoring of applications should now be required. Similarly, while the Department recently completed a pilot study on exclusions from school, it has refused to extend this nationally. In the crucial area of selection for higher and further education, in 1991, following the publication of the CRE's report on the selection of medical students in St George's Hospital Medical School, the Universities Central Council on Admissions and the Polytechnics Central Admissions System decided to include an ethnic question in future application forms.

In the criminal justice system effective monitoring has only just started, and it was only in 1993 that the Lord Chancellor announced 'a co-ordinated system of ethnic monitoring across the criminal justice system ... to monitor systematically all stages between arrest and sentencing.'[11]

In many other service areas ethnic monitoring is now being introduced. In 1988, for example, the Department of Health agreed that there was a need for ethnic monitoring of compulsory admissions under the Mental Health Act, and in 1995 the National Health Service began to collect ethnic data on patient services and take-up. According to the Audit Commission's report on 1994/95 performance indicators, however, while just over half of local authorities had policies on equal opportunity in service provision their monitoring arrangements were inadequate in the great majority of cases.

CONTINUING LEVELS OF DISCRIMINATION

In view of all this it is not surprising that discrimination continues to be a significant barrier to equal opportunity. It is not easy, however, to estimate just how high this barrier is in each area, whether it has become lower over the past decade, and whether it is more of an obstacle for some ethnic groups than for others. To a certain extent these questions are addressed elsewhere in this book, but it will be seen that our evidence is incomplete and, in some crucial aspects, out of date.

Individual complaints are no indicator of levels of discrimination, since the number of people who complain is minute compared with the number who suffer discrimination, and the number of successful complaints is even less. In 1985 the Policy Studies Institute (PSI) concluded that 'at a conservative estimate' there were 'tens of thousands of acts of racial discrimination in job recruitment each year'.[12] In the same year the CRE received fewer than 200 applications for assistance in complaints relating to job recruitment.[13]

Levels of racial disadvantage are also an unreliable guide, since discrimination is only one of the factors involved. Differences in educational achievement, for example, may be due in part in some cases to differences in command of English, and the factors of class and gender constantly need to be taken into account. One of the most remarkable features of recent surveys – summarised in other chapters in this book – has been the differences emerging *between* ethnic minority groups. It is out of the question that these differences can be wholly explained by different levels of discrimination.

Nevertheless, while the facts of racial disadvantage cannot provide us with the answers about levels of discrimination, they can certainly raise questions and give cause for concern. While falling short as proof of discrimination, they can often point very clearly towards it. Conversely, and unfortunately theoretically, the disappearance of racial disadvantage would be a powerful indicator that racial discrimination had ceased to be a serious and widespread problem.

The surest evidence about levels of discrimination comes from testing and research. The most extensive tests in recent years have been those carried out by the PSI into job recruitment in 1984. These established that, when responding to a press advertisement of a vacancy, a white applicant was a third more likely to receive a positive response from the employer than an Asian or Afro-Caribbean applicant with similar qualifications and experience. Comparing these results with previous tests conducted in 1973/74, the PSI concluded that there was no evidence of a decrease in the extent of racial discrimination over the previous decade.[14] Unfortunately there has been no similar exercise by the PSI in the 1990s. In a much smaller testing exercise conducted in 1992, however, Nottingham and District Racial Equality Council found, according to their own analysis, that a white applicant's chance of being invited for an interview were twice as high as those of an Afro-Caribbean or an Asian applicant.[15]

The private rented sector of housing is also susceptible to testing and, in 1990, having used this method, the CRE was able to report that one accommodation agency in five was discriminating against the ethnic minority testers and one hotel in twenty.[16]

One of the most important pieces of recent research has already been referred to: the study by Roger Hood on behalf of the CRE of sentencing patterns in the crown courts of the West Midlands.[17] This was all the more striking because it identified and measured discrimination by members of the judiciary, a group of people trained over many years to confine their consideration to the pertinent facts of the case and to ignore such irrelevancies as the ethnic origins of the accused. Before that the two enquiries which had the greatest impact were the CRE's formal investigations into the selection of students at St George's Hospital Medical School, published in 1988, which showed that each year about sixty ethnic minority candidates were not invited for interview as a result of racial discrimination; and into housing allocation by the London Borough of Hackney, published in 1984, which showed massive discrimination against ethnic minority households. There was evidence from other research which showed that St George's and Hackney were not isolated instances,[18] but the more recent research by Tariq Modood and Michael Shiner into student admissions generally reveals little if any racial discrimination,[19] while the performance of local housing authorities has undoubtedly improved over the past decade.

In employment research and formal investigations, whether into recruitment on the new Beaumont Leys Shopping Centre in Leicester, the recruitment of chartered accountants, the employment of graduates, promotion to management in London Transport, employment patterns in the hotel industry, or admissions to articles by law firms, have all revealed ethnic minority disadvantage, in some cases clearly attributable to discrimination, and in almost every case accompanied by weaknesses in equal opportunity policies or no such policies at all.[20]

In spite of the gaps in our information, it is clear that, for all the progress that has been made, much more is needed than voluntary effort if discrimination is to be effectively eliminated. We must therefore look to contract compliance and law enforcement.

CONTRACT COMPLIANCE

Since 1969 all Government contracts have contained a standard clause requiring contractors to conform to the provisions of the race relations legislation currently in force relating to discrimination in employment and to take all reasonable steps to ensure that their employees and sub-contractors do the same. This in effect has been a dead letter, and in the

White Paper on Racial Discrimination which preceded the Race Relations Act 1976 the Government declared its intention 'that it should be a standard condition of Government contracts that the contractor will provide on request to the Department of Employment such information about its employment policies and practices as the Department may reasonably require'. Though contract compliance has been a powerful lever of change in the United States, and though it has been introduced in respect of religious discrimination in Northern Ireland, the Government has done nothing to fulfil this intention.

LAW ENFORCEMENT: INDIVIDUAL COMPLAINTS

Complaints are an essential avenue of redress for aggrieved individuals, but they do not provide the basis for a strategic attack on racial discrimination generally. It has already been noted that very few people complain and that fewer still complain successfully. Throughout the operation of the 1976 Act successful cases in any one year have rarely exceeded fifty, and within these figures non-employment cases have rarely reached double figures. In 1988, for example, there were three, in 1990 two.[21] Most complaints are very narrowly focused, few relate to indirect discrimination, and their incidence is inevitably random.

There is evidence which suggests that complaints on their own have little or no effect on a respondent's policy unless they are followed up by advice and assistance from the CRE.[22] This work, on a selective basis, has long been part of the CRE's strategy, but it places a heavy demand on its resources and it has not always been rigorously carried through. The CRE now claims some success, however, and clearly some complaints, like those against the armed forces, do help to change practices generally. Not surprisingly, most companies ascribe their adoption of equal opportunity policies to factors other than complaints.[23]

Because of the difficulties of proof, complainants have always needed strong legal support. In the United States the enactment of civil rights legislation was in response to a powerful civil rights movement, which was then poised and ready to help complainants. In the absence of such a movement in the United Kingdom most complainants turned, and still turn, to the CRE for assistance in bringing their cases. In the words of McCrudden, Smith and Brown, the CRE became 'the major source of fully competent free representation', and a 'twin track system' emerged with complainants who went to the CRE having a much better chance of success than complainants who did not.[24] The CRE has always endeavoured to stimulate the development of alternative sources of support, but only recently does it appear to have had any success.[25]

The CRE has also argued that legal aid should be available for complainants in the Industrial Tribunals. At first the Government rejected this argument, then altered its position in the context of its general review of legal aid policy, but now appears to have gone back to its original position.

Other changes recommended by the CRE, such as the establishment of a special Discrimination Division of the Industrial Tribunals to deal with all discrimination cases, whether employment or non-employment, have also been rejected by the Government. But one change, forced on it by a judgment of the European courts in a case of sex discrimination, has been the removal of the upper limit on awards that can be made under the Race Relations Act. This will boost settlements as well as awards, and will certainly add to the deterrent effect of the Act.

LAW ENFORCEMENT: FORMAL INVESTIGATIONS

It was because of the inadequacy of individual complaints as a basis for tackling discrimination that the 1968 Race Relations Act was replaced by the Act of 1976. Although the old Race Relations Board had the power to conduct investigations under section 17 of the 1968 Act, it could do so only when it had evidence to suspect discrimination. As in its work with complaints, it was essentially a responsive organisation. What was needed, it was argued, was an organisation with the power to conduct wide-ranging enquiries on a strategic basis into those organisations and areas where equal opportunity was most needed, regardless of whether or not it had received a complaint or allegation. The newly-created CRE was therefore given the power to conduct formal investigations for any purpose connected with its statutory duties and, if it found discrimination, to issue a non-discrimination notice requiring it to be stopped.

The CRE was determined to make full use of these powers and, within its first five years, it started forty-six investigations. The difficulties which it ran into have been described in detail by McCrudden, Smith and Brown[26] and by Anthony Lester in the preceding chapter of this book.[27] Very briefly, the CRE tried to do too much too quickly, and the effects of this were exacerbated by the delays and resistance of some respondents and by the extraordinary complexity of the law.

Even worse, because of the defective drafting of the law, the CRE's powers of investigation were severely cut back. At the outset it was thought that the CRE could conduct three types of investigation:

1 a general investigation;
2 an investigation into a named person, i.e. a specified organisation, without any suspicion of unlawful discrimination; and

3 an investigation into a named person where unlawful discrimination was
   suspected.

The first type of investigation amounted to little more than a research
exercise, since the CRE had no power to issue a non-discrimination notice
as a result of its findings. It could be valuable in exposing patterns of
discrimination, but it could not be described as law enforcement. It was
the second type of investigation that was regarded as the great breakthrough, since it gave the Commission power to conduct enquiries on a
strategic, not a responsive, basis, and it was this power that the courts
struck down. As a result the CRE had to rely on the third type of
investigation, which, except for the important additions of sub-poena
powers and the power to issue a non-discrimination notice, amounted to
no more than the section 17 investigations which were open to the old Race
Relations Board.

Although this curtailment of the CRE's powers was contrary to Parliament's intentions when the Act was passed, and although the Commission
has made a very strong case that these powers should be restored, the
Government has simply replied that it 'does not believe it would be right
to give the Commission power to investigate named persons where it has
no suspicion of wrongdoing'. As a result a named person investigation
cannot be the kind of 'audit' favoured by McCrudden, Smith and Brown –
'serious, routine, helpful, a little painful, ultimately backed up by the law,
but not carried out as a legal offensive' – but has to start on an accusatory
basis.[28]

The Government has accepted one major proposal in the CRE's review
of the Act: 'Where there is agreement between the Commission and a body
on specific practices to be adopted, the Commission should have the power
to accept legally-binding and enforceable undertakings by that body to adopt
these practices.' In this way the CRE will be able to cut through all the
complexities of formal investigations and the issue of non-discrimination
notices. This change, of course, will also make life more comfortable for
respondents, but even so the appropriate legislation has not yet been placed
before Parliament.

A NEW FRAMEWORK FOR TACKLING RACIAL DISCRIMINATION

At the core of the Commission's review of the Act was the proposed
introduction of a legal framework for tackling racial discrimination on the
same lines as the framework for tackling religious discrimination in
Northern Ireland.[29] Employers above a specified size would be required to

carry out ethnic monitoring, to make the results available to the public, and to submit them, if required, to the CRE. They would be under a duty, where appropriate, to draw up affirmative action programmes with specified goals, and the CRE, like the Fair Employment Commission in Northern Ireland, would have the power to issue directions. Moreover, the relevant Secretary of State would have the power to prescribe ethnic monitoring in housing, education and other service provisions.

The requirement to conduct ethnic monitoring and to set targets would not place an additional burden on employers, since it is no more than what they should be doing already. And the requirement to make this information available to the CRE would add no more than the labour and cost of printing and posting an extra copy of the relevant documents. More important, there can be no valid reason why the law against racial discrimination in the United Kingdom should be any weaker than the law against religious discrimination in Northern Ireland. The Government, however, has rejected this proposal, once again not meeting the Commission's arguments in any detail.

THE CRE'S PRESENT POLICY

The CRE's first review of the Act failed to elicit any written response from the Government. The Home Office had no wish to strengthen the Act, and even if it did, as Peter Newsam points out in the final chapter in this book, any attempt to do so would almost certainly have failed and might even have been counter-productive. The response to the second review was little more than a paper exercise to ensure that the Commission could not complain again that it had not received the courtesy of a reply.

There are three main themes which stand out in it. First, the present arrangements for dealing with racial discrimination are generally satisfactory and no major change in the law is needed. Second, voluntary action is nearly always preferable to law enforcement. Third, 'whenever possible, the Commission should adopt a conciliatory approach when promoting good equal opportunities'.

It is against this background that we need to consider the first three of the seven 'priority goals' spelt out by the CRE in its Annual Report for 1994.[30] The first goal in its list is that 'anyone who is seeking redress against racial discrimination should be able to get help in bringing a case'. This help may range from advice to full legal representation, and it may be provided by the CRE or by some other organisation. But the CRE is not fighting every case to the finish. In the same year as it announced its priority goals, 1994, the number of successful cases which it supported was twenty-one, the lowest for more than a decade. Settlements, however, amounted to

£513,347, compared with £146,463 in 1987, and in 1995 the CRE claimed as one of its major achievements that 'early intervention by Commission staff resulted in more settlements, and more cases being withdrawn'.[31] The CRE has been disappointed that because of the confidentiality of many settlements it has been unable to publicise them and so achieve a wider effect.

The CRE's second goal is 'to use our power to conduct formal investigations as a weapon of last resort; and to persuade more employers and organisations instead to enter into voluntary agreements to take action for equality'. In 1995 the CRE reported that it had now entered into several such agreements as an alternative to mounting formal investigations. So the CRE is now using named-person investigations mainly as a threat, to be held in reserve in case its promotional work is unsuccessful. As for general investigations, neither they nor research are referred to in the Commission's priorities. In view of the central role that they have played in exposing racial discrimination in the past and supporting the case for stronger legislation, this can only be regretted.

The third goal, 'tackling institutional discrimination', relates solely to promotional work. The CRE wants to capture people's 'hearts and minds' so that they do the right thing 'because *they* believe in it, not because the Commission says they should'.

In short, over the past twenty years, confronted by the Government's refusal to strengthen the law, the Commission has shifted away from law enforcement towards promotional work, and within law enforcement it has shifted away from formal investigations to complaints work and voluntary agreements. It is much closer to the old Race Relations Board and the old Community Relations Commission than anyone could possibly have imagined in 1976. The 'conciliatory approach' which was so derided then is now heavily relied on.

CONCLUSION

Circumstances have changed. Employers and others are much more open to equal opportunity arguments, and a primary reliance on voluntary action, backed up with the threat of a formal investigation and supported by individual complaints, stands a much better chance of success today than it would have done twenty years ago. Yet even within the present framework much more can be done through formal investigations and research. More radically, a new framework is needed along the lines laid down in the Commission's second review of the Act, incorporating both contract compliance and the Northern Ireland model. Until that is done we cannot claim that the challenge thrown out by Peter Newsam as Chair of the CRE in 1985 has been met. We know how to overcome racial discrimination. 'What remains in question is the strength of society's commitment to bring it about.'

NOTES

1 CRE, *Annual Report 1985*, p. 1.
2 See p. 32 above.
3 See p. 109 below.
4 CRE, *Local Authorities and Racial Equality: a Summary Report* (1995), pp. 22–23.
5 CRE, *Connections Information Sheet*, no. 6: March 1996, p. 8.
6 CRE, *Cautions v. Prosecutions: Ethnic Monitoring of Juveniles by Seven Police Forces* (1992).
7 Roger Hood, *Race and Sentencing: A Study in the Crown Court* (OUP, 1992).
8 CRE, *Local Authorities and Racial Equality: A Summary Report* (1995), p. 13.
9 CRE, *Large Companies and Racial Equality* (1995).
10 See p. 141 below.
11 CRE, *Annual Report 1993*, p. 29.
12 Colin Brown and Pat Gay, *Racial Discrimination: 17 Years after the Act* (PSI, London, 1985), p. 31.
13 CRE, *Annual Report 1985*, p. 12.
14 Brown and Gay, op. cit., p. 31.
15 Alan Simpson MP and John Stevenson, *Half a Chance, Still? Jobs, Discrimination and Young People in Nottingham* (Nottingham and District REC, 1994), pp. 15–16.
16 CRE, *Sorry It's Gone: Testing for Racial Discrimination in the Private Rented Sector* (1990).
17 See n. 7 above.
18 See, e.g., Nottingham and District Community Relations Council, *Stacking the Decks: A Study of Race, Inequality and Council Housing in Nottingham* (1981); Deborah Phillips, *What Price Equality? A Report on the Allocation of GLC Housing in Tower Hamlets* (GLC, 1986); CRE, *Race and Housing in Liverpool* (1984); CRE, *Homelessness and Discrimination* (1988); I.C. McManus and P. Richards, 'Admission to medical schools', *British Medical Journal* 1985: 290, pp. 319–20.
19 See p. 102 below.
20 CRE's formal investigation reports on Beaumont Leys (1985), Accountants (1987), Graduates (1987), London Transport (1990), and the Hotel Industry (1991); David Halpern, *Entry into the Legal Professions. The Law Student Cohort Study Years 1 and 2* (PSI, 1994); Michael Shiner and Tim Newburn, *Entry into the Legal Professions. The Law Student Cohort Study Year 3* (PSI, 1995).
21 See the table in the Commission's *Annual Report 1994*, p. 8, for cases assisted by the Commission.
22 McCrudden, Smith and Brown, *Racial Justice at Work: Enforcement of the Race Relations Act 1976 in Employment* (PSI, 1991), pp. 44, 256.
23 CRE, *Large Companies and Racial Equality* (1995), pp. 12–13.
24 McCrudden, Smith and Brown, op. cit., pp. 276–7.
25 CRE, *Annual Report 1994*, p. 8.

26 McCrudden, Smith and Brown, op. cit., pp. 48–77.
27 See p. 26 above.
28 McCrudden, Smith and Brown, op. cit., p. 268.
29 CRE, *Second Review of the Race Relations Act 1976* (1992), pp. 38–44.
30 CRE, *Annual Report 1994*, p. 5.
31 CRE, *Annual Report 1995*, p. 4.

4 Ethnic diversity and racial disadvantage in employment[1]

Tariq Modood

INTRODUCTION

The post-war migration to Britain from the Caribbean and the South Asian sub-continent, while based upon imperial ties, was very much driven by economic imperatives. The rebuilding of the war-shattered economy created a demand for labour that could not be satisfied by the British population alone. The demand was particularly acute in the National Health Service, in public transport and in many sectors of manufacturing; qualified and unqualified workers, especially young single men, were invited from the Caribbean and the sub-continent to fill the vacancies. Early studies of these migrants in the British economy show that, regardless of their social origins and qualification levels, Caribbean and Asian people were largely confined to low-paid manual work, and that racial discrimination in recruitment was widespread, even after being outlawed (Daniel, 1968; Smith, 1977). The PSI Third National Survey, undertaken in 1982 found that while some progress in relative job-levels and earnings among these non-white groups had occurred, they were disproportionately suffering from the high levels of unemployment, despite some groups participating in the burgeoning self-employment sector (Brown, 1984). Moreover, racial discrimination in the labour market seemed as prevalent if not as overt as before (Brown and Gay, 1985). The Labour Force Surveys of the late 1980s (Jones, 1993) and the 1991 Census (Ballard and Kalra, 1994) confirmed the trends of the early 1980s: the minorities were upwardly mobile, expanding in self-employment but had much higher levels of unemployment than whites. It was abundantly clear, however, that each of these conditions applied to some rather than all Caribbean and Asian ethnic groups (Modood, 1991). Economic differences between migrants have become much more pronounced and much better substantiated by statistical data than was the case at the time of the Third Survey.

In the 1970s and 1980s theorists sought to explain racial inequality; the

Fourth Survey makes clear that what needs to be explained is racial inequality *and* ethnic diversity. For, in so far as there is a fundamental divide in employment by ethnicity, it is not a black–white divide, but a divide between white, Chinese, African Asian and Indian men on the one hand, and Bangladeshi, Pakistani and Caribbean men on the other. There are difficulties in creating a single measure that encompasses both sexes, but if both sexes are taken into account, there seems to be a tripartite division. The Chinese and African Asians are in broad parity with whites; the Indians and Caribbeans are somewhat disadvantaged, and the Bangladeshis and Pakistanis are extremely disadvantaged.

THE FOURTH NATIONAL SURVEY OF ETHNIC MINORITIES

The Policy Studies Institute and its predecessor, PEP, have been conducting surveys charting the changing position of Britain's ethnic minorities about once a decade from the mid-1960s (Daniel, 1968; Smith, 1977; Brown, 1984). The latest in the series, the Fourth Survey, undertaken jointly with Social and Community Planning Research (SCPR), was in the field in 1994. Besides detailed coverage of employment, the survey included many other topics, such as housing, health, racial harassment and cultural identity (Modood *et al.*, 1997).

The survey was based on interviews of roughly about an hour in length, conducted by ethnically matched interviewers, and conducted in five South Asian languages and Chinese as well as English. Over five thousand persons were interviewed from the following six groups: Caribbeans, Indians, African Asians, Pakistanis, Bangladeshis and Chinese. Additionally, nearly three thousand white people were interviewed, in order to compare the circumstances of the minorities with that of the ethnic majority. Further details on all aspects of the survey are available in Modood *et al.*, 1997.

UPWARD MOBILITY AND RACIAL DISADVANTAGE

The findings of the Fourth Survey depict a pattern of inequality, but also of a divergence in the circumstances of the main minorities. Many aspects of this diversity are not new and, especially the radically differing economic-educational profiles of African Asians and Indians on the one hand and Pakistanis and Bangladeshis on the other, were apparent in the 1970s (Smith, 1977). They were somewhat obscured in the 1980s when attention was focused on the disproportionate impact of unemployment upon the ethnic minorities. This combined with a tendency to over-generalise from the condition of the worst-off groups to the minorities *as such*, led sociologists to continue to assert that the ethnic minorities were 'at the bottom of the occupational and income scale'(Anthias and Yuval-Davis, 1992: 62). This chapter will present the findings of the Fourth Survey on job-levels and earnings, and examine whether the differences between minorities are consistent over time and, if not, whether they are narrowing or widening. For example, are some groups experiencing more mobility across job levels than others?

Job levels: men

Table 4.1 presents male job levels as found in the 1982 and 1994 PSI surveys. For the sake of comparison with 1982 the self-employed are not included, even though the 1994 survey found that self-employment disproportionately contributed to the presence of the South Asians and the Chinese in the higher job categories. The table shows that the period 1982–1994 was one of structural change and that all groups, though in differing degrees, participated in the change. The main change is a movement from manual to non-manual work. In 1982 a fifth of white and African Asian male employees who were in work were in the top employment category, in 1994 it was over a quarter, though with whites overtaking the African Asians. The Caribbeans and Indians, starting from a much lower base have roughly doubled their representation in the top category of employees, but mobility for Pakistani employees has been more modest and may even have been proportionately downwards for Bangladeshis. There is no 1982 data for the Chinese but the 1994 survey confirms the Census records, that of the groups under discussion the Chinese are most represented in the top non-manual category.

For white men it seems that this upward movement has come from contraction in skilled manual and foremen work, whereas for the minorities junior and intermediate non-manual work has grown, and the proportions engaged in semi and unskilled manual work has declined. With the exception of the African Asians, in 1982 about four-fifths of employed South Asian and Caribbean men were in manual work, now it is about two-thirds. For the Caribbeans the loss is evenly spread across the manual categories, for the South Asians, especially the Indians, it is their presence in the semi-skilled jobs that has declined. The group whose employment profile has shifted most substantially in this period are Indian men. At the start of the 1980s they were preponderantly in manual work, like the Caribbeans, Pakistanis and Bangladeshis; however, while these three groups are still largely in manual work, the Indian profile is now much closer to that of the whites, African Asians and Chinese. As has been stated, the Caribbeans, Pakistanis and Bangladeshis, too, have experienced some movement up the occupational hierarchy but their overall position continues to be a disadvantaged one compared to the other groups.

Table 4.1 Job levels of male employees in 1982 and 1994 (per cent)

	White '82	White '94	Caribbean '82	Caribbean '94	Indian '82	Indian '94	African Asian '82	African Asian '94	Pakistani '82	Pakistani '94	Bangladeshi '82	Bangladeshi '94	Chinese '94
Professional/manager/employers	19	30	5	11	11	19	22	26	10	14	10	7	41
Other non-manual	23	21	10	20	13	28	21	31	8	18	7	22	26
Skilled manual and foremen	42	31	48	37	34	23	31	22	39	36	13	2	5
Semi-skilled manual	13	14	26	26	36	22	22	17	35	28	57	65	20
Unskilled manual	3	4	9	6	5	7	3	3	8	4	12	4	8
Non-manual	**42**	**51**	**15**	**31**	**24**	**47**	**43**	**57**	**18**	**32**	**17**	**29**	**67**
Manual	**58**	**49**	**85**	**69**	**75**	**52**	**56**	**42**	**82**	**68**	**82**	**71**	**33**

Source: Modood et al., 1997.

Table 4.2 Job levels of full-time female employees in 1982 and 1994 (per cent)

	White '82	White '94	Caribbean '82	Caribbean '94	Indian '82	Indian '94	African Asian '82	African Asian '94	Pakistani '94	Chinese '94
Professional/manager/employers	7	21	1	4	5	3	7	14	7	38
Intermediate and junior non-manual	55	58	52	76	35	61	52	66	60	55
Skilled manual and foremen	5	3	4	2	8	2	3	3	3	–
Semi-skilled manual	21	17	36	18	50	32	36	17	29	7
Unskilled manual	11	1	7	1	1	3	3	–	–	–
Non-manual	**62**	**79**	**53**	**80**	**40**	**64**	**59**	**80**	**67**	**93**
Manual	**37**	**21**	**47**	**21**	**59**	**37**	**42**	**20**	**32**	**7**

Source: Modood et al., 1997.

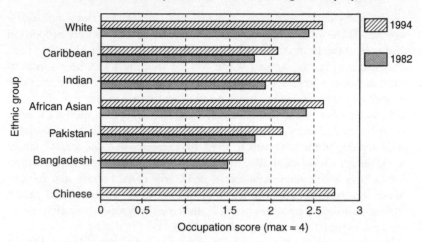

Figure 4.1 Relative improvement in male employees' job levels, 1982–94

Source: Modood *et al.*, 1997

Note: Based on an average job-levels score derived from the following scale:
4: Professional, managerial, employers
3: Other non-manual
2: Skilled, manual and foreman
1: Semi-skilled manual
0: Unskilled manual

A good way of capturing this lessening of racial disadvantage among male employees is by scoring the job levels on a common scale. One can then derive an average for each ethnic group for 1982 and 1994, and measure the degree of movement.[2] This is presented in Figure 4.1, from which it can be seen that all the minority groups made more relative improvement in this period than whites, though only African Asians have achieved parity with whites (the Chinese are best off in 1994 but there is no 1982 data for them).

It is important to bear in mind that in this period there was also growth in self-employment. It particularly benefited ethnic minority men; both within the non-manual and manual job levels self-employment marks an upward movement for ethnic minority men. This is particularly important, because of the importance of self-employment in the economic profile of certain groups: a third of all Chinese, Indian, African Asian and Pakistani men in paid work rely on self-employment (Modood *et al.*, 1997).

Job levels: women

The women's pattern of movement across job levels has some parallels with that of the men, especially in the growth of non-manual work, which was greater for women than men, and for some minorities more than white women (Table 4.2). While women continue to be in a smaller proportion than men in the professional/managerial/employer category, there has been a significant increase among white women in these jobs; the position of African Asian women seems to be slightly better than in 1982, but the other minority women are much more poorly represented in this category, and Indians possibly worse than a decade ago. The exception are the Chinese, who were not included in the 1982 survey, but were very much concentrated at the top end of the job levels in 1994. Intermediate and junior non-manual work has grown substantially since 1982 for all minority groups for whom data allows a comparative analysis, and Caribbeans, Indians and African Asians are now disproportionately in this category. Pakistani and Indian women full-time employees are still, however, disproportionately manual workers, especially at the semi-skilled level.[3]

If we measure the movements in women's occupational levels through scoring the job levels on a common scale, as we did for the men, we get the results displayed in Figure 4.2. This shows that Caribbean women have made the most progress, closely followed by white and African Asian women. The result is that white and African Asian women maintain the relatively advantaged position they had in 1982, but that Caribbean women

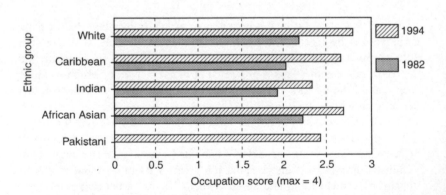

Figure 4.2 Relative improvement in female employees' job levels, 1982–94
Source: Modood *et al.*, 1997.

Note: Based on an average job-levels score derived from the following scale:
4: Professional, managerial, employers
3: Other non-manual
2: Skilled, manual and foreman
1: Semi-skilled manual
0: Unskilled manual

have almost caught up with them. Indian women have made less progress and are on the whole in a similar position to Pakistani women (the latter are much less likely to be in employment, and in fact were too few in 1982 for comparison with 1994). The position of Chinese women is much the best of all women.

Our findings about job-levels are consistent with the general trends of upward mobility, and of movement from manual into non-manual work, identified in successive Labour Force Surveys (Jones, 1993) as well as in the 1991 Census; though they are not as sanguine about the presence of Pakistani and Bangladeshi men, and ethnic minority women in general, in the top jobs category.[4] This upward movement in which the minorities share disproportionately even where they have not achieved parity comes out clearly in a recent study which examines the progress of ethnic minorities over a period of twenty-five years (Iganski and Payne, 1996). By comparing LFS data for 1966 with 1991 they are able to show that there has been a substantial decline in the differentials between whites and each of the main ethnic minority groups.

Earnings: men

An analysis of earnings tells a similar tale. Earnings data is a useful alternative way of looking at equality in employment, especially as job-levels analysis uses some very broad categories, and so there is always a risk that such analyses may miss the inequalities that may exist within each category. Earnings offer a more precise comparative measure, but suffers from their own limitations. People have a reluctance to state their earnings to researchers and may not give accurate answers. There was, in fact, quite a high refusal rate for the earnings questions in the Fourth Survey among South Asians. Nevertheless, given the Survey's large sample sizes, it offers one of the best, if not the best, sources of data on comparative earnings.[5] Table 4.3 compares the mean weekly earnings of full-time male employees of different ethnic and religious groups. It shows that the average for ethnic minority men was below that for white men, but there was in fact parity between whites, African Asians and Chinese, with the Caribbean men a bit behind, Indians even more so, and the Pakistanis and Bangladeshis a third or more below whites. The inclusion of religious groups in Table 4.3 allows one to see that the addition of Indian and African Asian Muslims to Pakistanis and Bangladeshis raises the Muslim mean weekly earnings from what it might otherwise be.

This comparative position of African Asians and Hindus compared to other South Asians is a striking new development which has not been properly recorded before. At the time of the PSI Second Survey of Racial

Table 4.3 Male employees' earnings

Mean weekly earnings	White	Caribbean	Indian	African Asian	Pakistani	Bangladeshi	Chinese	Hindu	Sikh	Muslim	All ethnic minorities
(£)*	336	306	287	335	227	191	(336)	338	249	223	296
Comparison to earnings of whites (%)		−9	−15	same	−32	−43	same	same	−26	−34	−12
Weighted count	541	255	154	152	76	42	72	162	84	140	751
Unweighted count	493	179	169	144	113	78	42	154	84	223	726

Source: Modood et al., 1997.
Base: Male full-time employees
* Means calculated from mid-points of 16 earnings bands.
Bracketed figures indicate cell size of less than 50.

Table 4.4 Female employees' earnings

Mean weekly earnings	White	Caribbean	Indian	African Asian	Pakistani/ Bangla-deshi	Chinese	Hindu	Sikh	Muslim	All ethnic minorities
(£)*	244	267	252	254	(181)	(287)	258	223	(221)	259
Comparison to earnings of whites (%)		+10	+3	+4	−26	−26	+5	−9	−9	+6
Weighted count	345	278	103	90	34	48	93	65	46	552
Unweighted count	337	206	94	72	36	28				

Source: Modood et al., 1997.
Base: Female full-time employees
* Means calculated from mid-points of 16 earnings bands.
Bracketed figures indicate cell size of less than 50.

Minorities in 1974, it was clear that the African Asians, who at the time were recent refugees from East Africa, were much better qualified, had a better facility in English and were more likely to be in non-manual work than Indians; correspondingly, Indians were in a much better position than the Pakistanis (Smith, 1977). On the other hand, perhaps partly because of their recent arrival in Britain, and perhaps because of their larger numbers in white-collar work in which overtime and shiftwork premiums were not available, their median gross male weekly earnings were 15 per cent below that of whites, and 10 per cent below Indians, and were in fact the lowest for all groups (Smith, 1977: 83). The PSI Third Survey in 1982 found that while average earnings for Asian men were nearly 15 per cent below those of white, there was little difference between Indians and African Asians, or between Hindus and Sikhs, both these pairs of Asian groups being much better off than Pakistanis and, especially, Bangladeshis (Brown, 1984: tables 109 and 114). The position now is that while the tripartite earnings differentials between whites, Indians and Pakistanis seem to be still in place as they have been for two decades, African Asian men have moved from the bottom to the top of these relativities. Two decades ago they were averaging less than the Pakistanis, a decade ago they were equalling Indians, and now they seem to have caught up with the whites. Similarly, a decade ago Hindu and Sikh men averaged the same earnings, but now Hindus have more than a quarter more than Sikhs. The earnings position of African Asians found here is, as the reader will appreciate, consistent with earlier findings about their job-levels. As a group they were always highly qualified and were largely in the professions, administration and business in East Africa. After the period of being political refugees and rebuilding their livelihoods and establishing themselves in Britain, they seem to have made considerable progress in re-creating their prosperity.

Earnings: women

The position of full-time women employees was very different to that of men's. Female weekly earnings were considerably lower than men's in all ethnic groups, but the biggest gender gap was among whites (Table 4.4). As a matter of fact, the average earnings of ethnic minority women were better than for white women, though it is unlikely that this extends to Pakistani or Bangladeshi women (the cell size is too small for certainty). This is an important finding which shows the limits of the idea of 'double discrimination', the view that besides the general disadvantage of women, non-white women suffer an additional inequality in comparison to white women (Bhavnani, 1994).[6] The highest average earnings were of Caribbean women (though possibly of Chinese women: the Chinese sample was rather small).

The differential between groups of women, however, was less than in the case of men. Interestingly, there was no difference in the averages for Indians and African Asians, and yet the earnings for Sikh women were significantly less than for Hindus.

Finally, as with job levels, so with earnings, it is important to bear in mind that some minority groups are disproportionately involved in self-employment, a category that has not been included in the analysis. In fact the survey found that while white male employees earned more than their self-employed counterparts, the reverse was true of ethnic minorities except African Asian men (Modood *et al.*, 1997: 121). The mean earnings for self-employed Indians and Chinese were over a fifth higher than those of whites, while for Pakistanis they were a fifth lower. Yet as Pakistani self-employed males earned more than employees, in general self-employment contributed to narrowing the earnings gap. As with paid employment, ethnic minority women in self-employment on average earned more than their white peers (though the sample sizes are relatively small).

ECONOMIC MOBILITY AND RACIAL DISADVANTAGE

There is then an overall trend of progress in the job levels and earnings of ethnic minorities and a narrowing of the differentials between the ethnic majority and the minorities. As all the ethnic minorities have higher, sometimes much higher, levels of participation in post-compulsory education (Modood *et al.*, 1997: 76–80), and increasing levels of admission into higher education (18–27-year-old Asians, excluding Bangladeshis, are more than twice as likely to be in higher education than their white peers), it is most likely that the minorities will continue to improve their relative position in the economy. The differentials between minorities may also become more pronounced as some groups consolidate the relatively advantaged profile they have begun to develop.

If today the ethnic minorities cannot be collectively described as being disproportionately confined to low-skill, low-paid work it may be because they are returning to their pre-migration occupational levels. It is sometimes asserted that migrants 'have tended to be from the poorest and most underprivileged groups of their countries of origin' (Anthias and Yuval-Davis, 1992: 77). This is almost certainly not the case. An analysis of 1972 data from the Nuffield Social Mobility Survey found that nearly a quarter of the non-white migrants had professional class origins, predominantly higher professional, which was twice the proportion of the native English; and over half had social origins in either the petty bourgeoisie or the farming classes (the figure for the English was 16 per cent) (Heath and Ridge, 1983).

The analysis shows that there was, however, a serious downward social mobility as people of professional origins failed to secure professional posts, and the petty bourgeoisie was 'proletarianised': children of self-employed traders, artisans and farmers met the demand for labour in British factories (Heath and Ridge, 1983). An earlier PSI study, too, found that the initial effect of migration was downward social mobility as the overwhelming majority of migrants could only get manual work, including persons with academic qualifications, even degrees, and who may have been in white-collar work before migration (Smith, 1977). The Fourth Survey suggests that among the first generation, Indian men were among the most qualified, and one might conjecture, therefore, suffered particularly from the racial bias operating in entry into non-manual work. The initial downward mobility was accepted because it still offered much higher earnings than in the countries of origin, but it is not surprising that those individuals who have been able to gradually resist the proletarian character ascribed to migrant labour and their families should have endeavoured to do so. It is, therefore, not inappropriate to see the above-average upward social mobility among some minorities as a process of reversal of the initial downward social mobility produced by migration and racial discrimination in the early years of settlement in Britain.

Yet this certainly has not developed to a point where there is an ethnic parity or where the concept of racial disadvantage is redundant. Table 4.5 sets out the extent of the employment disadvantages of ethnic minority men compared to white men. Six key indicators of advantage/disadvantage have been chosen, and for this analysis employees and self-employed are combined. The figures in Table 4.5 are derived from treating the position of whites as a baseline against which the minorities are given a score. Where the positions are the same, this is represented by a 1; where a minority group is under or over-represented relative to whites a figure is given showing the scale of the under- or over-representation. Table 4.5 shows that most, but not all, the groups are still disadvantaged, but not evenly so. There is in fact only one circumstance in which all the minorities are disadvantaged: all minorities are substantially under-represented in the most elite jobs, namely as employers and managers in large establishments. This could be said to be a 'glass-ceiling' that equally affects all non-white men.

Beyond that the differences between the minorities are as important as their position in relation to whites. For by the rest of the measures the Chinese are more advantaged than whites, and the African Asians are broadly similar to whites. The Indians are somewhat disadvantaged, but are closer to whites than to the remaining three minority groups who, despite any progress they may have made, continue to be significantly

Table 4.5 Employment disadvantage of ethnic minority men[1]

	Chinese	African Asian	Indian	Caribbean	Pakistani	Bangladeshi
Employers and managers in large establishments	0.5	0.3	0.5	0.5	0.3	0.01
Professionals, managers and employers	1.5	1.0	0.8	0.5	0.6	0.6
Supervisors	0.9	0.8	0.6	0.7	0.4	0.4
Earnings	1.0	1.0	0.9	0.9	0.7	0.6
Unemployment rates	0.6	0.9	1.3	2.1	2.5	2.8
Long-term unemployed[2]	–	(1.6)	3.1	5.9	7.7	7.7

Source: Modood *et al.*, 1997.

Table 4.6 Employment disadvantage of ethnic minority women[1]

	Chinese	African Asian	Indian	Caribbean	Pakistani	Bangladeshi
In paid work[3]	1.1	1.0	0.9	1.0	0.3	0.1
Professionals, managers and employers	1.9	0.8	0.7	0.3	0.8	—
Higher and intermediate non-manual	—	1.0	1.0	1.1	—	—
Supervisors	1.4	0.7	0.8	0.9	1.1	—
Earnings	1.1	0.8	0.6	1.1	0.6	—
Unemployed	0.7	1.3	1.3	2	4.3	4.4

Source: Modood *et al.*, 1997.

1 Disadvantage is expressed as a relation to whites, who are taken to represent 1. A figure below 1 gives, therefore, the degree of under-representation in that category compared with whites of the same sex. The figures include the self-employed.
2 Based on all women aged 16–60 not in retirement, full-time education or long-term illness.
3 Those unemployed for more than two years as a proportion of economically active in ethnic group, relative to white men.

disadvantaged. Caribbean men at some points are in a similar position or more advantaged than Indians but are significantly more disadvantaged in relation to job levels and unemployment. The Pakistanis are in all respects more disadvantaged than the Caribbeans except that, due to their much higher level of self-employment, which as we have seen yields on average low incomes, they score slightly higher for presence in the professional, managers and employers category. Finally, the Bangladeshis are as a group the most disadvantaged. Ethnic minority men fall therefore into two broad groups: those who are close to parity with whites (the Chinese, African Asians, Indians), and the others who are significantly disadvantaged. It is also possible to represent these six groups in three bands, with the Indians and Caribbeans occupying the middle band.

Table 4.6 offers a similar analysis of employment disadvantage for women. The key measures used in Table 4.6 are not the same as those used for men but reflect the fact that the low participation rate of some groups of women is an indicator and source of disadvantage. Moreover, too few women are managers and employers in large establishments to generate large enough sample sizes for analysis. Table 4.6 shows that the scale of differentials between women of different ethnic groups is much smaller than is the case for men, but otherwise the ethnic groups are stacked up in a similar order. There are, however, two distinctive features in the comparative circumstances of women. First, the low economic activity rates for Pakistani and Bangladeshi women create a division between these groups of women and all others which does not exist for men. It could though be said to have some parallel with the high levels of Pakistani and Bangladeshi male unemployment, which exists too among women from these groups, for what both Pakistani and Bangladeshi men and women have in common is very low levels of paid work, especially as employees. The second difference in employment disadvantage between men and women is that the position of Caribbean women relative to white and other women is much better than Caribbean men's. While Caribbean women are grossly under-represented in the top jobs category and have a high rate of unemployment, they are strongly represented in intermediate non-manual work and, as a result, have an above-average share of supervisory posts and above-average earnings.

If we combine the position of the sexes, the position of the minorities in employment relative to whites seems to fall into three bands:

1 disadvantage confined to top jobs in large organisations: the Chinese and African Asians;
2 relative disadvantage: the Indians and Caribbeans; and
3 severe disadvantage: the Pakistanis and Bangladeshis.

EXPLAINING DIVERSITY

Racial disadvantage, then, continues to be a fact even if it does not apply to all ethnic minority groups. This disadvantage is partly attributable to discrimination in employment. Controlled tests, whereby white and ethnic minority persons respond to advertised vacancies for which they are equally suitable, have been conducted since the 1960s and tend to reproduce the result that at least one-third of private employers discriminated against Caribbean applicants, Asian applicants or both (Daniel, 1968; Smith, 1977; Brown and Gay, 1985; Simpson and Stevenson, 1994). Discrimination is found not just in face-to-face encounters, or telephone calls, but has also been found in tests using written applications where it is clear from the applicant's name or biographical details that they are or are not white (Noon, 1993; Esmail and Everington, 1993). The Commission for Racial Equality continues every year to publish findings of direct or indirect discrimination in the practices of specific employers and sometimes whole professions or industries such as accountancy (CRE, 1987) or hotels (CRE, 1991). The number of complaints of racial discrimination made by individuals to the CRE and to industrial tribunals rises most years. The Fourth Survey found that the belief that some employers discriminate is held by 90 per cent of white people and three-quarters of minority ethnic persons. One in five of the minority ethnic respondents said they had been refused a job on racial grounds, nearly half of whom had had this experience at least once in the previous five years ((Modood *et al.*, 1997: 131).

Nevertheless, with a diversity in the structure of inequality which cannot be explained simply by differences in qualification levels, nor simply by racial bias, the question has been raised as how to 'explain the disparity between groups which share similar skin colour' (Robinson, 1990: 284). Robinson suggests three possible lines of inquiry exist. One approach 'stresses the differential incorporation or marginalisation of the groups and the impact that this might have upon the desire for social mobility in a society which is perceived as alien' (Robinson, 1990: 284). Malcolm Cross, for example, has distinguished between class exclusion and class segmentation as two different socially structured forms of racial inequality (Cross, 1994). While high levels of representation among the unemployed and low-pay is a symptom of class exclusion, class segmentation takes place when a group is allowed to enter the higher occupational classes, but is confined to an inferior sub-set of the higher occupations (Cross, 1994: 232). Cross believes that the Caribbeans are subject to class exclusion, while the racism against Asians within British employment practices has the effect of incorporation through segmentation of the existing class structure.

The distinction between class segmentation and class exclusion may be an important one, but Cross's application of it through an Asian–Caribbean dichotomy is not feasible. Pakistanis and Bangladeshis fit much better Cross's definition of the excluded as given above, especially as the high levels of Pakistani unemployment pre-date those of the Caribbeans and consisted of actual job-losses as the textile and related industries collapsed during the 1970s and early 1980s. In contrast, for the Caribbeans, un-employment rose more gradually as successive cohorts of school leavers found that the supply of jobs, especially for those without qualifications, had dried up. Hence, Robinson found that while 5 per cent of all workers who had a job in 1971 did not have one in 1981, 8 per cent of Caribbeans did not, but 19 per cent of Pakistanis did not (Robinson, 1990: 280). The reason why Cross thinks that the longer-term prospects of the Pakistanis and Bangladeshis are of class segmentation rather than exclusion is because, in contrast to the Caribbeans, economic marginalisation has not led to socio-political alienation. The Pakistanis and Bangladeshis are still committed to economic advancement; the young will acquire, he believes, qualifications that will enable them to compete for the kind of jobs that will be available. The impact of racism and economic disadvantage seems, however, to have blunted the motivation of a sizeable proportion of younger Caribbeans (Cross, 1994: chaps 8 and 10). While there is some truth in this contrast, the prediction that Pakistanis and Bangladeshis will develop a similar class profile to other South Asians grossly understates the current scale of the disadvantage of Pakistanis and Bangladeshis, and takes no account of the cultural differences between South Asians (Modood, Beishon and Virdee, 1994); nor of a political alienation, sometimes expressed in terms of a political Muslim identity, which is itself a product of, and further stimulates, anti-Muslim prejudice (Modood, 1990); nor of anxiety about a possible trend of criminalisation among young Pakistanis and Bangla-deshis, which in some ways parallels the experience of young Caribbean males (Nahdi, 1994).

In any case the position of young Caribbean men (and to some extent women) is itself paradoxical: among the highest rates of unqualified and unemployed and yet also among the highest average earnings (Modood *et al.*, 1977). It is possible that the high earnings averages are a product of the high unemployment, for by taking out of the earnings sample more potentially lower earners, the sample is biased compared to other groups in favour of higher earners, especially among manual workers. Yet it does not have this effect upon Pakistanis and Bangladeshis, who too have high rates of unemployment among 16–34 year olds. It is more likely that the paradoxical findings are pointing to an economic polarisation among young Caribbean men, who are to be disproportionately found both among the long-term unemployed and the middle band of earners. Indeed, in this respect the Caribbeans may be becoming more like the Pakistanis and Bangladeshis, rather than vice versa. For the aspect of these latter groups that probably suggests to Cross that they will progress like the other South Asians is the presence within them of a highly qualified professional and business class. Yet this class is not new among Pakistanis and Bangladeshis: it was picked up in the PSI Surveys of 1970s and 1980s (Smith, 1977; Brown, 1984), and what is remarkable is that it has hardly grown between 1982 and 1994 (see Table 4.1). Indeed, if the unemployed are added back into the figures on which the analysis is based, in contrast to other groups there is no growth at all among Pakistanis and Bangladeshis, in the proportion of men in the top jobs category.[7] At a time of general upward mobility for men, this would be a relative decline. The Fourth Survey suggests that in relation to qualifications of migrants, the internal polarity among those from the sub-continent, with a disproportionate number having degrees and a disproportionate number having no qualifications and many speaking little English, was in strong contrast to the relative homogeneity of the Caribbeans (Modood *et al.*, 1997). This tendency among Caribbeans of disproportionate grouping around the middle is also found in Robinson's longitudinal study of social mobility between 1971–81 (Robinson, 1990), as also in the findings about earnings in this chapter. The paradoxical statistics about young Caribbean men may be pointing to a post-migration, indeed, a relatively recent, internal polarisation among Caribbeans, while the class divisions among Pakistanis and Bangladeshis and the divisions between these two and the other South Asian groups, have deepened by the collapse of those industries that provided jobs to the Pakistanis in the 1970s, but in fact stretch back to pre-migration origins.

So while Cross is right not to want to conflate the disadvantaged profiles of Caribbeans with the disadvantaged profiles of Pakistanis and Bangladeshis, the differences in question cannot be captured by his differential use of exclusion and segmentation, and give no grounds for his Caribbean–Asian dichotomy, nor for projecting an optimistic view of upward social mobility for Pakistanis and Bangladeshis. If one wanted to explore these questions further, one could perhaps proceed by asking how differently post-industrial long-term unemployment would impact on excluded groups if one but not the other was composed of tightly-knit, hierarchically organised families and communities. Such a reformulation would not be a basis for reliable predictions (for there are too many other variables to take into account, especially in relation to changes in the economy), but it would bring one closer to raising some of the issues that lie behind Cross's discussion. It also leads us to a form of explanation identified by Robinson.

A second possible explanation for the disparity between minorities 'stresses the groups' histories prior to migration, and the traditions and resources they can therefore mobilise to gain mobility' (Robinson, 1990: 284). This is an approach that has been most developed to explain the phenomenon of immigrant self-employment, as found in many countries, especially in North America, and which is often critical in facilitating upward social mobility (Waldinger, Aldrich and Ward, 1990), and connects with a sociological tradition that arose through studies of European migration to the large American cities in the early part of this century (Lal, 1990). While the resources in question are of a complex sort and relate to culture, religion and gender, one simple measure is qualifications. There does seem to be a strong correlation between the qualifications of the first generation and the extent of current disadvantage depicted in tables 5 and 6 (Modood *et al.*, 1997). This lends particular support to the general view that the post-migration social mobility of groups consists of the re-creation of a comparable class profile the group had in the country of origin before migration. We have, of course, seen that similar qualifications do not yield similar occupational advantages for all groups, and that it is likely that some of the differences are explained by forms of direct and indirect discrimination.

This relates to the third possible explanation of disparities mentioned by Robinson: that different groups are stereotyped differently, perhaps influenced by the roles allotted to groups during British colonial rule (Robinson, 1990: 285). An important piece of research on middle managers' perceptions of minority workers and their ethnicity in the early 1980s found that stereotypes (not always negative) related to two groupings, Caribbeans and South Asians, and that radically different stereotypes were held of the two groups. The most common view expressed of Caribbean workers was that they were lazy, happy-go-lucky, or slow; while the most common view of Asians was that they were hard workers (Jenkins, 1986). It has been argued that similar antithetical images of the main non-white groups are in fact pervasive in commonsense and media representations (Bonnett, 1993). In the last decade or so, it has increasingly been argued that contemporary racism cannot be understood in terms of an undifferentiated colour-racism, but that additionally groups are racialised, and praised or condemned, on the basis of alleged cultural traits rather than any kind of biology (Barker, 1981; Gilroy, 1987; Cohen, 1988), and that groups such as South Asian Muslims suffer a distinctive and complex kind of racism (Modood, 1992 and 1996). The Fourth Survey found that nearly half of South Asians who complained of racial discrimination in recruitment believed that their religion was a factor in the discrimination; and so did a quarter of Caribbeans, further suggesting the complex nature of discrimination as perceived by those who believe they have direct experience of it (Modood *et al.*, 1997: 132–3). The survey also found that all groups now believe that the most prejudice is directed at Asians and/or Muslims (Modood *et al.*, 1997: 133–4).

It has to be said that it would be wrong to expect racial disadvantage, both its decline and its persistence, to be only or even primarily explained in terms of 'race', discrimination or ethnic differences. There is a general agreement that the most important fact is of economic restructuring. The changes in job levels for the minorities, no less than for the majority population, are above all a consequence of the continuing loss of jobs in manufacturing especially those that require low levels of skills, in favour of the service sector, which has seen a continuous growth in higher-level jobs and lower-level part-time work. It is this fundamental and continuing shift, together with the demographic shortages that have increased job opportunities for women and some minorities, that is the cause of the differential advantage and disadvantage experienced by the different minority groups, and is the context in which the more specific factors that have been discussed are played out.

CONCLUSION

Ethnic minorities in Britain can no longer be said 'to be at the bottom of the occupational and income scale'. For while this description is true of some minorities, others are less likely to 'at the bottom' than white people. The commonality between the ethnic minorities is that they are less likely than white people to be at the top, but some minorities are now well-represented near the top and in the middle. In general, it may be said, however, that the ethnic minorities are reversing the initial downward mobility produced by migration and racial discrimination in the early years of settlement in Britain. This is happening, despite the persistence of racial discrimination and the emergence of new forms of prejudice, such as that against Muslims. Nevertheless, while some groups are, therefore, re-establishing their pre-migration middle class profile, other minority groups or sub-groups are among the most marginal and disadvantaged people in Britain. The confluence of the continuing severe disadvantage of Pakistanis and Bangladeshis with the rise of an anti-Muslim prejudice marks one of the biggest challenges to racial egalitarians in Britain today. While the disadvantage of Pakistanis and Bangladeshis actually pre-dates the rise of anti-Muslim prejudice, the latter threatens to exacerbate the former, and to prevent the formation of goodwill required to act against the chronic disadvantage of Pakistanis and Bangladeshis.

NOTES

1 This chapter is based on work undertaken at the Policy Studies Institute on the Fourth National Survey of Ethnic Minorities. This large project was funded by the Joseph Rowntree Charitable Trust, the Department of Health, Department of Environment, Department for Education and Employment and the Economic and Social Research Council. I have benefited from the assistance of colleagues and the comments of an advisory group at all stages of the project. For full acknowledgements and details, see Modood *et al.*, 1997.

2 The scoring schemes used in Figures 4.1 and 4.2 inevitably have some degree of arbitrariness. Their main justification is that they reflect the differences in earnings (see Table 4.23, Modood *et al.*, 1997).

3 The low economic participation level and the high unemployment level of Pakistani women probably accounts for their having a jobs profile different from the men. Thus, for example, Pakistani men have relative to Indian men a much smaller proportion in non-manual work, whereas this is reversed in the case of Pakistani women relative to Indian women. This strongly suggests that economic participation by Pakistani women is more likely to take place in the non-manual sector; their proportionately lower presence in manual jobs was not simply the result of the higher rates of unemployment in manual work, for in fact, compared to other groups the unemployment rate for Pakistani women in non-manual work is much higher (Modood *et al.*, 1997: 94). The explanation probably is that Pakistani women who seek paid work outside the home are likely to have the language skills, educational qualifications and career aspirations to make them want non-manual work; and to the extent that they lack these, they are more likely to be keeping house than be in paid manual work outside the home. The former women are more likely to be from the minority of Pakistani families of urban origin.

4 Compared to our survey the 1991 Census reports that women of all ethnic minorities except the Chinese have a greater presence in the top jobs category, with the result that there is little difference between South Asian and white women. The Census found also that there was a smaller proportion of Caribbean than other women in the top category, but it shows them as being as well represented as white women, and much better than all other groups, among employers and managers in large establishments (3 per cent) (OPCS, 1993: table 16; Abbot and Tyler, 1995: table x). South Asian and Chinese women in contrast were more likely to be professional workers. The difference between our findings and the census may be that our survey includes more women from the 'hard to find' categories such as those with poor English, and as they are more likely to be in manual work (though they are even more likely to be economically inactive) their inclusion will depress the percentage of women of certain minorities in the top category.

5 The earnings question was asked with the use of a show card, with sixteen bands of earnings, each of which was labelled with a random letter of the alphabet. Respondents were asked to state the letter which labelled the band in which their gross weekly earnings fell. While there was a good response from some groups, there was a high refusal rate among South Asians, about a quarter of whom, excluding Bangladeshis, declined to indicate their earnings. The comparative earnings analyses offered here need to be read with this limitation in mind. The non-respondents in each ethnic group were spread across the job levels, though

the relatively few white and Chinese non-respondents were more likely to be non-manual employees, and South Asians' rate of refusal was higher when they chose to be interviewed in English only. It is possible, therefore, that the aggregate average earnings presented here are a little reduced as a consequence of the composition of the non-respondents.

6 It has been argued that the female full-time employees' earnings differentials in the analysis of the 1982 data were misleading, for minority women worked longer hours and were in fact not earning more than white women on an hourly pay comparison (Bruegel, 1989: 52; Bhavnani, 1994: 84). Maybe this was so in 1982, but the finding of the 1994 survey is that ethnic minority women in full-time work do fewer hours than whites; an hourly pay analysis would, therefore, widen the gap. In fact, the same applies to men.

7 The 1991 Census though does suggest growth.

REFERENCES

Abbott, P. and M. Tyler (1995) 'Ethnic variation in the female labour force: a research note', *British Journal of Sociology* 46(2), pp. 339–51.

Anthias, F. and N. Yuval-Davis (1992) *Racialised Boundaries: Race, Nation, Gender, Colour, Class and the Anti-Racist Struggle*, Routledge.

Ballard, R. and V. S. Kalra (1994) *The Ethnic Dimensions of the 1991 Census: A Preliminary Report*, Census Dissemination Unit, University of Manchester.

Barker, M. (1981) *The New Racism*, Junction Books.

Bhavnani, R. (1994) *Black Women in the Labour Market: A Research Review*, Equal Opportunities Commission.

Breugel, I. (1989) 'Sex and race in the labour market', *Feminist Review* 32, pp. 49–68.

Bonnett, A. (1993) *Radicalism, Anti-Racism and Representation*, Routledge.

Brown, C. (1984) *Black and White Britain. The Third PSI Survey*, Policy Studies Institute.

Brown, C. and P. Gay (1985) *Racial Discrimination: 17 Years After the Act*, Policy Studies Institute.

Cohen, P. (1988) 'The perversions of inheritance: studies in the making of multi-racist Britain' in Cohen, P. and Bains, H. S. (eds) *Multi-Racist Britain*, Macmillan.

Commission for Racial Equality (1987) *Chartered Accountancy Training Contracts: Report of a Formal Investigation into Ethnic Minority Recruitment*, London.

——(1991) 'Working in hotels: report of a formal investigation into recruitment and selection', London.

Cross, M. (1994) *Ethnic Pluralism and Racial Inequality*, University of Utrecht.

Daniel, W. W. (1968) *Racial Discrimination in England*, Penguin.

Esmail, A. and S. Everington (1993) 'Racial discrimination against doctors from ethnic minorities', *British Medical Journal*, 306, pp. 691–2, March.

Gilroy, P. (1987) *There Ain't No Black in the Union Jack*, Hutchinson.

Heath, A. and J. Ridge (1983) 'Social mobility of ethnic minorities', *Journal of Biosocial Science Supplement*, 8, pp. 169–84.

Iganski, P. and G. Payne (1996) 'Declining racial disadvantage in the British labour market', *Ethnic and Racial Studies* 19(1), Routledge.

Jenkins, R. (1986) *Racism in Recruitment*, Cambridge University Press.

Jones, T. (1993) *Britain's Ethnic Minorities*, Policy Studies Institute.

Lal, B. B. (1990) *The Romance of Culture in an Urban Civilisation*, Routledge.

Modood, T. (1990) 'British Asian Muslims and the Rushdie affair', *Political Quarterly* 61(2), pp. 143–60.

Modood, T. (1991) 'The Indian economic success: a challenge to some race relations assumptions', *Policy and Politics*, 19(3).

Modood, T. (1992) *Not Easy Being British: Colour, Culture and Citizenship*, Runnymede Trust and Trentham Books.

Modood, T. (1996) 'The changing context of "race" in Britain', *Patterns of Prejudice*, 30(1), January.

Modood, T., S. Beishon and S. Virdee (1994) *Changing Ethnic Identities*, Policy Studies Institute.

Modood, T., R. Berthoud, J. Lakey, J. Nazroo, P. Smith, S. Virdee and S. Beishon (1997) *Ethnic Minorities in Britain: Diversity and Disadvantage*, The Fourth National Survey of Ethnic Minorities, Policy Studies Institute.

Nahdi, F. (1994) 'Focus on crime and youth', *Q News* 3(3),15–22 April.

Noon, M. (1993) 'Racial discrimination in speculative applications: evidence from the UK's top one hundred firms', *Human Resource Management Journal* 3(4), pp. 35–47.

OPCS (1993) *1991 Census: Ethnic Group and Country of Birth (Great Britain)*.

Robinson, V. (1990) 'Roots to mobility: the social mobility of Britain's black population, 1971–87', *Ethnic and Racial Studies* 13(2), pp. 274–86, Routledge.

Simpson, A. and J. Stevenson (1994) *Half a Chance, Still? Jobs, Discrimination and Young People in Nottingham*, Nottingham and District Racial Equality Council.

Smith, D.J. (1977) *Racial Disadvantage in Britain*, Penguin.

Waldinger, R., H. Adrich, and R.Ward (1990) *Ethnic Entrepreneurs*, Sage.

5   The impact of immigration policy on race relations

Sarah Spencer

'This country has a proud record on good race relations. I am determined
to do everything that I can to maintain that record. Firm control of
immigration is vital to achieve that objective', Michael Howard, Conservative Home Secretary, told the House of Commons in December 1995.[1]
Defending the measures in his Asylum and Immigration Bill, the Home
Secretary's oft repeated assertion that firm immigration controls are
necessary for good race relations was no different from that used by his
Labour predecessor when the foundations of current immigration and race
relations policy were laid in the 1960s. 'Immigration', Roy Jenkins said,
'should not be so high as to create a widespread resistance to obstruct the
integration process',[2] while his colleague, Roy Hattersley, coined the
memorable phrase: 'Without integration, limitation is inexcusable; without
limitation, integration is impossible.'[3]

The bi-partisan consensus that firm immigration control is the prerequisite of good race relations rests on the assumption that the hostility
which some white people feel towards black and Asian people would be
exacerbated if they believed that their entry into the country was not
effectively controlled. The assurance that immigration controls *are* effective
is intended to reassure that section of public opinion that the number of
(black and Asian) immigrants will not rise more than is absolutely
necessary. Mr Howard's Bill, now law, was only the latest of a series of
measures since 1962 which were intended to convey that assurance. As this
maxim is the premise on which these legislative measures are based – rather
than, for instance, any rational assessment of the economic and social impact
of immigration, it is perhaps time to examine whether it is justified. Has
immigration policy made a positive contribution towards community
relations over the last thirty years – or not? Will the 1996 Asylum and
Immigration Act genuinely contribute to positive attitudes or 'cause untold
damage to race relations' as the Labour Opposition contended?[4]

PUBLIC OPINION

If immigration controls do have an influence on public opinion, they do not do so in a vacuum. Many factors may influence attitudes and one would not expect a direct cause-and-effect relationship. Nevertheless, it can be said with certainty that government has not succeeded in its objective of assuring the public that immigration is firmly controlled. The extent of hostility to black and Asian immigrants did decline during the 1980s but in 1994 a majority of people still thought that the United Kingdom should allow in fewer Asian people (60 per cent) and West Indians (54 per cent) although only a minority (30 per cent) were concerned about the number of settlers from Australia. Forty-four per cent thought that there should be restrictions on political refugees.[5] In 1991, almost one third of white people (29 per cent) thought that the ethnic minority population was over 10 million, about four times the actual figure; over half (52 per cent) thought that it was more than double the actual figure, and while 48 per cent of white people disagreed with the view that 'past immigration has enriched the quality of life in Britain', 30 per cent did agree.[6]

Could it be said that the policy has nevertheless contributed to positive attitudes towards resident members of minorities? The evidence again is not encouraging. A survey in May 1996 found that 59 per cent of black people and 39 per cent of Asians had experience of racism, over one-fifth of them experiencing physical rather than only verbal abuse. One-third of white, Asian and black people thought racism more of a problem now than it was five years ago. Of white people, 31 per cent admitted to being at least slightly prejudiced, 4 per cent (representing 1.5 million people) to being very prejudiced, and 28 per cent thought 'most' white people would mind if an Asian person moved in next door.[7] Although it has become less socially acceptable to express negative views about black and Asian people within the United Kingdom, fewer inhibitions constrain expression of such views about immigrants, foreigners and, in recent years, refugees.

It could be argued that attitudes are nevertheless more positive than they might have been had firm immigration controls not been introduced. It is certainly true that there was some anti-immigrant feeling prior to the 1962 Commonwealth Immigrants Act, when modern immigration controls began.[8] Nevertheless, researchers have questioned the extent to which politicians themselves contributed to that sentiment. Jim Rose, in his seminal study of the events of the time, suggested that the emphasis on the need for control 'helped to create the anxieties it was intended to calm, with the curious result that public concern was eventually prayed in aid of policies that had helped to create it', and Shamit Saggar that the new curbs on immigration 'did not so much follow popular sentiment as actually precede and create it'.[9]

While we cannot, therefore, deduce what attitudes would have been had immigration policy been different, we can say that it has not succeeded either in reassuring the public that immigration is under control, nor led to significantly more positive attitudes towards black and Asian people than existed thirty years ago.

FIRM CONTROL

The public's lack of confidence is not justified by the facts. The number of temporary *visitors* has increased, for business, tourism and to study, over one-third of them from the United States. The number permitted to settle in the United Kingdom, however, has declined significantly over the last two decades, from a peak of over 90,000 in 1972 to 55,500 in 1995. The origin base of immigration to settle has broadened during that time; only 45 per cent now come from the New Commonwealth. The majority of those who are accepted for settlement are the wives, husbands or children of those already settled here.

Statistics mask the complex picture on the ground. On the one hand, labour immigration continues to compensate for labour or skill shortages as it did when modern immigration began in the 1950s, although work permits are now almost entirely for professional and managerial staff. On the other hand, spouses and children in the Indian sub-continent who apply to exercise their right to come to the United Kingdom wait up to six months for their first interview. Forty-five per cent of husbands had their applications rejected in 1995, as did 25 per cent of wives and 45 per cent of children (even taking into account the outcome of successful appeals). Dame Elizabeth Anson, the Independent Monitor who reviews cases in which visitors are refused permission to come to the United Kingdom (against which there is no appeal) found in her 1996 report that too many applicants were being refused entry to visit relatives, attend weddings and funerals or assist with new babies:

> I did see a number of compassionate cases, people refused entry to visit dying or very ill parents or children and it was not apparent in the interview or the refusal that the entry clearance officer had considered the compassionate reasons.[10]

The number of people claiming asylum has risen dramatically from around 4,500 per annum in the mid-1980s to 44,000 in 1995. However, only a small percentage are granted refugee status – 5 per cent in 1995, some 1,300. A further 15 per cent (4,400) were given 'exceptional leave to remain'. Eighty per cent of those whose applications were considered, 21,300 people, were refused permission to stay.[11]

Public fears that immigration is out of control are thus not justified. It has become increasingly difficult to enter the United Kingdom and numbers have fallen significantly over the last twenty years. Nevertheless, the public has not been reassured.

FAILURE TO REASSURE

It is reasonable to suggest, given the current level of public opposition towards immigration, that a complete failure by government to control the entry of foreigners would lead to a rise in public concern. Yet it is also apparent that the ever-tightening controls since 1962 have failed to reassure some sections of the public or to lead to positive attitudes towards members of existing minorities. The reasons why immigration policy has failed in this, its primary objective, are not hard to discern.

Contradictory message

First, the message sent to the public by immigration policy, that particular kinds of foreigners would not be welcome members of British society, is in direct contradiction to the message relayed by government race relations policy – that existing members of minority communities in Britain should be accepted as equal members of society. Roy Hattersley, former Minister and Shadow Home Secretary, himself now recognises that the inherent contradiction in this argument makes it untenable:

> Good community relations are not encouraged by the promotion of the idea that the entry of one black immigrant to this country will be so damaging to the national interest that husbands must be separated from their wives, children denied the chance to look after their aged parents and sisters prevented from attending their brothers' weddings. It is measures like the Asylum and Immigration Bill – and the attendant speeches – which create the impression that we 'cannot afford to let them in'. And if we cannot afford to let them in, those of them who are here already must be doing harm.[12]

There are two related points here: that the *content* of policy, in seeking to keep out particular kinds of people, is damaging; and that the *presentation of policy*, the arguments and language used to justify it, are damaging in reinforcing the negative attitudes which the policy is intended to dispel.

Content

It has never been officially acknowledged that immigration control is primarily intended to exclude black and Asian people. Such overt discrimination would breach the United Kingdom's obligations under international human rights law. The term 'immigrant' in common parlance, however, has always been confined to people of colour so that politicians could appear to talk about immigrants in general while leaving no one in any doubt that it was black and Asian people to whom he or she was referring. Cabinet discussions in the 1950s, released under the thirty-year-rule, have revealed the more candid discussions which were then held in private.[13]

Home Office immigration statistics provide detailed figures on immigrants from the New Commonwealth (black and Asian) but not for those from other regions; internally no statistics are collected on former immigrants, only on ethnic minorities. The media is thus provided with some facts on black and Asian immigrants, and on subsequent generations, but not on those immigrants from the United States or Japan, for instance; facts which would provide a broader picture of the United Kingdom's immigrant population.

The way in which the 1962 and 1968 Commonwealth Immigrants Acts, the 1971 Immigration Act, 1981 Nationality Act and interspersed changes in the Immigration Rules were effectively designed to restrict the entry of black and Asian people is well documented, as is the discrimination in the way in which the law is administered and discretion exercised.[14] In order to protect that legislation from challenge under the race discrimination legislation, immigration law and its enforcement were and remain exempt from its provisions.

The 1996 Act formed part of wider provisions to limit access for asylum seekers, illegal immigrants and some temporary visitors to employment, welfare benefits and public services. It was accompanied by changes to social security provisions in February 1996 and administrative changes designed to encourage public service officials to check on individuals' eligibility to receive a particular service and to inform the immigration authorities of any suspicion that the individual might not be in the country lawfully. The content of the 1996 measures, and their presentation to the public, are used to illustrate the argument in this chapter.

Research has established that public awareness of the new proposals was resulting in inappropriate checks being made on lawful black and Asian residents even before the new provisions came into force.[15] Many critics, including the Secretary of State for Employment, had argued that Clause 8 of the Bill, introducing penalties on employers who employed illegal immigrants, would lead to discriminatory checks and the rejection of applicants from resident ethnic minorities, as has happened in the United States under similar legislation.[16]

There are two points at which discrimination may take place. The first is when the employer decides which applicants should be checked. If checks are not to be made on *all* new applicants, those who look as though they could be foreign may be selected. Such a choice will inevitably focus on 'non-white' applicants, including those born or legally resident in the United Kingdom.

The second point at which discrimination may take place is when the employer decides whom to employ. If the employer is not certain whether or not the individual is entitled to work, perhaps because the documentation does not make it clear, he or she may decide that it is too much trouble to make further investigations. If the job applicant is white, the employer may feel able to give them the benefit of the doubt and give them the job. If the applicant is not white, the employer may be less likely to take this risk and therefore reject their application.

Responding to the Government's Consultation Paper outlining these proposals, the Commission for Racial Equality therefore argued that the effect of the measure would be to justify and reinforce attitudes of hostility and suspicion towards members of ethnic and national minorities.[17]

Gerald Kaufman, a Manchester Labour MP, argued that such views were already being voiced:

> Our Asian and black constituents are being talked about as potential invaders of our country, and as potential bogus applicants for housing benefit and for social security benefit. They are being talked about as though they cannot hear what we are saying, and as separate, different and inferior.[18]

The United Nations Committee on the Elimination of Racial Discrimination, having examined the United Kingdom's report on its record on discrimination in March 1996, expressed its concern that most of those affected by the new legislation and regulations would be persons belonging to ethnic minorities.[19] One Conservative MP echoed this concern during the passage of the Bill:

> [W]hich people will be most affected? It will be those from Sri Lanka, Sierra Leone, Nigeria and Ghana. Although one has no intention of involving race, inevitably the perception will be that those are the people whose benefit will be withdrawn ... it will be perceived that they are causing the problem.[20]

An enquiry into the potential impact of the Bill and associated provisions, chaired by Sir Iain Glidewell, a recently retired Lord Justice of Appeal, concluded that there was a considerable body of evidence that the Bill would increase discrimination and damage race relations.[21] It had been suggested to the enquiry, by both the CRE and the Runnymede Trust, that the

Government had chosen to introduce the new measures because of perceived electoral advantage. They pointed to the leaked 'Maples Memorandum', a strategy paper written by the deputy chairman of the Conservative Party in 1994 based on market research among potential Conservative supporters. It had noted that such people had 'very right wing views on crime and immigration' and that the party's electoral strategy should therefore support, or appear to support, such views. The existence of such a strategy was indeed confirmed by Andrew Lansley, head of the Conservative Party Research Department, in September 1995: 'Immigration, an issue we raised success-fully in 1992 and again in the 1994 European election campaign, played particularly well in the tabloids and has more potential to hurt.'[22] The Opposition parties, the enquiry was told, were vulnerable in the face of such a strategy and this affected their willingness to pursue reasonable and ethical alternative policies.[23]

Presentation

It has been in the *presentation* of immigration policy that politicians have reinforced so forcefully the message that particular kinds of foreigners are unwelcome in the United Kingdom. The strategy of successive governments has not been to reassure the public that existing controls are adequate, nor to remind the public of the substantial economic and social contribution which immigrants have made. On the contrary, successive governments have accepted that public concern about immigration is legitimate, as Mrs Thatcher did in her famous intervention on Granada TV in 1978 when she spoke of 'The British people's "fear" of "being swamped" by people with "alien cultures"'.[24] An opinion poll taken after the broadcast revealed that the percentage of the public who thought that immigration was an 'urgent issue facing the country' rose from 9 per cent to 21 per cent.[25]

Once government decides to appease rather than assuage public concern, new measures have to be proposed to show that something is being done. Loopholes are identified, rule changes proposed, appeal rights abolished, time-limits shortened, defences removed. When new measures are an-nounced, examples must be given of the 'abuse' at which they are directed. Those 'abusing' the system, 'clogging up the appeals procedure' or 'taking advantage of our goodwill' are referred to in negative terms; new catch-phrases such as 'bogus refugee' are introduced to lead public opinion towards acceptance of the proposed controls.

This term, so frequently used during the passage of the 1996 Bill, merits examination. The Government argued that, as only 4–5 per cent of asylum seekers are granted refugee status, the vast majority of those who apply are bogus. However, to use the term 'bogus' – meaning, to use the

Oxford dictionary definition, that these are 'sham, fictitious or spurious' refugees – is to ignore the fact, well understood by government, that only those refugees who fall within the narrow UN definition of refugee can claim that official status. The UN definition covers only those who have a 'well-founded fear of being persecuted for reasons of race, religion, nationality, membership of a particular social group or political opinion'.[26] This definition *excludes* the vast majority of people who are recognised by the public to be genuine refugees – those fleeing civil war, famine, ecological disasters and so forth. While some of the 44,000 people who applied for asylum in the United Kingdom in 1995 were not refugees by any definition, to describe all of those who fall outside of the narrow UN definition as 'bogus' is plainly not justified.

The language used during the Parliamentary debates on the 1996 Bill illustrates the dramatic change in political discourse about refugees which has taken place since the number of asylum seekers rose in the late 1980s and government brought them within the scope of immigration legislation in 1993. Gone are the days when the primary objective of political leaders was to extol Britain's generosity in helping victims of persecution. The Home Secretary and Conservative MPs spoke of 'a great deal of abuse', of 'money being wasted on people who do not deserve it, do not need it and have no right to it', of 'wage rates for labouring jobs (being) undercut by bogus applicants who are working for a cheap price'; and, envisaging open racial strife if immigration were not cut back further, of 'several urban Yugoslavias . . . undreamt of and unimaginable barbarism'. The term 'bogus' was used perjoratively by Conservative and Labour MPs to describe asylum seekers no less than forty-seven times during the Second Reading debate.[27]

There can be no surprise that the language of political discourse was quickly adopted by the popular press and in turn by the public. The *Daily Express* article on the Bill in November 1995 began:

> Why asylum seekers are besieging Britain. Hundreds pour in each day for handouts but few are in genuine danger. Britain is now seen as a 'soft touch' for asylum seekers. They are arriving at the rate of 1,000 a week and join the queue of 70,000 already living here on benefits while their applications are considered.

It could, alternatively, have been argued that the rise in asylum seekers' dependence on benefits was due to the extensive delays in resolving their applications. At the end of October 1995, 60,000 applicants were awaiting a decision; of these 49,000 had already been waiting eleven months, 23,000 had been waiting since 1993 and 13,000 since 1991.[28]

Significantly, articles in the press also reiterated the line that firm immigration control is necessary to preserve good race relations. Bruce Anderson, writing about the Bill in *The Times* asserted:

Tough immigration laws are essential for good race relations. . . . There is no reason for racial tension in this country. We do have a small percentage of citizens of non-European stock, most of whom are doing very well. A minority do have and cause problems, but these are by no means insurmountable. The desirable process of helping them to assimilate would be made much harder if the fears of the white majority were to be aroused by uncontrolled immigration. It has been widely understood since the mid-1970s that good race relations depend on strict immigration control. The right of asylum is one of the last remaining means of undermining that control,[29]

while the *Daily Mail* argued 'it is in the best interests of all Britons that feelings should not be inflamed by an influx of illegal immigrants or sham asylum seekers'.[30]

Even children have taken on board the change in public attitudes towards asylum seekers. Lord Dubs, when Director of the Refugee Council, reported the experience of a primary teacher in Hillingdon who was approached by one of her 8-year-old pupils, a refugee from Ethiopia: 'What does the word bogus mean?' she asked. 'Why do you want to know?' the teacher replied, thinking that this was an unusual word for such a young child to know. 'Because it is what they are calling me in the playground' she said.

That this anecdote was not an isolated incident was confirmed in evidence to the Glidewell enquiry about children in Newham schools: 'I was horrified by the things I heard young children talking about. When we raised the issue of asylum seekers and refugees they talked about them in the context of being bogus – welfare scroungers, beggars, dirty and disgusting.'[31]

Thus, the more effectively government defended its proposals, the more effectively it reinforced the impression that immigrants and asylum seekers are a problem, and one which is not adequately controlled.

There were signs that the Prime Minister recognised this danger when he initially responded with interest to the proposal from the Leader of the Opposition that the Bill be referred to a Special Standing Committee of the House, a procedure which enables draft legislation to be considered in a more informed, less politically charged, forum. John Major was quoted as saying that, if he did decide to refer the Bill to a Special Standing Committee. 'it would be because I am concerned with good race relations' and that: 'I do not want to deal with that problem in a way that encourages our political opponents to raise the race issue . . . and unsettle people who do not deserve to be unsettled.'[32] The Prime Minister's judgement on this issue was, however, outweighed by opposition within his party, and the proposal rejected.[33]

National identity insecure

The first reason that immigration policy has not contributed to an improvement in attitudes towards members of minorities is that the message of immigration policy – that black and Asian people should be kept out of Britain where possible – blatantly contradicts the message of race relations policy, that they are welcome members of British society. Moreover, government strategy has not been to reassure the public that existing controls are adequate, but to stress the need for yet further controls, thus legitimising fears that existing controls have indeed not been sufficient. The popular press has echoed the Government's line and the myths, inflammatory language, as well as genuine concerns, have thus become the currency of public debate.

There is, however, a second and more fundamental reason why the public has failed to be reassured. Post-war immigration to Britain has, it appears, contributed to a national identity crisis.[34] Having lost its imperial, military, economic and sporting prowess, Britain is no longer confident of its role and cultural identity. Some British, or more accurately, English people, doubting whether their culture is resilient enough to survive perceived dilution by other cultures, feel threatened by immigrants who may have different customs and values and do not, in Lord Tebbit's terms, adopt England's cricket team as their own.

There has been a clear resistance to updating Britain's self-image to accommodate the multicultural reality of British society and its history. The notable absence, during the VE day celebrations in 1995, of a celebration of the major contribution made by Indian and Caribbean soldiers in Britain's armed forces during the Second World War was one visible example. Mrs Thatcher's description of Europe's shared history, during her Bruges speech in 1991, was another:

> From our perspective today surely what strikes us most is our common experience, for instance the story of how Europeans explored, colonised and – yes without apology – civilised much of the world – is an extraordinary tale of talent, skill and courage.[35]

Later in the speech she spoke of our 'common Christian heritage'. This is not a description of Europe's common experience in which Europe's minority communities can feel included. It is an approach which has been reflected in the shift in education policy away from a celebration of multiculturalism back towards a narrow focus on white British history, literature and Christian religious worship; and was encapsulated by the editor of *The Daily Telegraph* writing in *The Spectator* in 1993:

> We want foreigners as long as their foreignness is not overwhelming ... Britain is basically English speaking and Christian and if one starts to think it might become Urdu speaking and Muslim and Brown, one gets angry and frightened.[36]

Bhikhu Parekh explains that the notion of a *single* national identity is, however, untenable. Identity implies a distinct, homogenous, common culture, marked by common values, shared understandings and loyalties. The reality, in a society with class, gender and regional differences, is very different. Moreover, like individuals, a nation does not have one identity but many: 'an individual is a bearer of multiple, evolving and dialectically related identities. To attribute identity to a community of millions spread over vast expanses of space and time makes even less sense.'[37]

Nevertheless, the sense of national anxiety is real. It is an unease which has wider implications, not least in public attitudes towards the European Union. On that issue, as on immigration, the statements of political leaders have tended to fuel rather than assuage public anxiety.

The question for a future government must, therefore, surely be this: in what way should immigration policy and its presentation be changed in order to ensure that it does, *inter alia*, contribute to an improvement in public attitudes towards immigrants and members of resident minorities in future?

STRATEGY FOR REFORM

The fact that current immigration policy, and its presentation by government, are damaging race relations does not mean that all immigration controls should be withdrawn. Given the strong fears of immigration which now exist within sections of the public, such a move would provoke fierce opposition and be political suicide for any government. Moreover, there is a second objection to any such proposal.

Immigrants who settle in the United Kingdom must be entitled to the same civil, political, social and economic rights and benefits as other residents. To suggest otherwise would be to concede a future two-tier society of those who really belong, and those who do not. Employment is not available for all who need it and social and economic rights – to use the health service, to education, to welfare benefits or student grants – are expensive. If the United Kingdom were to remove immigration controls and allow unlimited entry, those resources would have to be shared out among a significantly larger population. The question is, therefore, what kind of immigration controls the United Kingdom should have, and how to ensure that their impact on race relations is a positive one.

Objectives

I have argued elsewhere, with others,[38] that immigration policy should be designed to achieve specific, stated objectives which should include, but not be restricted to, improving race relations. The preamble to the Canadian Immigration Act 1978 which sets out the objectives which the Act is intended to achieve, is a good model. Included in the objectives is the need to: 'enrich the cultural and social fabric of Canada; facilitate reunion between Canadians/permanent residents and their relatives abroad; foster the development of a strong and viable economy, and fulfil international legal obligations.'

Such objectives, defined as positive goals to be achieved, are far removed from the defensive, largely negative, tone of the United Kingdom's aims as set out in the Report of the Immigration and Nationality Department. These are to:

- allow genuine visitors and students to enter the United Kingdom;
- give effect to the 'free movement' provisions of European Union law;
- continue to admit the spouses and minor dependent children of those already settled in the United Kingdom;
- meet the United Kingdom's obligations towards refugees under international law, while reducing the scope and incentive for misusing asylum procedures;
- subject to the above, restrict severely the numbers coming to live permanently or to work in the United Kingdom;
- detect and remove those entering or remaining in the United Kingdom without authority; and
- maintain an effective and efficient system for dealing with applicants for citizenship.

The Government seeks to pursue this policy firmly and fairly and it is applied without regard to the race, colour or religion of the person seeking entry to the United Kingdom or applying for citizenship.[39]

The Government acknowledged in 1971 that: 'Immigration law in this country has developed mainly as a series of responses to, and attempts to regulate, particular pressures rather than as a positive means of achieving preconceived social or economic gains'[40] and no government since has seen fit to change this approach. If immigration policy is to have a positive impact on race relations it must do so.

Research and consultation

In order to identify the objectives appropriate for this country, government should encourage research on the social and economic impact of immigration, and on the impact of current controls, to provide an informed base for public debate and policy development. Many governments draw on such research in developing policy and to make and to justify policy decisions.

Whereas in countries as diverse as Australia and Germany, governments know the macro- and micro-level impact of immigration on the labour market, its effect on public expenditure or on the teacher–pupil ratio, such information is not available to British policy-makers. Home Office officials cannot advise the Home Secretary whether the deportation of the parent of a British child has an adverse effect on that child's life chances, whether current visa policy deters wealthy tourists from the Middle East or whether illegal immigrants are more likely to be working in the hotel and catering industry or in construction, because no research has been conducted to find out.

In Australia, the Bureau of Multi-cultural, Immigration and Population Research (BIMPR) was set up in 1989 after an official enquiry argued that the government needed research data in order to sell the rationale for immigration policy to an increasingly sceptical public.[41] Speaking at an IPPR seminar on the role of research in developing immigration and refugee policy in October 1995, the Deputy Director of the BIMPR, Lynne Williams, said:

> Immigration and the treatment of refugees are both extremely emotive issues. There exist a wide range of opinions often based on very little research or facts but rather on perception and feelings. What BIMPR, with its charter to 'raise the level of debate on immigration and population related issues' has tried to achieve is to reduce the emotionalism in the various immigration related debates. The most important contribution of research is that it has enabled consensus to be reached on many of these important emotive issues.[42]

The head of the Canadian government department responsible for similar research, Meyer Burstein, said:

> Research enables the government to give greater attention to educating the public by providing the facts. There is a consensus that research has improved the level of public debate. It has had an impact on decision-making and on the quality of decisions.[43]

Research is necessary equally in the United Kingdom to find out the impact of current policy and to provide data to assess future policy options.

It is necessary, in order to separate unfounded prejudice from legitimate concern, to enable political leaders to refute misinformation and disinformation in the press, to inject balance into a public debate in which the currency can become that of disputed fact rather than prejudice based on ignorance.

Canadian immigration ministers have a statutory duty to consult the public on the form which immigration policy should take. The Government leads and informs that debate. Employers, trade unions, minority groups, inner-city residents, welfare professionals, ordinary members of the public – all have a chance to voice their concerns and priorities. Policy is more informed and publicly acceptable as a result. Organisations and individuals in the United Kingdom would undoubtedly equally welcome such an opportunity to express their views. The outcome of the consultation exercise could be evaluated, along with the evidence from research studies, by a Royal Commission rather than, in the first instance, by government. Such a strategy might help to reduce the political heat of the debate and enhance the possibility of achieving a consensus on the key issues.

Reform immigration and asylum controls

There are many additional reasons to reform immigration and asylum controls beyond the need to ensure a positive impact on race relations. That requirement should be only one of a series of policy objectives to which reform should be directed. A second objective is that the United Kingdom should ensure that its immigration and asylum policy meet international human rights standards – the right to family life and to a fair hearing under the European Convention on Human Rights, to seek asylum under the Geneva Convention on the Status of Refugees, to avoid discrimination under the UN Convention on the Elimination of Racial Discrimination, among many others. These commitments should be seen as minimum standards, a prerequisite to good practice, not as obstacles to be side-stepped by entering reservations, as the United Kingdom has frequently done, to exempt its immigration and nationality legislation. They should be the first yardstick against which an individual's application to enter and reside in the United Kingdom should be measured: do they have right, under international law, to enter the United Kingdom? Where international law provides insufficient detail, government should be guided by the views of the supervisory bodies which monitor these commitments.

If an individual does *not* have a right to enter the United Kingdom, a second question should arise. Would he or she nevertheless make a valuable contribution – economic, cultural or social – from which the United Kingdom would benefit? This should be a further objective of immigration policy, to ensure that immigration meets positive economic and social objectives, recognising the contribution which selective immigration can make, whether to replenish skill shortages, to the world of entertainment or to sport. (A policy which welcomed people with skills would, nevertheless, need to take into account the impact of their emigration on their country of origin.)

Were immigration policy to be organised in this way, the criteria for *rejecting* an individual would be clear and objective: he or she had neither a right to enter under international human rights law, nor a clear economic or cultural contribution to make. The degree of discretion exercised by immigration officials, and hence the scope for discrimination, would be significantly reduced. If a visitor were to be refused on the grounds that the immigration official did not accept the individual's assurance that they would leave at the end of their visit – as happens many times each day – evidence must be cited to substantiate that suspicion. Only in this way, and with the restoration of appeal rights, can the discretion, which enables Americans to visit with impunity while those from Africa and Asia are regularly turned away, be curtailed.

Presentation of policy

National political leaders currently have the greatest impact on public attitudes towards immigrants. There can be no doubt about this. Unlike the 1960s, there are no significant pressure groups or extreme right parties advocating anti-immigrant programmes. Government sets the tone of the debate which the popular press echoes. Much of the material used by the press, as we have seen, comes from government and the immigration service. Given this influence, a government which chose to have a *positive* influence on public attitudes towards immigrants and members of minorities would be in a powerful position to do so.

Government should, first, inject balance into the debate by ensuring that information about the *positive* social and economic contribution made by immigrants and members of minorities is regularly drawn to public attention. The goal should be that the association of 'immigrant' with social problems should be counteracted in the public mind by an awareness of the immigrants and their descendants who have become Nobel Prize winners, pioneers of medical science, masters of industry, pop stars, Olympic medallists and valued friends. The public should be aware that without immigrants neither our health service nor transport system would be viable. They should know, because the Government has ensured that they do, that the refugees who came to Britain have a *higher* education and qualification level than those already settled here[44] and that children from Indian, Chinese and Black African families are *more* successful at school than those from white families.[45]

The need to inject this balance into the debate is slowly being recognised. The CRE published a path-breaking report in 1996 to draw attention to the vast and varied contribution made by members of minorities as part of its campaign to change public opinion.[46] Bob Ayling, Chief Executive of British Airways, is on record as saying: 'As a country we have thrived, improved and become more wealthy by taking the best of the immigrant community and utilising their skills',[47] and a representative of the Peabody Trust told the Architecture Foundation Debate in July 1996 that: 'Migrants to this country should be seen as an asset rather than a problem – London's economic growth has been based on the absorption of different nationalities.'[48] Jack Straw MP, as Shadow Home Secretary, opened his contribution to the Second Reading debate on the Asylum and Immigration Bill with the words: 'Britain has been immeasurably enriched by the contribution that has been made to its economy and its society by successive generations of immigrants',[49] but this is not an approach which has as yet been promoted by the most influential voice in forming public opinion, the Government.

Not only does government need to stress the positive, it must avoid unnecessary negative, emotive, language. Tensions must of course be acknowledged, problems identified and solutions recommended. All can be done without the use of terms which inflame public sentiments and raise, rather than assuage, public concern.

All branches of government must sing the same tune. It is futile for the race relations section of the Home Office to be promoting positive approaches if the Immigration and Nationality Department or its Minister is creating a very different impression.

The Home Office should ensure that *all* government statements relating to immigrants, asylum seekers and members of minorities are cleared centrally to ensure that the presentation of policy is consistent.

The main political parties are organised internally to enable instant rebuttal of negative slurs by their opponents. Government should similarly be organised to facilitate instant rebuttal of misinformation about immigrants and minorities. When an article claims that immigrants are abusing the social security system, receiving unfair priority in allocation of public housing or over-represented in certain crime figures, government, at national or local level, should be ready with the facts, fairly analysed and presented.

Does this issue warrant government according such high priority to changing public opinion? The other chapters in this book have provided the evidence that it does. The happiness and the security of members of minority communities are violated by discrimination, racial abuse and physical attacks. The well-being of the rest of the population is undermined by ensuing public disorder, whether provoked by white racists or by alienated black and Asian youth. Our common prosperity is weakened by the exclusion of black and Asian talent when they are victims of discrimination, and by the exclusion of immigrants whose skills we need but who cannot obtain work permits from a system designed only to protect the indigenous workforce and to keep numbers down.

What message should the UK Government be seeking to portray about immigrants, refugees and members of minorities as we approach the millennium? Let us reject, once and for all, the message of *tolerance*. Tolerance is what we feel for those whom we disapprove of, or dislike, but nevertheless feel obliged to be civil to. People who have a right to be in the United Kingdom, or are here because they have a specific contribution to make, do not want to be 'tolerated'. As former Labour MP Gerald Kaufman has put it: 'good race relations does not mean whites tolerating blacks; good race relations means people of all ethnic origins cooperating to create a harmonious society.'[50]

Government should be promoting a message of welcome and appreciation. It should stress that people from overseas have much to offer this country, as their predecessors had before them. The United Kingdom cannot provide jobs and homes to all of those who would like to live here and controls are therefore needed which select people, objectively, according to their rights under international law and, in the absence of such rights, on the basis of the contribution which they can make. Those who are allowed to enter are to be regarded as full and welcome members of society, adding to the country's vitality and prosperity.

The UK Government could not change the content and presentation of its immigration and asylum policy in isolation from its European Union partners. The European Commission, at least, would have no difficulty with the programme of reform outlined here. It has urged member states to give due weight to international human rights standards and to ensure that the public are fully aware of the economic and social contribution which immigrants make.[51] Nor should the greater reliance on objective criteria for selecting immigrants, the reduction in official discretion and strengthening of appeal rights present any difficulties for other member states. Nothing in these recommendations would weaken the United Kingdom's immigration controls, only make the decisions fairer and more transparent. The United Kingdom could in this way, and in the tone of its presentation of immigration policy, seek to lead a European trend towards immigration controls which contribute to, rather than detract from, positive public attitudes towards immigrants and members of existing resident minority communities.

CONCLUSION

The justification for British immigration policy for the last thirty years has been that firm, fair immigration controls are essential for good race relations. Despite the fact that immigration controls have been firm, however, resulting in a significant decrease in immigration since the 1970s, opinion polls show that successive governments have failed to reassure the public that immigration is under control. A significant section of the public remain opposed to immigration, critical of existing minority communities and, in recent years, hostile to asylum seekers claiming refuge in the United Kingdom.

The failure of immigration policy to achieve its stated objective is not hard to explain. The underlying message of that policy, that black and Asian foreigners are not wanted in the United Kingdom, directly contradicts the overt message of successive governments' race relations policy, that non-white residents in Britain are welcome, equal members of society who should be treated with respect. Past immigration legislation has been discriminatory in effect and there are realistic fears that the most recent measure, the 1996 Asylum and Immigration Act, will lead to discrimination in the provision of jobs and services.

Moreover, in their presentation of immigration policy, governments have not sought to reassure the public that immigration is under control, nor to remind the public of the significant economic and social contribution which immigrants and refugees continue to make to British society. On the contrary, governments have repeatedly identified ostensible weaknesses in immigration controls, proposed new measures to remove the loopholes, and sold the new measures to the public by drawing attention to alleged abuse of the system, using emotive language and imagery. The popular press has echoed the Government's line and the negative language has become the currency of public discourse on immigrants and asylum seekers.

Public attitudes to immigration do not develop in isolation. Part of the wider context is the crisis of identity in a country no longer confident of its role and cultural identity. Those who cling to images of the United Kingdom's past feel threatened by foreigners who challenge their dream of a mono-cultural country that never was. A country, like an individual, has many identities which change over time. The United Kingdom must up-date its self-image to accommodate its multicultural complexity.

This is not to argue that all immigration is positive and that controls should therefore be withdrawn. Public opposition would ensure that such a move by government was political suicide. Moreover, all United Kingdom long-term residents must be entitled to equal rights and benefits. To remove all immigration controls would thus open the exchequer to expenses and lead to demands on the labour and housing markets which could not be met. The question is, therefore, what kind of immigration controls *does* the United Kingdom need and how should they be designed to ensure that their impact on race relations is a positive one?

The strategy I outlined began with identifying positive objectives for immigration policy which, I suggested, should include a commitment to fulfil the United Kingdom's obligations to international human rights standards. Once that objective has been met, control should ensure that immigration contributes to the country's wider economic and social objectives. Meeting those objectives would contribute to ensuring that immigration policy had a positive impact on race relations – by removing discriminatory practices and ensuring that decisions on entry, residence and citizenship were based on objective criteria.

I argued that, prior to determining the objectives and the detail of policy, government should encourage and sponsor research on the social and economic impact of immigration to assess the effect of existing controls and examine options for the future, as is done in many other countries. Government should consult the public and interested parties – a Royal Commission would be one forum in which to do this. Government could lead the ensuing debate, informed by the results of research which would make it possible to separate unfounded prejudice about immigration from genuine concerns which need to be addressed.

Finally, I argued that government must undertake a radical shift, a complete U-turn, in its presentation of immigration policy. Government is the *primary* influence on public attitudes towards immigrants and it should use this influence to positive effect. First, it should inject balance into the debate by ensuring that the public is reminded of the positive contribution which immigrants, and subsequent generations, make to British society. Second, it should organise itself internally to enable instant rebuttal of negative misinformation in the press, using the research findings to provide an informed base to subsequent debate. Third, it should ensure that no branch of government inflames public opinion by using language which distorts public images of immigrants. That is, it should adopt a comprehensive communications strategy designed to ensure that the public debate on immigration is informed, balanced and fair. Roy Hattersley said recently:

The politics of race is enormously complex and pretty squalid. There is something about the British temperament that makes it antagonistic towards men and women who are different ... particularly towards foreigners who can be identified by their appearance and their habits. Therefore there is a potent well of prejudice to be tapped by politicians who say 'Rivers of blood', 'You're going to be swamped' ... and much to our shame there are votes to be gained from tapping that, not basic, but base instinct. Some parties are prepared to tap that base instinct and some parties . . . are frightened of it being tapped. I think it is as simple as that.[52]

Only a determined effort to change the terms of the debate on immigration, to inform and educate public opinion, will release government and opposition from the immigration politics of the past. Government would then be able to introduce the legislative and administrative reforms necessary to ensure that the United Kingdom's immigration and asylum policy meet its international obligations, make a positive economic and social contribution and facilitate, rather than detract from, good race relations.

NOTES

1 Second Reading of the Asylum and Immigration Bill, 11 December 1995, Hansard col. 711. The author acknowledges with thanks the assistance of Robert McGeachy in providing rescarch material from the Parliamentary debates on the Bill for this chapter.
2 House of Commons, 8 November 1966, 735 Hansard col. 1252.
3 Quoted in Rose, E. J. B., 1969, *Colour and Citizenship, A Report on British Race Relations*, Oxford University Press, p. 229.
4 Opposition spokesperson Doug Henderson, Second Reading of the Asylum and Immigration Bill, 11 December 1995, Hansard col. 788.
5 Jowell, R, *et al.*, (ed.), *British Social Attitudes*, the 12th report, Social and Community Planning Rescarch, 1995/6.
6 Runnymede Trust/*Independent* survey *Politics for All*, 1991.
7 *Racism in Britain*. A survey of the attitudes and experiences of black, Asian and white people for BBC Radio Five Live 'Race Around the United Kingdom', May 1996. Unpublished.
8 E.g. *Daily Express* survey after the Notting Hill riots showing high levels of support for immigration control, quoted in Layton Henry, Z., *The Politics of Immigration*, Blackwell, 1992, p. 73. *Survey of Race Relations in Britain* reported in Rose, J., *Colour and Citizenship*, 1969, op. cit., chap. 28.
9 Rose, E. J. B., *et al.*, 1969, *Colour and Citizenship*, OUP, p. 228; Saggar, S., in Benyon, J., (ed.), *Race and Politics in Britain*, 1992, Harvester Wheatsheaf, p. 175.
10 Anson, E., 1996, *Report by the Independent Monitor* (Asylum and Immigration Appeals Act 1993), Migration and Visa Division, Foreign and Commonwealth Office. 'Visitors wrongly refused visas', *Guardian*, 30 July 1996.
11 Salt, J. *International Migration and the United Kingdom*, Report of the United Kingdom SOPEMI correspondent to the OECD, 1995, pp. 20–22. *Control of Immigration: Statistics United Kingdom Second Half and Year 1995*, HMSO Cm 2935. *Asylum Statistics 1995*, Home Office Issue 9/96, 16 May 1996.
12 *Guardian*, Endpiece, 26 February 1996.
13 E.g. Sir Alex Douglas Home quoted in A. Dummett and A. Nicol *Subjects, Citizens, Aliens and Others, Nationality and Immigration Law*, Weidenfeld and Nicolson, London, 1990.

14 E.g. see Storey, H. 'International Law and Human Rights Obligations' in
   Spencer, S. *Strangers and Citizens, A Positive Approach to Migrants and
   Refugees*, 1994, IPPR/Rivers Oram Press; Dummett, A., and Nicol, A., *Subjects,
   Citizens, Aliens and Others: Nationality and Immigration Law*, 1990, Weidenfeld and Nicolson. One prominent example in the 1968 Act was the exemption
   from immigration control for individuals with a United Kingdom citizen
   grandparent. Few East African Asians could meet that requirement.

15 Commission for Racial Equality and Refugee Council Research Project,
   Submission to the House of Lords for the Committee Stage of the Asylum and
   Immigration Bill, April 1996.

16 E.g. see Fraser, J, *Lessons from immigration law reform in the United States:
   practical control measures to fight against the employment of illegal immigrants
   and the sanctions taken against their employers*, OECD Conference, Paris 1993.
   E.g., see Chief Executive of the Industrial Society, *Financial Times*, 23
   November 1995, and leaked letter quoted in the Second Reading debate on the
   Asylum and Immigration Bill, 11 December 1995, Hansard col. 775.

17 Response from the CRE to the Department of Employment Consultation Paper
   on Illegal Working, 30 January 1996, paras 29–30.

18 Second Reading of the Asylum and Immigration Bill, 11 December 1995,
   Hansard col. 746.

19 *Runnymede Trust Bulletin*, March 1996, no. 293.

20 Jim Lester, Second Reading, Asylum and Immigration Bill, 11 December 1995,
   Hansard col. 754.

21 *The Asylum and Immigration Bill, the Report of the Glidewell Panel*, April 1995,
   section 10.

22 *Observer*, 3 September 1995.

23 Glidewell Report, op. cit., section 5.1.2 'Playing the "race card"'.

24 *World in Action*, January 1978.

25 NOP poll, 1978, quoted in Saggar, S., *Race and Politics in Britain*, 1992,
   Harvester Wheatsheaf.

26 Article 1(2) of the 1951 UN Convention on the Status of Refugees, as amended
   by the 1967 Protocol.

27 Second Reading debate on the Asylum and Immigration Bill, 11 December 1995,
   Hansard cols. 699–795.

28 David Alton, MP, citing information provided to him by Home Office Minister
   Anne Widdicombe, in the Second Reading of the Asylum and Immigration Bill,
   11 December 1995, Hansard col. 736.

29 *The Times*, 8 December 1995.

30 Comment in the *Daily Mail*, 12 December 1995.

31 Sajida Malik, reported in House of Lords Committee Debate on the Asylum and
   Immigration Bill, 23 April 1996, col. 1050.

32 *Evening Standard*, 17 November 1995.

33 E.g. see 'Major v Howard in Asylum U-turn', *Daily Express*, and 'Right wing
   fury over suggestion of a deal', *Daily Telegraph*, 18 December 1995.

34 See, e.g., Christopher Husband's 'Crises of national identity as the "new moral
   panics": political agenda setting about definitions of nationhood', in *New
   Community*, 1994.

35 Quoted in Yasmin Alibhai-Brown, 'Community whitewash', *Guardian*, 28
   January 1991.

36 Quoted in Yasmin Alibhai-Brown 'Epilogue: prospects for the future' in Sondhi,
   R., and Solomos, J., *The Race Relations Act Twenty Years On*, forthcoming.

37 In 'Three theories of immigration' in Sarah Spencer (ed.), *Strangers and Citizens: A Positive Approach to Migrants and Refugees*, IPPR/Rivers Oram Press, 1994.
38 Sarah Spencer (ed.), *Strangers and Citizens: A Positive Approach to Migrants and Refugees*, Rivers/Oram Press 1994.
39 Home Office, 1995.
40 Home Office evidence to the Home Affairs Select Committee Sub-Committee on Race Relations and Immigration, February 1971.
41 *Immigration: A Commitment to Australia. The Report of the Committee to Advise on Australia's Immigration Policies* (Fitzgerald Report), 1988.
42 'The role of research in developing immigration and refugee policy: the Australian experience', presentation to IPPR Seminar on 26 October 1995, City Conference Centre, London.
43 Speaking at the IPPR seminar on 26 October 1996, op. cit.
44 Home Office Research and Planning Unit Research Report no. 141, *The Settlement of Refugees in Britain*, 1995.
45 Material from analysis of the 1991 census, *Independent*, 12 June 1996.
46 *Roots of the Future, Ethnic Diversity in the Making of Britain*, Commission for Racial Equality, 1996.
47 Quoted in *Equal Opportunities: Ethnic Minority Graduates and their Careers*, 1996, Hobsons, p. 5.
48 *The Architect's Journal*, 11 July 1996. George Peabody, the founder of the Peabody Trust, a major provider of affordable housing in London, was himself a United States citizen.
49 11 December 1995, Hansard col. 711.
50 Second Reading debate on the Asylum and Immigration Bill, 11 December 1995, Hansard col. 742.
51 Communication from the European Commission to the Council and Parliament on Immigration and Asylum Policies, February 1994.
52 The Rt. Hon. Roy Hattersley, MP, interviewed for Radio 5 Live 'Race Around the United Kingdom', May 1996.

6   Towards a learning society

Can ethnic minorities participate fully?

Tessa Blackstone

Access to power, relative prosperity, effective participation in political, social and economic life – what might be called full citizenship – is heavily dependent on education. For ethnic minority communities this is especially true in what is now termed a learning society. Without a reasonable level of education they face the double jeopardy of poor qualifications and discrimination. This will leave them particularly vulnerable to long-term unemployment, given the difficulty of being recruited for ever scarcer semi-skilled and unskilled jobs. Those who leave school at the first opportunity, and then fail to obtain further education or training, risk being left on the margins of society with potentially damaging implications for race relations in which stereotypes about blacks and Asians at the 'bottom of the pile' are reinforced.

Fortunately most ethnic minorities in Britain demonstrate more persistence in the pursuit of educational qualifications than those from similar social groups in the white community, which in the end is likely to pay off with respect to their achievement. However, generalisations about the overall educational performance of British ethnic minorities are exceedingly difficult to make. There is extraordinary diversity among the different ethnic groups in this respect, with gender and social class cross-cutting ethnicity in different ways. For example, according to the only nationally representative study in this field, girls in African–Caribbean groups have greater success than their male peers, but only when they come from manual backgrounds; in the Asian community girls do not outperform boys in any social group; among white pupils girls do better than boys in all social groups (Drew *et al.*, 1992).

This chapter examines the evidence on the relative educational achievement of minority children and young people. It draws heavily on a report written by David Gillborn and Caroline Gipps of the Institute of Education commissioned by OFSTED (Gillborn and Gipps, 1996). I am indebted to the authors who gave me access to a confidential draft before it was submitted and published. It is a superb piece of empirical analysis, bringing together all the findings from recent British studies. It is handicapped only by the absence of up-to-date nationally representative research on a sufficiently large and ethnically diverse sample of pupils, which includes data about social class and gender, for any truly definitive conclusions to be reached about the relative achievements of the main ethnic groups.

That said, it nevertheless provides a wealth of strikingly interesting material, some of which should be of concern to policy-makers in education, but some of which should give rise to optimism about the effects of schooling on British minorities. Concern is appropriate when particular categories are falling behind their peers with a consequent waste of potential and lack of access to later education and employment opportunities. Where this occurs it is necessary to try to identify the possible causes and, wherever possible, to intervene to encourage improvements in performance and, where required, to put an end to any racial discriminaton that may be occurring.

Most of the earlier studies on the achievement of black and Asian children either did not take into account social class or did not distinguish between the different South Asian groups – Indians, Pakistanis, and Bangladeshis. Moreover they are not able to measure progress over time. They are simply snapshots at one time in a pupil's school life. At the time of the Swann Report in 1985, the last major review of the educational experiences and achievements of ethnic minority children, it was generally accepted that African-Caribbean children were 'underachieving'. Indeed, the Committee of Inquiry into the Education of Children from Ethnic Minority Groups set up in 1979, originally under the chairmanship of Anthony Rampton and later Michael Swann, was established because of concern about 'West Indian' pupils' academic performance and adjustment to school. The Report's findings confirmed the earlier concerns: 'West Indian children as a group are underachieving in our education system.' In the light of the evidence before the Committee this was a legitimate conclusion. However, subsequent research has revealed just how complex a subject it is. There is not much consistency when a wide variety of measures of achievement, at different ages, in different parts of the country are examined. It is also hard to escape the conclusion that most of the differences found between ethnic groups, including white children, may well be an artifact of social class or, in some cases, knowledge of English.

Gillborn and Gipps, in their review, reject the concept of 'underachievement' as leading to negative stereotypes in which teachers are lured into lower expectations of ethnic minority children. Black 'underachievement' becomes a problem, which is widespread and beyond the teachers' control. If this perception becomes predominant, there is a danger of self-fulfilling prophecies at worst and, at best, little effort to intervene to try to mitigate problems that some of these children may manifest. Gillborn and Gipps argue instead for focusing on:

> the relative achievements of pupils in different ethnic groups, conscious that total equality of output may be neither possible nor equitable – if some ethnic groups have better attendance records, tend to spend longer on their homework and are more highly motivated (as some black and Asian groups appear when given questionnaire based assessments) we might expect that (all other things being equal) they would achieve rather better than less motivated groups.

They go on to argue that since there is not much reliable evidence about differences of this kind 'significant differences in the relative achievements of different ethnic groups may reasonably be taken as a cause for concern'. They may also mean that the educational opportunities of some groups are less good than others, with consequent effects on their life chances. All this is indisputable. Whether, however, focusing on relative achievements rather than underachievement will change teachers' expectations is more debatable.

Children who do not speak English at home are likely to be at a disadvantage when they start school. Effort which would otherwise be spent on learning to read and write has to be spent on mastering English. Although children quickly pick up a foreign language at this age teachers face initial problems of communication and anxiety may result for both pupils and teachers. Moreover, learning a language effectively may still not result in the same fluency as native speakers. The interaction between starting school as non-English speakers and the expectations teachers have of pupils in this category may depress reading performance throughout primary schooling. Certainly the research indicates that fluency in English is an important factor. Bangladeshi and Pakistani children do relatively badly at the primary stage. There is, however, also cause for concern about African-Caribbean pupils, particularly in London. Another aspect of the findings for primary children is that the gap in reading scores between different groups tends to grow over the primary years, pointing to the need for early intervention to stop pupils falling behind in the first instance (Sammons, 1995). Pre-school education can play an important part, especially for small children who do not speak English. For example, in Tower Hamlets nursery places for Bangladeshi children have risen. As a result there has been a striking improvement in the performance of these children, who are bilingual by the time they start their primary schooling. At the secondary stage, most of the research is based on performance at age 16 in GCSE examinations. The largest national study examining 16-year-old achievement, which analyses ethnicity as well as social class and gender, was unfortunately based on data collected in 1985. It is therefore very out of date. Also it does not distinguish between different Asian groups. However, the Youth Cohort Study is an invaluable source based on a large national sample of youngsters. Its findings demonstrate yet again what every student of the sociology of education learns at the outset of their studies: social class is strongly associated with achievement. Whatever the ethnic origin or gender of pupils, those from higher social class backgrounds do better than those from lower social class backgrounds. However, it also emerges that African-Caribbean pupils, of both sexes, do less well than other groups, but Asian groups do as well or better than whites of the same class and gender. What is urgently needed is a replication of this study using up-to-date data and distinguishing between Indian, Pakistani and Bangladeshi pupils.

Since the data for this study was collected, there has been a substantial improvement in the achievement of British 16-year-olds, as measured by the proportion of pupils gaining five or more A–C GCSE passes. In 1988 the proportion was around 30 per cent; by 1994 it had risen to 43 per cent. It is now a well-established fact that girls have improved at a faster rate than boys. It is possible that ethnic minority pupils may have improved faster than white pupils. Unfortunately there is inadequate national monitoring to be sure, but what evidence there is certainly suggests this has occurred with respect to Asian groups. No group is exempted from the general improvement in performance at GCSE. However, the gap appears to have widened between the most successful and the least successful groups, so those that were already doing well are now doing even better.

Gillborn and Gipps suggest the following general conclusions for each major ethnic group from their survey of the data:

1 *Indians*: these pupils are achieving levels of success 'consistently in excess' of white pupils in some urban areas and they have the best results among South Asian pupils.
2 *Pakistanis*: evidence about this group is peculiarly inconsistent. In London they appear to be performing relatively well but this may be a function of the social class structure of Inner London schools where many white pupils come from disadvantaged manual backgrounds. Elsewhere they seem to do less well than Indian pupils, about the same as Bangladeshis but better than African-Caribbean pupils.
3 *Bangladeshis*: earlier research in the Inner London Education Authority identified these pupils as most likely to obtain poor results. This was explained by their recent arrival in the United Kingdom, poor knowledge of English and the high proportion of manual workers in the Bangladeshi population (higher than in any other ethnic group). In Tower Hamlets,

where a quarter of Bangladeshi pupils in the United Kingdom reside, they now have higher average achievement than either white or African-Caribbeans, although all groups in this disadvantaged borough score significantly below national averages. There is a clear association between fluency in English and measures of achievement, suggesting that policies for additional support with English, adopted by Tower Hamlets, will pay off.

4 *African-Caribbeans*: although there are variations in how these pupils do compared with others in different parts of the country, most research shows consistently that they are relatively less successful than their white and Asian peers. This is particularly true of African-Caribbean males. When distinctions are being made between Black Africans and those from the Caribbean, the former appear to do better. This may be a consequence of both social class and gender. The failure of boys of Caribbean origin to reach their potential is especially worrying.

Clearly performance at school has implications for later education. However, the widening of post-school opportunities, with a greater range of alternatives than in the past, means that performance in school-leaving examinations at 16 does not have quite the significance it used to before a wider range of routes into study after school were established. Moreover, the huge increase in part-time study by mature students may also mean that a 'catching-up' process can take place among people in their twenties and thirties. Poor performance in GCSE at 16 can also be mitigated by staying on in full-time education after 16 to retake subjects in which the student has failed to get a good grade or to switch into vocational studies.

The national trend shows a steep increase in the numbers remaining in education, so that more than half of young people now stay in full-time education after the end of compulsory schooling, although participation rates fall with each year that passes after compulsory education ends. Participation rates are highly affected by social background: indeed pupils from non-manual homes are likely to stay on whatever their GCSE results.

The evidence on the participation of ethnic minorities is crystal clear: between the ages of 16 and 19 all ethnic minority groups are more likely to be at school or college than white young people; indeed research shows that once attainment has been taken into account, ethnic origin is the most important variable determining staying on. Not surprisingly, however, social class is related to staying on in each ethnic group, so that the higher the social class, the higher the numbers of those staying on. Nevertheless an analysis of 1991 census data reveals that in every case (with the exception of Black Caribbeans from professional backgrounds) ethnic minority pupils are more likely to stay on than whites from the same social class (Drew,

Gray and Sporton, 1994). Remarkably whites from professional back-grounds are less likely to stay on than Black African, Indians and Bangladeshis from skilled backgrounds. And whites from skilled manual backgrounds are less likely to stay on than Black Caribbean, Black Africans, Indians and Pakistanis and Bangladeshis from semi-skilled or unskilled backgrounds.

Interesting differences emerge when gender is taken into account. After the Chinese, the South Asians from the Indian sub-continent tend to be the most persistent 'stayers on' with a majority still in full-time education three years after compulsory schooling. However, in each of the three main South Asian groups participation rates are higher (and markedly so for Pakistanis) among males than females. As Gillborn and Gipps point out, however, this should not be interpreted as meaning that girls in the Asian community are seriously disadvantaged in relation to other girls. In all groups they are more likely to stay on than white girls and markedly so in the case of Indians. But in contrast to whites and Black Caribbeans, where girls are more likely to stay on than their male peers, they are less likely to do so than males in their own communities.

The reasons for higher staying-on rates by the ethnic minorities need to be studied. In the absence of proper research, we can only speculate about them. Cultural as well as structural factors seem likely to be at work. There appears to be a greater commitment to education on the part of parents, with more encouragement to stay on and possibly greater parental impact on the young person when this encouragement is provided. It is possible that white working class parents who do provide encouragement to their children to remain in education are more likely to be resisted than are Asian parents. If parental authority is weaker in some groups than others, this could explain some of the differences. The collapse of the youth labour market could also have a differential effect on different groups if, for example, it is more difficult for those of African-Caribbean origin to get jobs than, say, whites. Staying on will look like a better option than unemployment for many young people.

Racism in the wider community may also be a spur to young blacks and Asians to demonstrate their worth by getting educational qualifications – qualifications which will also improve their chances of going into higher education or getting a job. Indeed one of the few studies which has examined the reason why ethnic minority young people stay longer in education found that Indian, Pakistani, Chinese and Black Africans were still at school or in Further Education in order to get into higher education; they wanted qualifications which would lead to professional jobs (Shaw, 1994). In the six TEC Areas covered by the study all the apprentices taken on were white. This is an alternative route for white youngsters which is either unavailable for black and Asian youngsters because of discrimination or is rejected by them because they aspire to professional and white collar jobs. Both white and Black Caribbean young people were less likely to be aiming for university than other groups.

In spite of the poorer showing of some ethnic minority groups in terms of achievement in the compulsory sector, a willingness to stay on in education is likely to strengthen their position in gaining access to higher education. This must, however, be qualified if the courses they pursue are not those which normally gain entry to universities. African-Caribbean young people are in fact more likely to take vocational qualifications; Asians on the other hand are more likely to take A-Levels; indeed by the age of 18 they are the most highly qualified group (Drew *et al.*, 1992). What is also quite clear, from all the available data, is that proportionately more young people from the ethnic minorities *apply* to do a degree, than is the case for young whites.

Work done at the Policy Studies Institute by Tariq Modood and Michael Shiner suggests, however, that admissions by no means mirror applications (Modood and Shiner, 1994). Admission rates vary considerably between different groups. The data they analysed relates to 1992 before the poly-technics became universities and they examined applications and admissions on both sides of the binary line. Outcomes were markedly different in the two types of higher education institution. Starting with the universities they found that a substantially higher proportion of white applicants were admitted while a lower proportion of black applicants (both those of African and Caribbean origins) were admitted. Before accusations of discrimination in admission procedures are made, it is necessary to check on the qualifications of different ethnic groups to see whether and how they vary. It is also important to know whether they tend to apply for courses on which it is particularly difficult to get a place because they are over-subscribed and have higher entry requirements.

Both of these appear to operate against ethnic minority students trying to get into a university. In 1992 more than 20 per cent of applications from ethnic minorities were for medicine and law, three times that of whites, and these were the most difficult subjects in which to get admission. Conversely, education courses, which are the easiest to get into, had much lower numbers of applications from ethnic minorities. Mean average A-Level scores were lower for ethnic minority applicants than for whites, moreover they were more likely to have gained A-Level points from re-sits than white students. Admission tutors often seem to prefer those who were successful in their A-Levels first time round.

Nevertheless, even when these differences between whites and ethnic minority applicants were taken into account some, but not all, ethnic groups were less likely to get in than whites. Black Caribbeans and Pakistanis were less likely to get a place. On the other hand Chinese and 'Asian-other' were more likely to get a place. The 'under-admission' of some ethnic minority groups is perplexing and must be a cause for concern. On the other hand other groups – Black African, Indians and Bangladeshis – were not significantly under-admitted, when choice of course and level of academic performance were taken into account. Straightforward discrimination against blacks and Asians in general does not seem to occur. The authors also point out that their data is based on applications and firm offers *accepted* not offers made. If more Black Caribbeans and Pakistanis rejected university offers in order to go to their local polytechnic, this could explain at least part of the difference.

Regrettably there is recent evidence that in part of the university sector, the medical schools, discrimination is still occurring. After the Commission for Racial Equality's formal investigation into St George's Hospital Medical School following serious allegations of discrimination, it is discouraging to discover that in nearly half of all British medical schools ethnic minority applicants fare less well than white applicants (McManus *et al.*, 1995). However, the disadvantage has diminished since 1986. An astonishingly high proportion of applications are from ethnic minority groups (26 per cent). They are less likely to be accepted because they are less well qualified and apply later. However, once such differences have been taken into account, they are still less likely to be offered a place than white applicants. Bias in favour of white students appears to take place when offers are made prior to taking A-Levels. A second study confirms that some medical schools may still be guilty of discriminatory practice (Esmail *et al.*, 1995). It found that there was little evidence of bias among applicants with the highest A-Level grades, but that white students in the next tier down had a better chance of obtaining a place than their non-white peers with similar scores. The authors of both studies comment that medical schools may be inadvertently trying to cut down on ethnic minority entrants because of the disproportionate number of applications from these groups. As they rightly imply, there is no justification for this; potential students should be selected on the basis of merit.

When applications to the polytechnics were examined, the research showed that minority group students were more likely to have received and accepted an offer for a polytechnic than their white counterparts. However, further analysis, which took into account other variables including academic qualifications, showed that only Black Caribbean and Indian applicants continued to be significantly more likely to have gained admission to a polytechnic than their white equivalents.

In conclusion, when the universities and polytechnics are taken together, none of the ethnic minority groups had less chance of admission than whites. Further research is needed to determine whether more ethnic minority students actually choose to go to the 'new' universities, as they now are, rather than the old universities. They may do so for a variety of reasons; geographic proximity (many new universities are located in inner cities close to large ethnic minority populations); more vocationally oriented courses; larger numbers of ethnic minority students than in what might appear 'white only' old universities.

The greater propensity of British ethnic minorities to seek and obtain access to higher education is good news. By the early 1990s the Bangladeshis were the only major minority group which was under-represented in relation to whites in the polytechnics. In the universities Chinese, Black Africans and Indians were all over-represented although Black Caribbeans were still under-represented. Circumstantial evidence also suggests that more ethnic minority students, who missed out earlier, are now entering the universities as part-time mature students. In doing so, they are studying the hard way, but those who came through this route will have demonstrated to themselves and others that they have the determination and grit to succeed against the odds. This has important implications for their employment potential once employers become more aware of the special qualities of mature graduates who have combined study with a job.

The growing proportion of graduates in the ethnic minority community should not, however, lead to complacency about the education of blacks and Asians in Britain. Even if this trend is maintained or perhaps accelerates, as it well might, there is a danger that the ethnic minorities could be divided between a well-educated group at one end of the spectrum and a very poorly-educated group at the other. In other words, they could be disproportionately represented at the extremes: among graduates and among those with no qualifications at all. There is, for example, an alienated poorly-qualified group of African-Caribbean males, some of whom have been excluded (expelled or suspended) from school, others who have had poor attendance records and none of which follow the pattern of many of their peers, staying on beyond compulsory schooling. This is the group to which I was referring in the opening sentence of this chapter.

The fact that there is plenty of positive evidence about the educational achievement of the ethnic minorities does not mean that policies are all working well and that no action needs to be taken to improve them. The burgeoning research on differences in the way schools affect pupils' progress suggests that some secondary schools are more effective than others for certain ethnic groups, although unfortunately little light so far has been thrown on the reasons (Nuttall *et al.*, 1989). What is needed is research which focuses on those schools which appear from quantitative analysis to be more successful in this respect, to try to discover what distinctive characteristics they have and what might account for their success.

More qualitative research, which looks closely at the interaction between pupils and teachers would be valuable in this context. For example, do teachers' expectations about, say, Asian girls or African-Caribbean males, have a damaging effect on this interaction? In both instances there is case study research whose findings suggest that teachers have negative views of these pupils. Asian girls suffer from stereotypes about their passivity and docile nature (Brah, 1992); African-Caribbean boys suffer from stereotypes about being undisciplined and troublesome (Mac an Ghaill, 1988; Gillborn, 1990). It is, however, perfectly possible that these stereotypes are not baseless and hostile but a genuine reflection of gender and ethnic differences. Teachers are only human and, like the rest of us, observe differences in behaviour by different social groups, generalise about them and, at times, may alter their own behaviour to take into account what they observe (Foster, 1992).

Intervening quickly to stop disciplinary problems getting out of hand can be interpreted as over-controlling behaviour in relation to black boys or as sensible action to help order in the classroom. However, most thoughtful teachers would probably agree that they should avoid making assumptions about their pupils as individuals, based on negative stereotypes about the gender and ethnic group to which they belong. To expect bright assertiveness and ambition from Asian girls or a willingness to conform to certain basic school requirements and to control aggression on the part of African-Caribbean boys, is more likely, in any case, to produce these responses than the low expectations imposed by strongly-held stereotypes of the kind described above. Case study material suggests that Moslem girls are in any case increasingly successful in negotiating a model which incorporates both British and Asian cultures. Many of them have middle class aspirations about careers supported by their ostensibly working class families. The stereotypes may after all be based on a misunderstanding of Asian girls in Britain and of how they perceive their future.

If what Gillborn and Gipps describe as the 'considerable gulf between the rhetoric of equal opportunities and the daily reality experienced by many black pupils' is to be avoided, work is needed in schools to create greater awareness among teachers of the dangers of negative evaluations. A variety of approaches may be helpful. These include targetted support for black pupils in trouble: even pupils who have had great difficulty in adapting to school, to the extent of being excluded, can, it appears, be given the chance of remaining in education with good results with the right help. They also include working with pupils collectively to bring about change in an open and self-aware way, which involves them in the project and motivates them. Breaking down peer-group hostility to being ambitious to learn, or to succeed in learning, ought to be part of such an approach. Involving parents and the local community is not always at all easy, but there is plenty of research about effective schools which suggests it pays off. It is reasonable to assume it will also produce positive results with black and Asian parents.

During the 1980s a number of local authorities developed what became known as anti-racist policies in schools. These were designed in part to counter violence and harassment in schools and in part to incorporate the culture of the ethnic minority communities into the school through what became known as multicultural approaches to the curriculum and multifaith approaches to religious education and to the daily act of worship required by law in our schools. Both had the broader object of supporting black and Asian pupils and of securing the best possible levels of achievement from them. Whether they have had much success in denting racial harassment is unclear. There have been too few studies of this phenomenon to be sure. What the evidence does suggest is that South Asian pupils are much more likely to be victims of harassment and violence than African-Caribbeans. They may be more vulnerable both because they appear to be weaker and more distinctive from the white majority in terms of language, eating habits, religion, dress and other customs. When slighter build among some South Asian groups is added to differences of the kind just listed, it may help to encourage bullying by pupils who might be more nervous about harassing larger pupils who pose a greater physical threat. Paradoxically, the behaviour of white pupils is a cause of both concern and hope for the future. Clearly there is a worrying level of racist behaviour, especially in secondary schools, as well as a great deal of racial tolerance between pupils from different ethnic backgrounds and many close friendships forged between pupils from different ethnic groups.

Anti-racist policies have been demonised on the Right and disregarded as unfashionable in certain quarters in recent years. They have been written off as ineffectual or typical of early 1980s' political correctness in Labour education authorities. It is perfectly possible, however, to reach a quite different conclusion, which is that they have not worked because they have not been tried, at least not on a wide enough scale and not sufficiently sensitively. This conclusion would lead not to abandoning them, but to redoubling efforts to make them work better and to disseminate them more widely.

Obviously racism in the wider society will affect the attitudes of both teachers and their pupils. Any suggestions that this means that there is nothing schools can do to address racism should be resisted. What it does mean, however, is that it would be naive to expect anti-racist policies in schools to wipe out racist attitudes. Racist behaviour on the streets, on the football terraces and racist attitudes expressed at home are likely to influence young people and affect their behaviour at school. At the same time schools provide the best opportunity there is for intervention to promote tolerance and to prevent the expression of racial prejudice among young people. Turning a blind eye when pupils indulge in racial taunts and name-calling, on the grounds that it is relatively harmless, is an easy way out for teachers to take. It is, however, dangerous to be passive in such circumstances for it can lead pupils to assume that it is acceptable. Moreover incidents that start as the exchange of verbal abuse, which is both insulting and hurtful, can degenerate into racially-motivated violence.

However, the most constructive approach is to include anti-racist policies firmly within whole school behaviour policies and individual development plans, which should be published by all schools, rather than separating out anti-racism for special treatment. A crude and unsubtle approach to anti-racism can make matters worse by playing up people's colour as a crucial differentiating factor, when in fact it might be better to play it down. Encouraging the assumption that colour is an individual's defining characteristic is not likely to be helpful. Race and ethnicity interact with class, gender, religious identity and other cultural characteristics. The fact that race is so visible is important but it does not in itself make it the overriding differentiating factor (Gilroy, 1990).

Anti-racist policies have also tended to assume, at least implicitly, that racism is a white 'crime' confined to them and implicating all whites in racist structures and racist behaviour because they are the majority. Conversely blacks are perceived as oppressed victims with no attempt to concede group differences within the minority community. It is unsubtle and simplistic, often with moralistic overtones, which are likely to be resented by white young people. Anti-racist policies need to be based on a proper understanding of the complexity of our multi-ethnic society. As Gillborn has cogently argued:

> It is vital to break with victim/criminal stereotypes of minority youth and reject angels/devils categories which:
> a   regard racism as a 'whites only' preserve; and
> b   require the maintenance of fictions about the essential 'goodness' of minority groups, as if they were not subject to the same depth and variation as other people. By engaging with the variability and complexity of social relations, antiracism can build genuine support and involvement across race and class barriers.
>
> (Gillborn, 1995)

Above all it is vital to avoid those approaches which lead to polarisation around racial identities as if they were set in concrete, rather than fluid and subject to many influences which shape and change them. Young people are also more likely to respond to attempts to involve them in examining their own attitudes and how they are formed, with teachers taking a lead in doing the same, rather than directly lecturing them about why racism is unacceptable. This is why integrating the unacceptable nature of racism into general policies about behaviour is the best approach. Talking down to pupils as if they are the only people guilty of stereotyping and discrimination will not work either. Pupils are perfectly aware of racism in the wider community, and indeed in their own homes. This needs to be addressed in a sensitive way by teachers. Where this happens, with proper attention given to the complexity of what is at stake, pupils are more likely to respond positively.

Successful anti-racist policies in schools, set in the context of development plans and behaviour policies, are of profound importance in helping to create a tolerant, cohesive multiracial society. They will not, however, in themselves bring about equal success in learning to read or the same level of achievement in GCSE exams or equal proportions from different ethnic groups entering higher education. These are also shaped by the way children interact with their parents and their teachers, by their own perceptions of the rewards of educational success and by material factors.

The nature of the curriculum itself is perhaps less influential than has sometimes been claimed. The relative educational success of some Asian groups suggests that although the secondary school curriculum may arguably be a reflection of a dominant British culture, not all minority group children are excluded with debilitating effects on their capacity to learn. Nevertheless, to question some of the claims of multiculturism does not excuse the demands made, for example, by some evangelical Christians for religious education to be Christian. To concede these demands can only lead to some pupils feeling excluded. However, the debate about multicultural and multifaith approaches to the curriculum requires a chapter of its own and I have not sought to address it here. A multicultural curriculum is in any case largely about educating white children.

Nor unfortunately have I been able to cover other important problems concerning the education of ethnic minority pupils, such as exclusions from school. The fact that Black Caribbean children are almost six times more likely to be excluded from school than white pupils is a matter of grave concern. Exclusion from school is usually temporary and may be only for a few days. Where it is permanent, meaning that the pupil can never return to the same school and alternative arrangements have to be made, recent Department for Education statistics show that two-thirds of those excluded never return to another mainstream school. While numbers are too small to have a serious impact on the overall performance of Black Caribbean boys (and more boys are excluded than girls), it is worrying that they are growing.

Both more research, to get to the bottom of why this is happening and more thought, on other solutions to disruptive pupil behaviour, are needed.

To conclude, in much earlier work I undertook on gender differences in educational achievements, I always stressed that the differences in perform-ance within each gender were much greater than the differences between them, and the same must be said of ethnic group differences. There is enormous diversity in what pupils achieve within every group. It is, as I have tried to show, nevertheless possible to discern distinct patterns between ethnic groups. The patterns that emerge are a cause for some celebration. What they show is the remarkable extent to which many children and young people from British ethnic minorities have overcome language and other barriers to succeed in the sometimes somewhat alien education system they have entered. Their willingness to persevere, remaining at school or college in higher proportions than their white peers, is particularly striking.

If this trend continues, it will have an important effect on job opportunities and career prospects for young blacks and Asians in this country as qualifications become a more and more important route into rewarding employment. Better access to skilled jobs is central in preventing the marginalisation of young people from the ethnic minorities. Thus it links into many of the other themes explored in this volume. Without the full participation of all groups in the education system, we cannot have a truly meaningful learning society. The battle to secure the best possible education for all our young people must be fought with renewed vigour. It can be won, as many black and Asian youngsters are proving by their own extraordinary efforts.

REFERENCES

Brah, A. (1992), 'Women of South Asian origin in Britain: issues and concerns' in P. Braham, A. Rattansi and R. Skellington (eds) (1992), *Racism and Antiracism: Inequalities, Opportunities and Policies*, London, Sage.

Drew, D., Gray, J. and Sime, N. (1992), *Against the Odds: The Education and Labour Market Experiences of Black Young People*, England and Wales Youth Cohort Study, Report R and D no. 68, Sheffield, Employment Department.

Drew, D., Gray, J. and Sporton, D. (1994) 'Ethnic differences in the educational participation of 16–19 year olds', unpublished paper presented to the OPCS/ESRC Census Analysis Group Conference, University of Leeds, September.

Esmail, A., Nelson. P., Primarolo, D. and Toma, T. (1995), 'Acceptance into medical school and racial discrimination', *British Medical Journal*, vol. 310, February, 501–2.

Foster, P. (1992), 'Equal treatment and cultural difference in multi-ethnic schools: a critique of the teacher ethnocentrism theory', *International Studies in Sociology of Education*, 2(1): 89–103.

Gillborn, D. (1990) *'Race,' Ethnicity and Education: Teaching and Learning in Multi-Ethnic Schools*, London, Unwin-Hyman/Routledge.

Gillborn, D. (1995), 'Renewing antiracism', in *Challenge, Change and Opportunity*, Runnymede Trust, London.

Gillborn, D. and Gipps, C. (1996), recent research on the achievements of ethnic minority pupils, Office of Standards in Education, London, HMSO.

Gilroy, P. (1990), 'The end of anti-racism', *New Community*, 17(1): 71–83.

Mac an Ghaill, M. (1988) *Young, Gifted and Black: Student–Teacher Relations in the Schooling of Black Youth*, Milton Keynes, Open University Press.

McManus, I. C., Richards, P., Winder, B. C., Sproston, K. A. and Styles, V. (1995), 'Medical school applicants from ethnic minority groups: identifying if and when they are disadvantaged', *British Medical Journal*, vol. 310, February, 496–500.

Modood, T. and Shiner, M. (1994) *Ethnic Minorities and Higher Education: Why are there Differential Rates of Entry?*, Policy Studies Institute in collaboration with UCAS, PSI Research Report 786.

Nuttall, D. L., Goldstein, H., Prosser, R. and Rasbash, J. (1989) 'Differential school effectiveness', *International Journal for Educational Research*, 13: 769–76.

Sammons, P. (1995) 'Gender, ethnic and socio-economic differences in attainment and progress: a longitudinal analysis of student achievement over 19 years', *British Educational Research Journal*, 21(4): 465–85.

Shaw, C. (1994) *Changing Lives*, Policy Studies Institute.

7 The media and race relations

Yasmin Alibhai-Brown

BACKGROUND

Until the late 1980s the influence of the media on race was discussed in relatively simple terms. Most people were in broad agreement that the media *did* influence and reinforce public opinion and periodically journalists were willing to accept that on race, the media had the potential to affect attitudes and behaviour. In 1970 Harold Evans, then editor of the *Sunday Times*, submitted that:

> newspapers have effects at two reciprocal levels of ethnic tension. By the information they select and display and opinions they present, they have effects at ground level on the creation of stereotypes and the stimulation to behaviour. Because of the volatility of the subject, they have also swift effect at ground level on the creation of policy. . . . The Press must recognise that what it prints or broadcasts about ethnic groups can directly affect ethnic tension. Any organisation not in league with the devil . . . must then recognise the commitment which follows. It must have a positive policy to avoid unnecessary damage. These are responsibilities which many in the press refuse to acknowledge.'[1]

In the past, according to researcher Karen Ross, media critics also took a more deterministic view of the impact of television, which was seen as 'an agent of social control feeding its audience with established propaganda'.[2] With race, the influence exercised was more complex and subtle but nevertheless tangible, wrote Stuart Hall in 1981:

> How we 'see' ourselves and our social relations *matters*, because it enters into and informs our actions and practices. Ideologies are therefore a site of a distinct type of social struggle. This site does not exist on its own, separate from other relations, since ideas are not free-floating in people's heads. The ideological construction of black people as a 'problem population' and the police practice of containment in the black

communities mutually reinforce and support one another. Nevertheless ideology is a practice. . . . It is generated, produced and reproduced in specific settings (sites) – especially in the apparatuses of ideological production which 'produce' social meanings and distribute them throughout society, like the media.[3]

Most critics also believed that television, radio and newspapers had and promoted a 'white' perspective mainly because ethnic minorities were largely excluded from key journalistic and technical jobs.

EMPLOYMENT AND TRAINING

In the early 1980s black and Asian people in broadcasting institutions were mainly seen serving in cafeterias or dealing with the debris after those who made the programmes had finished. Cherry Erlich, introducing one of the first monitoring exercises carried out by the BBC in 1985, referred to the impression given that the only black people who worked at the Corporation were 'caterers or cleaners'.[4] It was the same story at TVAM and other commercial channels. Equal opportunity policies were developed, but progress was slow. At a conference on Black People and the Media in 1988 Michael Day, then Chairman of the CRE, criticised the lack of information about employment within the media as a whole. 'It needs to be monitored', he said,

> not only recruitment but how people get on once they are there, because it is no good saying we've got 10 per cent ethnic minorities if all they are doing is sweeping floors . . . organisations are hardly going to change until ethnic minorities get into positions where the shots are called. . . . many organisations have impressive equal opportunities but where does that take them? Not very far. The disparity between practice, activity and policy aspirations is grotesque.[5]

Speaking at the same conference, Sadie Robarts, the Equality Officer of the Cinematograph Television and Allied Technicians, offered the following statistics:

> The ACTT, the film and television technicians union attempted a shop floor survey in 1986 and concluded that about 1.5 per cent of its members were black. In the London area, Thames Television, a company which has declared itself an 'equal opportunity employer' since 1977, has 40 black employees in its 2,000 plus workforce.[6]

Robarts argued that an improvement in employment policies would change perceptions and correct inaccuracies and false stereotypes. The CRE's report on *Television in a Multi-Racial Society* (1986) made a similar direct link: 'The portrayal of ethnic minorities in Drama, Light Entertainment and other programme areas depends to a large extent on the employment opportunities open to ethnic minority artists.'[7]

There was a widespread belief that if black people began to enter the industry and rise within it, not only would it be impossible to make offensive 1970s programmes like *Love Thy Neighbour*, *Till Death Us Do Part* and *It Ain't Half Hot Mum*, but there would be changes, long overdue, in the way factual programmes dealt with ethnic minorities and Third World issues. Marc Wadsworth, one of the few black journalists in news and current affairs in the early 1980s, affirmed this in 1988 when he wrote:

> The white Eurocentric ethos of the British media, is the nub of the problem. Black points of view whether from people here or abroad get virtually no coverage except, as Anne Dummett notes, 'randomly through bitty television programmes where black people's concerns are normally identified in the white producer's terms'.[8]

In the same year Zeinab Badawi, a highly experienced Channel Four reporter, described her anxieties about the way Africa was represented on British television:

> Earlier TV coverage of Africa was born of a negative attitude towards Africans, and gave rise to negative effects. Africans were seen as colonised people. Their own culture, identity and history were not really recognised as being valid or important. ... With the end of empire one might have hoped for change, and certainly there is evidence of a more enlightened and positive approach ... [However] cultural superiority is still presupposed, only now it is much more subtle.[9]

A recent study on British television and global affairs, published by the Third World and Environment Broadcasting Project, confirms this view.[10]

Newspapers and weekly political magazines were deemed to be even more unenlightened. As late as 1990, there were only twenty ethnic minority journalists out of a total of 6,000 working for the national papers.

For those seeking to change portrayal and coverage, therefore, the employment of ethnic minorities was seen as the key. The Black Media Workers' Association, publishing its first research report in 1983, asserted that ethnic minority recruitment into the media would achieve wide tranformations. Racist practices, it believed, could only be 'challenged and eliminated' if there were more black people 'actually involved in reporting and editing, programme-making, and developing images of black people for public consumption'.[11]

It was widely recognised, however, that these changes could not be brought about overnight, and as an interim measure it was believed that if white people could be trained to become more aware of discrimination and portrayal they would start working in more sensitive and informed ways. The BBC, much to its credit, even commissioned programmes to reveal the extent to which broadcasters were guilty of unconscious prejudices. Following two of these, *The Black and White Media Shows I* and *II* (BBC2, 1984/85), Michael Grade, then controller of BBC1, acknowledged that there was a problem to be addressed.

It was during this period of introspection and change that London Weekend Television and, subsequently, the BBC, actively recruited black and Asian employees, trained their white staff in equal opportunity recruitment practices and looked at the way they catered for ethnic minority Britons.

THE MEDIUM AND THE MESSAGE

The received wisdom about the print sector in the early 1980s was that the tabloids tended to sensationalise news, to use racist language and to promote xenophobia while the broadsheets behaved in more responsible ways. The right-wing papers were unsympathetic to multiculturalism and anti-racism while the papers of the centre or left were more supportive.

An examination of some of the key events bears out these assumptions. The attacks in the right-wing tabloid press on 'loony' councils and the stories of 'race spies' banning the use of black bin liners and Baa Baa Black Sheep showed how predictable and rampantly hostile this section of the press had become. Such reports were brilliantly analysed by Chris Searle in his booklet, *Your Daily Dose: Racism and The Sun*; almost every issue of *The Sun*, he wrote, carried an example of such reporting, 'usually employing crude and populist humour as well as distortion and inaccuracy'.[12] Research from Goldsmiths College in London, published in 1987, proved that many of these 'reports' were entirely without foundation.

What also began to emerge with some force at this time was the new racism of the right, which no longer voiced views about racial or cultural inferiority but the more acceptable worries about the erosion of British values and of a historical core identity. According to Nancy Murray, a researcher for the Campaign against Racism and Fascism, there was nothing new in the Thatcherite right using 'race' as 'the focus of a cohering patriotism'. That was simply being 'true to its Powellian heritage'. 'But what is new is the emphasis on rolling back the gains of anti-racism in the name of traditional freedoms, national pride and the liberation of the white majority.' The press, she went on, 'has been a major platform' for the propagation of these views.[13]

Immigration and inner city disturbances in particular began to be discussed in these terms. *The Sun*, for example, ran an editorial in June 1986 attacking Labour's proposals to end discriminatory immigration laws, claiming that this country could not afford any increase in immigration. Six days later an editorial was asserting the right of all white South Africans to settle in this country if they needed to because they were 'our' people, 'the children and grandchildren of British settlers'.[14] Those who attacked multiculturalism, like Ray Honeyford in Bradford, were treated as heroic patriots.

During this period, compared with sections of the press, there was much less blatant racism in broadcasting. However, television and radio were guilty of excluding and marginalising ethnic minorities. There was rarely the sense that Britain was a dynamic, multicultural society. Ethnic minorities would feature only if they were held responsible for some crisis, and in news and current affairs the set of assumptions which underpinned reporting often lacked any genuine understanding of black communities. Tony Freeth, a freelance reporter and director, came to the conclusion that there was nothing 'neutral', 'balanced' or 'objective' about the way in which TV portrayed black people.[15] The ground-breaking programme *It Ain't Half Racist Mum* (BBC2, 1979), made among others by Freeth and presented by Stuart Hall, had shown the effect of this on documentaries. Controversially, it also challenged the biased way in which studio debates and discussions were conducted even when they were led by highly regarded broadcasters like Robin Day.

Six years on the *Black and White Media Shows* revealed that not much had changed.

In drama and entertainment the picture was not much better. The CRE, after a study in 1986, concluded that opportunities for ethnic minority actors were:

> still very limited and restrictive in both frequency and variety of roles. Most of the fiction roles given could be descibed as 'comic' or 'villainous' and it was doubtful whether the majority of roles could have been said to contribute towards racial harmony ... there were very few ethnic minority appearances in comedy programmes or sit-coms. For the most part, where appearances were noted in this type of programme these were negative and stereotyped.[16]

The CRE did acknowledge, however, that some progress had been made, mentioning in particular programmes like *Skin*, *The Chinese Detective* and *Empire Road*. But these were still a rarity.

CURRENT STATE OF THE MEDIA

Many features of the earlier period remain stubbornly in place. Immigration is still discussed in terms of numbers and problems, black families are still pathologised and Asians are in general only considered worthy of media interest if they can be shown to be culturally 'backward', if they are victims of racism or, less frequently, if they have made good as hard working immigrants. Shami Ahmed, for example, the millionaire Asian businessman who started off with a market stall, is seen frequently on television and recently even presented *Dosh*, a series on Channel Four.

But in the 1990s only the most pessimistic would argue that nothing has changed. Much obviously has, and in the direction that was sought by those who were campaigning back in the 1970s and 1980s. But, as well as old tendencies that still persist, there are now new problems.

It is important to remember the context within which race in the media must now be considered. There have been unprecedented structural changes in the media industry and enormous political shifts which have impacted on the way the media and race interact.

News International broke the power of the trade unions in the 1980s after the long-drawn-out strike at Wapping. It was not long before similar confrontations in the broadcasting industry reduced the influence of technical and journalistic staff in that sector. In the 1990s the BBC has set about restructuring itself mainly in order to cut costs. These changes have brought in intense competition, market forces, deregulation and a contract culture. There are few jobs for life, or even for a year, and volatility and insecurity are making it difficult to press for equal opportunities or even to compete fairly for work. Helen Auty, the Training and Equal Opportunity Adviser for London Weekend Television, described this in stark terms in 1991: 'It is very difficult to say to a manager you must take on suitably qualified black and ethnic people when in fact he has just lost 43 members of staff.'[17]

Ethnic monitoring has become increasingly difficult and reliable employment figures for both the broadcast and print sector are becoming harder to collate. The outlook appears bleak, says Dr Karen Ross: 'it is fruitless to predict what a deregulated media might look like in the future', but 'it will be a sad day if the precarious foothold that black media professionals have managed to obtain in the industry is blithely kicked away in the rush to embrace global EmpTV.'[18] But there are others, like Dr Lola Young, who believe that these changes need not be wholly bad news for ethnic minorities. She argues that as more and more niche markets are targeted by those who control broadcasting there might be more scope for ethnic minorities than is being assumed.[19] At the moment these opposing positions are just speculation and only time will tell.

ETHNIC MINORITY RECRUITMENT AND REPRESENTATION

There are now more black and Asian people working within the media than before, and not just on the lowest rungs of the ladder. The area which is showing greatest progress is television. Ethnic minority presenters are no longer a rarity and a cursory look at the titles at the end of programmes shows that there has been important penetration of talent from these communities in all areas of employment, even on the most highly regarded programmes like *Panorama* and *Horizon*. We take it for granted that series like *Black Bag*, *Black Britain*, *East* and *The Devil's Advocate*, all high quality programmes, appear regularly on our screens and that black and Asian people are presenters and reporters on these shows. Trevor McDonald, Shahnaz Pakravan, Zeinab Badawi and Moira Stewart are highly respected presenters and newscasters now catering to mass white and black audiences.

Progress in some areas highlights lack of progress in others. Popular programmes like *Eastenders* and *Cracker* have integrated casting as a matter of course, but *Coronation Street* remains resolutely white. Lenny Henry is now a household name, but others with talent like Meera Syal have not had the same exposure as their equivalents like Paul Merton or Jo Brand.

Dr Guy Cumberbatch recently conducted research on the portrayal of ethnic minorities for the BBC and for the Independent Television Commission. Compared with an earlier study in 1989/90 he found a much larger representation of ethnic minorities. In UK productions about 6 per cent of characters were from ethnic minorities, and of those appearing in serious factual programming 26 per cent. In fictional programmes the figure rose to 39 per cent, but there were only 40 Asian characters compared with 221 Afro-Caribbeans. Ethnic minority characters were much more likely to be seen as unemployed or working class, but the proportion appearing as criminals was lower than that for whites.[20]

More significantly, there has been some progress in getting ethnic minority people into key top positions in the industry. People like Samir Shah, head of BBC News and Current Affairs, Narendra Morar, the erstwhile head of Multicultural Programmes at the BBC and his long surviving equivalent, Farrukh Dhondy, head of Multicultural Programmes on Channel Four, and Trevor Phillips, Executive Producer at London Weekend Television, are, or were, individuals with real power and influence.

National Radio has been slower to change, but here too producers and editors are becoming conscious that in order to increase audiences they need to expand their appeal to diverse groups and one way they might begin to do this is by changing their employment profile. On Radio Four, as well as noticeable changes in personnel, there are now two well-established series given over to ethnic minorities – *In Living Colour* and *The Asian Perspective*. Mainstream documentaries and features deal more than competently with issues of race and multiculturalism. Ethnic minority presenters are beginning to appear on popular programmes like *You and Yours*. There are now ethnic minority reporters and even editors for the *Today* programme and one or two people like Marina Salandy Brown have become top executives. BBC Radio One, Four and Five Live periodically take the issue of race as a theme and give over hours of high quality broadcast time and resources. In 1996 the extraordinary Radio Five Live series *Race Around Britain* showed what radio broadcasting was and ought to be capable of. Over fifty first-rate and challenging programmes were broadcast over a period of nine days giving a real sense of how vibrant multicultural Britain was.

The print sector has been the most resistant to change both in terms of employment and coverage. The recruitment of journalists on national newspapers is not done through advertising but informal methods, and the exclusion of ethnic minority journalists continues to be a serious problem. In 1995, out of approximately 5,000 staff journalists on national newspapers, fewer than thirty were from the minority communities. Not a single editor, regular critic or columnist was black or Asian.[21] But even here there has been some change. The *Financial Times*, the *Daily Telegraph* and the *Daily Mail* have a number of black and Asian staff, as do the *Guardian* and the *Observer*.

On the whole, though, the picture is depressing, particularly as there seems to be no will to change on the part of most newspaper editors. Perhaps it is no accident that so many newspapers continue to peddle the worst xenophobic and racist messages in ways which you would not get on radio and television which are also more regulated.

The power of the press is significant. Print journalists set the agenda. What appears in the newspapers is picked up by the broadcasters who frequently recycle the material in more subtle and acceptable forms. British society has almost got used to the rampant racism of the tabloid and mid-market papers like the *Daily Mail* which through 1994 and 1995 constantly peddled stereotypes of refugees and asylum seekers as 'bogus', and 'scroungers' who had come to Britain to live off benefits. What has been less obvious is the extent to which what the *Mail* says is discussed on radio and television, often uncritically and in terms of whether this country should take 'bogus' refugees. Rarely if ever do we get programmes which question the idea that if people fail to fit into a particular set of criteria as defined by the Geneva Convention (like starving children from Somalia, for example) they must be 'bogus'. Broadcasters tend to follow these debates rather than direct them.

We have also seen the rise and rise of the brutally 'honest' columnist in

British newspapers. These voices are immune from responsibility or censure. Richard Littlejohn used to write for the *Sun* and produce thoughts like this in his column:

> What I can live without are British women married to Iraqis arriving back at Heathrow and Gatwick . . . in full Arab garb and complaining about Mrs Thatcher's 'aggression' in the Middle East. They have chosen to turn their back on Britain . . . they should be left to rot in their adopted country with their hideous husbands and unattractive children.[22]

Littlejohn has been the recipient of several press awards and has ended up with his own television show. He has also moved to the *Daily Mail* where he wrote recently about a Ghanaian who had seen a job advertisement in his village in a British newspaper which was over a year old:

> sadly by the time his letter was received the position had already been filled. He could always try suing for racial discrimination. It usually works and I'm sure the Commission for Racial Equality would be happy to assist. All he has to do is fly here and claim asylum and legal aid will be a mere formality.[23]

By no means the worst, Littlejohn nevertheless exemplifies the way columnists have obtained licence to disparage ethnic minorities and the institution that work for racial justice.

As described above, some areas of the media have transformed themselves. And even where there are few ethnic minority employees, as for example on the *Guardian* (where in 1995 there were about six ethnic minority staff), white journalists have shown themselves capable of understanding the deepest impulses of black and Asian communities and communicating these in a way that makes sense to readers from all ethnic groups. In fact the *Guardian*, the *Observer* and the *Independent* (which in 1995 had only one ethnic minority journalist) have tirelessly campaigned against unfair refugee legislation and against the use of race by politicians as a way of getting votes. Even the *Sun* can no longer be categorised simply as a 'racist' paper. In the past five years it has carried highly responsible stories on racial violence, mixed marriages and high achieving Asian children.

But other developments which might have been expected have simply failed to take place. Few if any custodians of high culture – book, film and theatre critics – are from the minority communities. Ironically even on popular culture – music, clothes, and the club scenes where many of the leading purveyors are black – the writers are universally white.

Radio and television show similar gaps. Among presenters and guests on the most highly regarded political or cultural programmes black and Asian people are invisible. *The Late Show*, which has acquired near mythical status as a highbrow arts programme, almost never has any black faces on screen. *Question Time*, *Without Walls*, *What the Papers Say*, and equivalent programmes on radio remain similarly almost exclusively white.

In fact there is little ethnic minority representation in the most influential sections of all three sectors of the media except as newscasters. Trevor Phillips chairing *The Midnight Hour* is an exception. Blacks and Asians never seem to chair mainstream programmes or write key editorials or comments where they can begin to challenge all the central assumptions that still frame coverage of race and multiculturalism.

The employment of ethnic minorities in key journalistic and editorial positions has not been the panacea it was assumed it would be. In too many instances it has helped to validate racist and prejudiced reporting. Those in positions of power have not, on the whole, made it their business to push for radical changes. Perhaps understandably, they have instead absorbed the underlying values of the white media to prove their worth. More dangerously we have examples now of black and Asian journalists and commissioning editors making racist programmes or writing inflammatory articles of the sort that white people tend these days to avoid. The highly respected series *Panorama* for example, made a programme on Muslims in Bradford entitled *Underclass in Purdah* (1994) which claimed many Muslims in that city were involved in illegal activities like drug trafficking and pimping. This sensationalist account was put out by an all-Asian team. Complaints were made to the Broadcasting Standards Council – which did uphold some of the complaints. Some people in the BBC defended the programme by claiming credibility on the grounds that it was made by Asian journalists. Ethnic minority editors defend themselves by referring to journalistic values. Samir Shah, for example, said in 1992: 'My own interest is not to make programmes that just propagandise or campaign for any particular community. . . . I don't think that is journalism.'[24]

As the 'tabloidisation' of the broadcast media gathers momentum, black and white broadcasters are increasingly putting across crude and lurid manifestations of black and Asian life. In the words of Karen Ross, 'There seems to be a definite and discernible trend in documentary programming, at least, whereby film makers invade and exploit particular communities for the sake of "good television" rather than for the purposes of genuine understanding'.[25] A series on black/white sexual relations, for example, *Doing it with You is Taboo*, had black women speaking out on why white women were not sexually desirable and also discussing the sexual prowess of black men. In 1996 the 'breakthrough' was Badass Television, which celebrates blacks behaving badly.

Some programmes, while approved of by white television producers, are seen very differently by black audiences. A number of black Britons were offended by *The Devil's Advocate* because they felt the presenter encouraged black stereotypes. In an interview for the *Observer*, when describing what it is to be an Afro-Caribbean, he proclaimed: 'I make children all the time. Why? I climb on top of them and make sex. . . . it's wonderful . . . it's not odd. My brothers and I have different mothers and my father was an Anglican priest.'[26]

It is not uncommon therefore these days to find black and Asian viewers who feel that both Channel Four and BBC ethnic programming has failed effectively to challenge the assumptions of British white society; that the editors have played safe by reproducing stereotypes and have only commissioned programmes that display the most negative aspects of black and Asian life. As the pressure to produce popular programmes grows, as people get more insecure in their jobs, this is likely to get worse.

The newspapers have, for some time, used black and Asian journalists to dig up the dirt within their communities. The *Daily Mail*, for example, which has carried out a vendetta against 'bogus' refugees and asylum seekers, often uses undercover black and Asian journalists for its investigations.

NEW ISSUES

Other problems have been emerging in the past five years in the way that race is dealt with in the media and, more worryingly, about how white people now feel about multiculturalism and British society. Highly intelligent liberal thinkers have started expressing views which would once have been unthinkable. Unexpected voices like those of Suzanne Moore, Fay Weldon, Melanie Phillips and others have been raised against what they perceive as threats to values they hold dear. Many began to feel these misgivings when the Rushdie affair blew up. Although there has never been any evidence to show that the majority of British Muslims supported the fatwa, because no survey was carried out, this is what commentators with influence assumed and still assume. There were hotheads and fanatical leaders who did of course declare their support, but their significance was overplayed because it served the purposes of the media. The late Kalim Siddique, infamous for his extremist views, is the only British Asian to have had eight full length newspaper profiles published of his life and views. His Muslim parliament had the backing of a few hundred people out of the one and a half million British Muslims. The fact that Muslims burnt *The Satanic Verses* triggered off memories of Nazism and totalitarianism. The comparison, though understandable, was false. This was a gesture by a group of people who felt frustrated by their sense of powerlessness, not an action by those bent on absolute power. As Tariq Modood wrote in May 1989:

Even when the Muslims began to take to the streets ... they were determined to be orderly and thereby doomed themselves to continuing invisibility. They found themselves silenced by the racially discriminatory judgements that lie at the heart of how race is reported and theorised about. Faced with this powerlessness, the unfortunate but true conclusion the organisers reached was that they would remain unheeded till something shocking was done. This led to the book-burning publicity stunt. That started a reaction with the libertarian-left, which when such stunts were interpreted through a prism lent by the Ayatollah, culminated in hysterical denunciations of the demonstrators as Nazis.[27]

The issue went far beyond a single book or author, or even the religious sentiments of a community. More than any other, it made white Britons confront the fact that multiculturalism was not merely about festivals and world music or even the exciting expansion of literature. Nor was it about cricket tests. Fundamental values were now being contested in a public arena.

Black and Asian people were no longer just clamouring for access but for influence and power in cultural and political life. For many white liberals, especially those who expected and had previously received praise and appreciation for doing the right thing, such conflicts were disheartening.

Out of all this, and other factors – the collapse of the left, and the emergence of a new generation unable to relate to the empire or the Second World War – a neo-conservatism has emerged, and nowhere is this being played out more clearly than in the media. Four separate and inter-connected threads are woven into this crisis of identity.

First, it is through using the label 'political correctness' that the disengagement of the left is taking place, says the critic Patrick White:

[PC] provides the present day realist with a neat way of mocking every political and ethical challenge back into the obscurity of its corner without even the remotest engagement with its claims ... it has become the reflex sneer of the right that is no longer prepared to argue its case. However it also has attractions for refugees from the collapsing Left, stepping out from behind all that ideological baggage to catch up with the opportunities of a world where everything seems to hang free.[28]

Second, reassessment is leading to a reassertion of liberal values, including freedom of expression and secularism. Too many writers to mention have been putting forward their beliefs in forms which have been described by some as 'liberal fundamentalism'.[29] Commenting on this the Muslim writers and academics Ziauddin Sardar and Merryl Wyn Davies wrote:

'Civilization as we know it' has always meant Western civilization. Civilized behaviour and products have been measured by the yardsticks of the West. . . . Colonial history and colonial Christianity did their utmost both to annihilate non-Western cultures and obliterate their histories. Now secularism in its post-modernist phase of desperate self-glorification has embarked on the same goal.[30]

Even if one allows for the hyperbole, there is more than a little truth in these remarks. In a more tempered voice Bhikhu Parekh asserts a view which is not dissimilar:

The post-Enlightenment world view, which through imperialism was foisted upon large parts of the world, has become *the* dominant paradigm: based on a specific view of the individual, of material interests, of rights, obligations and so on. What modernity has done is to destroy, obliterate, or simply laugh out of existence, a large variety of world views. . . . Liberalism has always remained assimilationist: others must become like us, my present is your future. It has always remained profoundly fundamentalist.[31]

Among the new champions of liberal values is Melanie Phillips in her influential *Observer* columns. Attacking anti-racist training for social workers, she launches this extraordinary assault: 'the anti-racism taught to social workers has nothing to do with promoting freedom and equality . . . [it throws out] tolerance and individualism . . . liberal ideas about intellectual inquiry being based on the rules of evidence are junked.'[32] She provides little evidence to justify this attack. When examined, social work training manuals and documents do not in any way indicate a contempt for the individual, tolerance or intellectual inquiry.

If the writers in the broadsheets are increasingly advocating cultural protectionism and pride, those writing for the tabloid press are going much further. The columnist Carol Sarlar, writing in the *People* in May 1996, had this to say about the suggestion made by the Commission for Racial Equality that children eating food with their fingers were as acceptable as children eating with knives and forks. 'There are also some cultures where they don't use loos; they just squat wherever they happen to be when the urge comes. So what should we do about that? Ban potty training?'[33]

Third, this battle of values is being fought most fiercely when Islam is being confronted. The Rushdie affair gave permission for those who had never quite felt at ease with Islam in their midst to lay down caution. Describing the contempt with which the British press treated Muslims at the time of the furore Bhikhu Parekh writes:

Neither the quality nor popular papers published the offending passages or invited Muslim spokespeople to state their case, or themselves made an attempt to read the books with their eyes. Instead they mocked the Muslims, accused them of 'intolerance' . . . Many a writer of impeccable liberal credentials openly wondered how Britain would 'civilize' them and protect their innocent progeny against their parents' 'medieval fundamentalism'.[34]

Even Roy Jenkins, the architect of our race relations laws and believer in cultural diversity, lamented the 'creation of a substantial Muslim Community' in this country.[35]

Once liberated the distaste snowballed. Connor Cruise O'Brien wrote in *The Times*: 'Muslim society looks profoundly repulsive, because it is repulsive from the point of view of Western post-enlightenment values.'[36]

What is disappointing is the way black and Asian people in the media have not managed to challenge any of these trends. In fact the anti-Muslim clamour was orchestrated in the ethnic minority programmes as much as it was elsewhere. People like Farrukh Dhondy and Tariq Ali, in their rush to support Rushdie, echoed the mainstream media. They did not adequately facilitate counter-arguments to be presented by offended Muslims, most of whom rejected the fatwa.

These three developments are closely connected to a fourth underlying, anxiety. There is a reassertion of Englishness, or a Britishness which reveals the extent to which people are feeling insecure about their historical identity. To see how that is affecting the media we have only to look at the ongoing cricket controversy. A few years ago Norman Tebbit pronounced that the true test of identity for a British person was which cricket team they supported. In July 1995 the *Wisden Cricket Monthly* published an article expanding this theory to the players, claiming that the desire to play for England was 'instinctive, a matter of biology', and that 'outsiders' were unlikely to put their hearts and souls into fighting for Britain. Even Matthew Engels, an experienced *Guardian* journalist, in part agreed with this thesis. He argued that in team sports those with a strong and unequivocal 'national identity' performed better than those without.[37] What all these men are grappling with is a British identity which takes them back into some glorious past and away from the complicated world of multiculturalism. They are simply examples of what Phillip Dodd describes as 'the national psyche which in most of its variants is a tale of backward-looking insularity, melancholy, decline and loss.'[38]

THE WAY FORWARD

Pressure needs now to be exerted on the print sector to introduce equal opportunity recruitment procedures. It needs to come from the ethnic minority communities, concerned politicians and journalists and organisations like the Commission for Racial Equality. The year 1997 has been designated by the European Commission as the European Year Against Racism and the role of the media is central to this.

Where they are not doing so already, the BBC and Independent television and radio companies need to carry out monitoring exercises on ethnic minority representation on key political and cultural programmes as well as the news. In particular programmes like *Any Questions*, *Question Time* and *Start the Week* need to be examined, and a real effort should be made to create a directory of influential black and Asian people who could be called upon by programme makers.

Seminars, debates and discussions should be instigated on the crucial areas of disagreement. A few years ago the CRE and Policy Studies Institute arranged seminars on pluralism and freedom of expression. There is a need for more such debates between liberal journalists and ethnic minority thinkers who are concerned about the future of this country and the values that would bind society rather than fragment it in the way we have seen happen in the United States.

Concerned journalists and editors should look at the way major events are covered and examine whether there are other ways of looking at subjects to do with ethnic minorities. Training for journalists needs to include discussions not just of stereotyping but of the point of view taken. When Paul Condon issued his statistics on black muggers, not a single newspaper, television or radio programme investigated the racial profile of other kinds of crime. Instead the debate got stuck on whether he was right to issue these figures. Opening up the subjects would benefit journalism as much as those who are consuming stories.

Meaningful regulation of the press is essential so that racist stories and comments are not allowed to go out without any redress.

Black and Asian media workers need to look at the way they are failing to change the ethos of the organisations they have entered and to take some action on this.

Better monitoring of employment figures can only be conducted if data collection is better managed. All media institutions should be required to collect and disseminate this information.

Ethnic minority targets should be incorporated into contracting and commissioning procedures.

Newspaper editors need to make more effort to recruit ethnic minority columnists and critics, where appropriate through the positive action allowed by the Race Relations Act.

SUMMARY

For many decades now concerns have been expressed about the role of the media in influencing race relations in Britain. Critics in the 1970s and 1980s argued that in general the media were failing to reflect the multicultural nature of this society and that they pandered to prejudices. Two solutions were put forward – the training of white media workers and employment, at all levels, of ethnic minority workers. Of the three sectors, television took up these recommendations most energetically. In the last few years there have been structural and other fundamental changes which have influenced the debate and made change more difficult. It would also be true to say that some of the solutions have not succeeded in the way that was envisaged. The way forward must entail an honest appraisal of existing strategies and take into account the wider shifts in British society.

NOTES

1 Harold Evans, 'A positive policy', *Race and the Press* (Runnymede Trust, 1970), p. 45.
2 Karen Ross, *Black and White Media* (Polity, 1996), p. 87.
3 Stuart Hall, 'The whites of their eyes: racist ideologies and the media', in Gail Dines and Jean M. Humez (eds), *Gender, Race and Class in Media* (Sage, 1995), pp. 19–20.
4 *Erlich Report* (BBC, 1986).
5 Michael Day, in Joe Harte (ed.), *Black People and the Media* (CRE, London Borough of Lewisham, 1988), pp. 26–27.
6 Sadie Robarts, in Joe Harte, op. cit., p. 51.
7 CRE, *Television in a Multicultural Society* (June 1986), p. 2.
8 Mark Wadsworth, speech at Black Media Workers Conference, London, June 1988.
9 Zeinab Badawi, 'Reflections on recent TV coverage of Africa', in John Twitchin, (ed.), *The Black and White Media Book* (Trentham Books, 1988), p. 134.
10 Adrian Cleasby, *What in the World is Going On? British Television and Global Affairs* (London, Third World Environment Broadcasting Projects, 1955).
11 Marina Salandy Brown, (ed.), *Black Media Workers Association Register*, (1983), p. 52.
12 Chris Searle, *Your Daily Dose: Racism and The Sun* (Campaign for Press and Broadcasting Freedom, 1989), p. 49.
13 Nancy Murray, *Anti-racists and other Demons: the Press and Ideology in*

Thatcher's Britain (Institute of Race Relations, Race and Class Pamphlet no. 12, 1989), pp. 2–3.

14 *Sun*, 10 and 16 June 1986.
15 Tony Freeth, 'Race on television: bringing the colonials back home' in Phil Cohen, Carl Gardener, (eds), *It Ain't Half Racist Mum* (Comedia, 1982), pp. 24–25.
16 *Television in a Multicultural Society*, op. cit., p. 4.
17 Helen Auty, *The Black and White Broadcasting Act* in CRE, Seminar Report (1991), p. 11.
18 Karen Ross, op. cit., p. 178.
19 Lola Young in *Race and TV in Britain, Channels of Diversity* (CRE Seminar Report, March 1996).
20 Guy Cumberbatch, 'Ethnic Minorities on Television' in CRE Seminar Report, *Channels of Diversity* (1996).
21 Yasmin Alibhai-Brown, *Independent*, 26 April 1995.
22 Richard Littlejohn, *Sun*, 18 September 1996.
23 Richard Littlejohn, *Daily Mail*, 4 July 1996.
24 Samir Shah, op. cit., p. 162.
25 Karen Ross, op. cit., p. 131.
26 *Observer Magazine*, 21 November 1993.
27 Tariq Modood, 'Goodbye Alabama', *Guardian*, 22 May 1989.
28 Patrick Wright, *Guardian*, 1 June 1993.
29 Richard Webster, *A Brief History of Blasphemy* (Orwell Press, 1990), p. 59.
30 Ziauddin Sardar and Merryl Wyn Davies, *A Distorted Imagination* (Grey Seal, 1990), p. 276.
31 Bhikhu Parekh and Homi Bhabha, 'Identities on parade', *Marxism Today*, June 1989.
32 *Observer*, 2 April 1989.
33 Carol Sarlar, *People*, 5 May 1996.
34 Bhikhu Parekh, 'The Rushdie affair and the British press', *Social Studies Review*, November 1989.
35 *Independent*, 4 March 1989.
36 Connor Cruise O'Brien, *The Times*, 11 May 1989.
37 Mike Marqusee, 'Fear and fervour', *Guardian*, 4 July 1995.
38 Phillip Dodd, *The Battle over Britain* (Demos, 1995).

8 Race and ethnicity in housing

A diversity of experience

Valerie Karn and Deborah Phillips

The position and experience of ethnic minorities in the housing market has been well documented by academics, local authorities, the Commission for Racial Equality (CRE) and non-governmental organisations over the last twenty-five years. The earliest accounts revealed how newly arriving immigrants had little choice but to occupy the bottom end of the market, ending up in poor private rental properties or, in the case of Asians, purchasing cheap, deteriorating inner city terraced housing abandoned by the suburbanising whites (Rex and Moore, 1967). Distinct ethnic clusters emerged in the inner cities, the product of a number of often inter-related factors, namely: the immigrants' poverty and lack of knowledge of the housing market, their job opportunities, their desire for clustering for social and cultural reasons, and the blatant discrimination of the early post-war years. The pattern at this time was one of racial deprivation, segregation and inequality.

The passage of time has brought some significant changes. Ethnic minorities now have access to a wider range of housing tenures, property types, and locations, and, on the whole, improved living conditions. The 1991 Census indicates that 'black' groups in particular are now well represented in public housing (see Table 8.1), a sector in which they were once acutely disadvantaged by formal and informal rules and direct discrimination. They are also well represented within the growing housing association sector. For those searching within the private housing market, access to finance and information has improved immeasurably since the early days of widespread institutional exclusion and vendor discrimination. What we now see is a diversity of experience among ethnic groups, reflecting racial, ethnic, class, generational and gender differences. The opportunities and barriers faced by ethnic minorities to a certain extent intersect with those experienced by the white population, so that it is unsatisfactory to describe or explain patterns of advantage and disadvantage in the housing market purely in terms of race/colour. These changes reflect the impact of race relations legislation, equal opportunities and anti-racist initiatives (mainly within the social housing sector), changes in housing demand from a socially, culturally, demographically and economically maturing population, generational differences in housing aspirations and strategies, and the role of ethnic minority creativity and empowerment in bringing advancement. Such developments have brought greater mobility to the ethnic population, to some extent loosening ties to particular locations and providing greater impetus for dispersal.

Table 8.1 Tenure by ethnic group of head of household, Great Britain, 1991

Ethnic group	Owner-occupiers	LA tenants	HA tenants	Private tenants	Renting with job	Total (=100%)
White	67	21	3	7	2	21,026,565
Black Caribbean	48	36	10	6	1	216,460
Black African	28	41	11	18	2	73,346
Black other	37	34	11	14	4	38,281
Indian	82	8	2	6	2	225,582
Pakistani	77	10	2	10	1	100,938
Bangladeshi	44	37	6	10	3	30,668
Chinese	62	13	3	17	4	48,619
Other Asian	54	14	4	24	4	58,995
Other other	54	19	6	18	2	77,908
All groups	66	21	3	7	2	21,897,322

Source: 1991 Census, Housing and Availability of Cars, Topic Report, Table 15 (OPCS/GRO(s), 1993)
Note: The ethnic groups are those used in the 1991 Census (for a discussion of the implications of these groupings, see Karn, 1997; Peach, 1996).

This positive pattern of change, however, provides only half the story. We can also see some disturbing continuities between the early post-war years and now. Our best national picture of the housing outcomes of this period is provided by the 1991 Census. This indicates that in all tenures, ethnic minority groups remain in a worse situation than whites in relation to housing quality, over-crowding, concentration in disadvantaged areas and levels of segregation (Karn, 1997; Peach, 1996). If we add to this that ethnic minorities are disproportionately represented among the homeless (LHU/LRC, 1989) and take into account the power of racial harassment and violence to shape housing options, it is clear that patterns of ethnic disadvantage in housing persist.

Of all the ethnic minority groups, Pakistanis and Bangladeshis live in the most deprived housing conditions in the worst locations. In 1991, over a fifth lived in properties which were assessed by the English House Condition Survey as the 'worst' in the country (DoE, 1993). Indians did better; only 12 per cent lived in such properties. Both the Pakistanis and the Bangladeshis are characterised by very high levels of overcrowding (30 per cent and 47 per cent respectively in 1991, compared with only 2 per cent of whites). Lending weight to the census, OPCS data indicated that nearly a third of Pakistani and Bangladeshi households had a deficiency of one or more bedrooms below the 'bedroom standard' for their household in 1991–93. Given the youthful age-structures of these populations, it seems likely that, in the short to medium term, living conditions will decline further as youngsters reach adolescence. Overcrowding among Indians was lower than that among Pakistanis and Bangladeshis, but was still much higher than among the white population. There were also considerable variations in housing types across the ethnic groups; in 1991 half the white households lived in detached and semi-detached properties compared with less than a quarter of Black Caribbean, Black African, Pakistani and Bangladeshi households. The South Asian groups were most likely to be found in the terraced housing so commonly associated with inner city living, a pattern which is broadly similar to that in the 1980s (Brown, 1984). The Black African population had the highest proportion of households living in purpose-built flats and bedsits, reflecting their metropolitan concentration and the high incidence of young people.

While the 1991 census indicated a diversity of housing conditions among ethnic minorities, with signs of some groups, such as the Indians, moving up the housing ladder, the persistence of housing inequality is clear.

So where does this leave our understanding of the position of ethnic minorities in the housing market of the 1990s? Three major themes emerge.

First, it is evident that improvements in the circumstances of ethnic minority populations have been partial. Some, but not all, Indians have advanced considerably, while other groups, notably the Pakistanis and Bangladeshis, still experience severe disadvantage. We need, therefore, to understand more about the processes underlying this fragmentation of ethnic minority experience.

Second, despite a wealth of literature, our understanding of some of the fundamental processes of ethnic differentiation in the housing market is scanty. In looking for explanations, researchers have debated the salience of minority choice versus constraint in housing outcomes, and the power of individual agency versus institutional discrimination in an endemically racist society. Over time, the focus of research has shifted away from explanations which blamed the individual, to those which see institutions and the state as powerful determinants of the pattern of racial disadvantage (e.g. Sarre *et al.*, 1989; Henderson and Karn, 1987). There is, nevertheless, still a need for better understanding of the ways in which racial inequalities are produced and reproduced, and why some groups have different housing careers from others. There is also a need for a greater understanding of the interaction of the housing and labour markets in shaping ethnic minority housing outcomes, and a closer analysis of the role of racial violence in restricting housing choices. Our understanding of particular processes in the allocation of resources in the housing market is inadequate.

Finally, we are also now having to confront another gap in our knowledge; one presented by a lack of recent research. Much of our current understanding is founded on material published in the late 1980s, which was based on fieldwork conducted in the late 1970s to mid-1980s. Very little new large-scale academic work on the subject has been initiated since then. At the same time, evidence from other sources has also fallen off as local authorities have given less priority to racial equality and the CRE itself has conducted fewer housing investigations.

The lack of continuity in research in this area has been particularly unfortunate because the last twenty years has been a period of radical change in the British housing system, with an escalation of the rate of change since 1980.

These major changes have been:

- the growth of home-ownership, particularly among lower and moderate income households;
- the rise and decline of large-scale slum clearance and the rise and decline of large-scale grant-funded improvement in inner cities;
- the transformation of council housing from an expanding rental tenure for the more privileged 'working class' into a declining 'welfare' tenure;
- the promotion of housing associations as mainstream rather than 'supplementary' providers of low income rental housing and as virtual monopoly builders of new rental housing;
- the decline in private renting and transformation to a tenure catering largely for short-term lets to younger people;
- the growth of homelessness and its dominance as an access route to social housing.

Our knowledge of the impact of these changes on ethnic minority groups is very sketchy and often based on assumptions about housing market behaviour rather than research data. The 1991 Census provides a good snapshot of outcomes, but can tell us little about processes. Yet these changes must have had both short- and long-term effects on the parameters within which ethnic minority groups, like the majority population, have been able to operate housing choices. This chapter looks at each of the areas of structural change noted above and examines their implications for the housing status and experience of ethnic minority groups.

THE GROWTH OF HOME-OWNERSHIP

The pattern of British housing tenure has been significantly restructured since the arrival of the first post-war migrants from the New Commonwealth. In 1945, only a quarter of households were owner-occupiers; by 1991 this figure had risen to 66 per cent. But the incidence of home-ownership is highly differentiated between ethnic groups (Table 8.1). In 1991, owner-occupation was greatest for the Indians (82 per cent), Pakistanis (77 per cent), whites (67 per cent) and Chinese (62 per cent) but fell to 48 per cent for the Black Caribbean, 44 per cent for the Bangladeshi and 28 per cent for the Black African groups.

Large though these differences are, they are smaller than a decade ago. Home-ownership rates among Indians and Pakistanis have remained roughly static, while those among Bangladeshis and Chinese have risen sharply and there has been a smaller rise among Black Caribbean households.

Once one starts to control for possible explanatory variables, such as gender, class, household type and regional location, the size of the differentials is markedly reduced. Gender, for example, has a striking effect on tenure within ethnic groups in that women heads of households are far less likely to own, even taking into account their socio-economic status. The high incidence of female heads of household in the Black Caribbean group partly explains the skew of this group towards rental housing (Peach and Byron, 1993: 422), pointing to the importance of both family structure and gender as powerful explanatory factors.

Earlier studies showed that home-ownership among ethnic minority groups was by no means always associated with above average incomes. Among South Asians in particular, low income home-ownership was a characteristic feature (Karn *et al.*, 1986). This was still the case in 1991; both Dorling (1997) and Phillips (1997) have found there was a much stronger positive association between home-ownership and occupational status among white, Chinese and Black Caribbean ethnic groups than South Asians, particularly Pakistanis and Bangladeshis (outside London).

There are also enormous local variations in tenure. In 1991, home-ownership levels for Indians varied, for instance, from 34 per cent in Tower Hamlets LB to over 90 per cent in suburban areas of the North and Midlands, and, among Black Caribbeans, from 12 per cent in Kensington and Chelsea to 96 per cent in suburban Leicestershire (Phillips, 1997). Dorling calculated that 24 per cent of variations in tenure between ethnic groups were accounted for by geographical differences. But taking economic position, household structure and geography together, this still leaves over two-thirds of the variations in tenure unaccounted for.

The 1991 Census gives us the opportunity to explore differences within, as well as between, ethnic groups. Compared with earlier studies, the census shows that there has been increasing fragmentation of ownership experiences:

> wider divisions have opened up within the ethnic minority groups in terms of social class and between the first generation of immigrants and the UK-born. We are now beginning to see some convergence of ownership patterns (both in terms of level of ownership and the quality of property purchased) between the later generations of ethnic minority group buyers and the white population.
>
> (Phillips, 1997: 14)

We are handicapped in studying differences in 'housing quality' by the fact that the census provides no data on the state of repair or age of property. It is impossible, for instance, to distinguish between run-down nineteenth-century terraces and newly constructed 'town-houses' in the owner-occupied sector. Phillips (1997) has attempted to overcome the deficiency in housing quality measures by creating a composite measure of quality in the owner-occupied sector, with the top category consisting of detached or semi-detached homes with central heating. She found that the home-owners most likely to live in these higher quality/higher status homes were the whites, Chinese and Indians and the least likely were the Pakistanis and Bangladeshis. This hierarchy of housing quality within home-ownership parallels the hierarchy of employment and occupations of ethnic minority groups. The only variable upon which Indian home-owners performed badly, though better than the Pakistanis and Bangladeshis, was overcrowding. This relates to the continuing large size of their households, and often survives, though in less acute form, a move to good quality accommodation in the suburbs (Law *et al.*, 1996).

Within ethnic groups Phillips also found a clear correlation between the social class of home-owners and the status of their property. But this association was much clearer for white and Indian owners in Social Classes I and II, of whom 62 per cent and 58 per cent, respectively, lived in centrally heated, detached or semi-detached houses, compared with 47 per cent of the equivalent Pakistanis and Chinese and 31 per cent of the Black Caribbeans. The high incidence of terraced housing among owners from ethnic minority groups is likely to be a function partly of price but also of the concentration of these groups into older, inner city areas.

The hierarchy of status of owner-occupied housing survives analysis by locality. The situation in suburban areas is particularly interesting because of the potential impact that moves to more modern housing in suburban areas could have on living conditions. White, Chinese and Indian owners appeared to experience greater improvements in housing status and quality with a move to the suburbs than did Black Caribbean owners. The latter still seemed to buy disproportionate numbers of terraced houses. The explanations of this are likely to be the youth of the black group, the high incidence of female headed households and possibly institutional discrimination and 'racial steering' (Phillips, 1997). As Karn writes,

> the phenomenon of 'racial steering' (and 'class steering') by estate agents is familiar to anyone who has ever moved to a new area and asked an agents advice about 'good places to buy'. The line between common sense advice and race and class stereotyping is very fine.
>
> (Karn, 1997)

There have been relatively few occasions upon which the CRE has been able to bring cases of racial steering. The most recent case was that of Norman Lester and Co. (CRE, 1990a). Actor tests, following complaints, found that the agency was discriminating against people selling in Asian areas, segregating purchasers on racial grounds, accepting discriminatory instructions from vendors, and discriminating against Asians in mortgage lending. The parallels with the findings of earlier studies of estate agent activity are strong (see Sarre *et al.*, 1989; CRE, 1988a).

Evidence of institutional discrimination in lending has been even harder to obtain because the building societies and banks have resisted ethnic record-keeping and actor testing of the process of purchasing is very problematical. Studies of lending have therefore had to rely largely on surveys. There were several pieces of research in the 1970s and 1980s (e.g. McIntosh and Smith, 1974; Lambert, 1976; Stevens *et al.*, 1982; Karn, 1983; Karn *et al.*, 1986; and Sarre *et al.*, 1989) which concluded that there was a strong case for much greater scrutiny of buying and selling practices and, in particular, the terms of mortgage lending to minority ethnic groups. A CRE investigation in Rochdale in 1985 found that lenders were avoiding the types of terraced houses that Asians were buying (CRE, 1985). However, this investigation, and the fieldwork for the academic studies, were carried out before deregulation, when there were mortgage shortages and when the building society cartel limited variety in charges. So the situation could subsequently have improved in terms of access to any mortgage at all, but deteriorated in terms of differential charging.

Overall, the evidence of the 1991 Census on home-ownership points to a variety of ethnic minority group experiences and in particular their 'creativity of response' (Cross, 1991: 311). The strategies adopted by households to provide themselves with housing, particularly owner-occupied housing, despite poverty and social exclusion, have been most impressive. Home-ownership appears to be providing a route to the suburbs for at least the more affluent minority groups.

However, more question marks probably hang over the success of inner city home-ownership in the 1990s, where a combination of deteriorating physical environments and unemployment may make owning more of a liability than an asset for some owners, particularly those on low incomes (Karn and Lucas, 1996). But even there home-ownership has given communities a degree of autonomy and identity which it would have been difficult to create in social rented housing.

DILEMMAS OF URBAN RENEWAL AND ETHNIC MINORITY HOME-OWNERSHIP

The heavy concentration of ethnic minority groups (especially Indians and Pakistanis) in pre-1919 owner-occupied housing in inner city areas means that urban renewal policies are particularly important to them, and, equally, their responses are crucial to the success of renewal initiatives. Much of the very worst housing is owned by Asians. The 1986 English House Condition survey showed that 9 per cent of households with heads born in the New Commonwealth and Pakistan were living in properties designated as 'unfit' and a further 22 per cent in property classified as 'in poor repair'. This compared with 4 per cent and 13 per cent of those of UK origin (DoE, 1988: 43).

In the late 1960s and early 1970s, ethnic minority home-owners were in the forefront of opposition to slum clearance, which they justifiably saw as breaking up their communities and jeopardising their hard-earned status as owner-occupiers. The subsequent shift to improvement policies was therefore generally welcomed. However, improvement policies have not produced the intended long-term up-grading of whole areas. Research by Ratcliffe (1992) suggests that ethnic minority households have probably been less likely than whites to have had either capital of their own to invest in improvements or access to grants. Various measures were introduced in the 1980s to promote renewal in the face of low participation rates by homeowners, notably enveloping and block improvement schemes. Ethnic minority home-owners were major beneficiaries of these, but the schemes proved too expensive to sustain in the deteriorating economic climate of the late 1980s.

Subsequently access to grants has become more difficult, with the introduction of means-testing for mandatory grants, ceilings substantially below the cost of improvement and cash shortages in local authorities. In doing appraisals of their renewal areas, many local authorities in the Midlands and North have concluded that, for the worst housing, clearance would be a more cost-effective option than renovation. But, once again, they face the fierce opposition of home-owners, Asians in particular.

On the evidence of the past, Asian and other low income owners do indeed stand to lose heavily through clearance. Not only do they suffer the breakup of their community and the disruption and economic and social costs of moving, but they typically benefit little in terms of improved quality of housing or security. It has been typical for owners in such areas to have to become tenants of local authority or housing association property after clearance because they cannot afford to buy another property (Karn and Lucas, 1996). However, there is usually a shortage of social rented housing in such areas, especially of larger houses and so a move away from the area is often required. Authorities have found many Asians unwilling to make such moves, fearing loss of contact with their communities and racial harassment.

For those who are able and willing to buy again, the property they can afford is typically only marginally better quality than the one they had before. They generally become more indebted and may even be involved in another round of clearance at a later date (Karn and Lucas, 1996).

In most renewal areas, Asian communities have gained much more political strength and organisation than they had in the 1960s, to defend their interests and oppose clearance. They arrange applications for mandatory grants, appeals against clearance, and negotiate about compensation levels and rental rehousing arrangements. This type of pressure led to a successful, DoE funded, pilot scheme in Saltley, Birmingham, for 'rebuilding grants', which have been incorporated into the 1996 Housing Act as 'relocation grants'. These grants provide for means-tested, top-up grants to home-owners in clearance areas to enable them to buy new, shared-ownership homes in the area. However, local authorities have to find the resources for these grants out of their HIP budgets, in competition with renovation grants, so the scheme, while potentially useful, can be seen as only an extension of the rehousing opportunities for some owners in clearance areas, not a wholesale solution to the problems of low-income, inner city home-ownership (Karn and Lucas, 1996).

THE TRANSFORMATION OF SOCIAL RENTED HOUSING

There are, potentially, four main topics to be addressed about minority access to social rental housing. The first concerns differential access to any housing at all, the second, the quality of housing and its surroundings, the third, segregation, and the fourth, equality of treatment in repairs and general management services. The latter, though undoubtedly potentially important has not been the subject of any research or CRE investigations so we are not in a position to discuss it further. We therefore consider the first two aspects only. (Segregation is considered more generally later.) We then go on to consider monitoring of racial equality in the social rented sector and the role of ethnic minority housing associations (EMHAs).

Representation of ethnic minority groups in social rented housing

Since 1980 it has been government policy to reduce the role of local authorities in the provision of social rental housing and to promote that of housing associations. This policy has been pursued through the Right to Buy, the virtual cessation of new building by local authorities and the transfer of estates to housing associations. In 1993, 95 per cent of all new social rented housing was produced by housing associations. However, because of financial constraints, rates of construction by housing associations have not nearly compensated for the loss of local authority construction; construction of social rented housing in 1993 was only 40 per cent of that in 1978. At the same time, the supply of private rental housing has continued to dwindle, so the post-1980 period has been marked by increasing shortages of rental housing and growing homelessness. The effect of this has been that, in the decade up to 1991, the proportion of households in Britain who rent from local authorities has dropped from about 30 per cent to 21 per cent, while the proportion renting from housing associations has risen only from 2 per cent in 1981 to 4 per cent in 1993.

The ethnic minority groups that most often live in council housing are the Black Africans, the Black Caribbeans and the Bangladeshis (Table 8.1). The Indians and Pakistanis are heavily under-represented. But in all groups, renting from the council is losing ground to home-ownership. The very high rates of local authority rental among Bangladeshis and Black Africans nationally reflect the concentration of these groups in inner London where the council sector is disproportionately large.

Housing associations cater for disproportionate numbers of ethnic minority households (Table 8.1), with the exception, as in the council sector, of the Indians and Pakistanis and the Chinese. Housing association properties are even more unevenly distributed geographically than council housing, with again high concentrations in inner London and larger urban areas but few in rural areas and small towns. All those groups most heavily represented in housing associations, namely the black groups and Bangladeshis, are particularly concentrated in London.

The over-representation of some ethnic minority groups within the social rented sector reflects their weak employment position, their household structure (e.g. single parents are especially well represented) and the particular household preferences and strategies of different ethnic groups. It is also a function of the high level of homelessness among ethnic minorities. As rental housing has become more scarce, priority for local authority and housing association lettings has increasingly gone to the statutorily homeless. Thirty-nine per cent of all council lettings in England in 1992/3 went to the homeless compared with only 10 per cent in 1977/8 and 20 per cent in 1984/5.

This pattern of allocation has had the effect of increasing the number of council and housing association tenants who are unemployed or on very low incomes. Rents rises have put the newer properties beyond the reach of low income earners; virtually the only people who can accept them are those on housing benefit. This places many tenants in a 'poverty trap', where obtaining a job means an inability to meet the rent. This problem is likely to be particularly acute for ethnic minority tenants, who have higher rates of unemployment. For instance, in 1991, among economically active white council tenants, 26 per cent were unemployed compared with over 50 per cent of Pakistanis and Bangladeshis and over 30 per cent of all other groups (Table 8.2).

The heavy reliance of some ethnic groups, such as the Black Caribbeans and Black Africans, on the social rented sector means that they are likely to suffer disproportionately from shortages of rental housing and from the adverse effects of the growing concentration of the poorest households in local authority and housing association estates (Page, 1993). One feels that it is not coincidental that improved access for ethnic minorities to social rented housing has come at a time when the sector has lost status and desirability, becoming a 'residual tenure' for 'residual groups'.

Quality of social rented housing

Studies of allocations of council housing over the past twenty-five years have shown that ethnic minority groups have received a disproportionate share of the least popular types of housing and least popular estates (e.g. CRE, 1984, 1988b, 1990b; Henderson and Karn, 1987; Phillips, 1986; Smith and Whalley, 1975).

In trying to use the 1991 Census to up-date our knowledge of the quality of council and housing association property occupied by ethnic minorities, we are severely handicapped by the absence of any measure of state of repair or the age of the property. However, Howes and Mullins (1997) have used types of housing as a proxy for quality in the local authority and housing association sectors and have found that white households continue to fare

Table 8.2 Economic activity and unemployment rates for heads of household by tenure and ethnic group, England and Wales, 1991

	All tenures*	LA tenants	HA tenants	Private tenants	OO	OO rate as % of LA Rate	OO rate as % of HA Rate
Per cent economically active	62	40	38	64	69	160	181
[Per cent of economically active unemployed]							
White	9	26	23	16	5	19	22
Black Caribbean	18	30	33	26	9	30	27
Black African	23	32	22	29	13	41	59
Black other	21	39	32	13	13	33	41
Indian	12	32	28	23	10	31	36
Pakistani	28	50	54	44	24	48	44
Bangladeshi	37	57	70	40	23	40	33
Chinese	10	35	-	23	4	11	-
Other Asian	11	31	41	7	7	23	17
Other other	15	26	23	26	9	35	39

Source: Howes and Mullins, 1997, Table 10.12 (based on 1991 Census, 2 per cent individual SAR)

* Excludes renting with a job.

much better than ethnic minority groups. However, as with the owner-occupied sector, there are large differences between groups. Black Caribbeans, Bangladeshis and Black Africans, in particular, have far fewer detached or semi-detached houses and more flats (Howes and Mullins, 1997). This pattern may partly reflect the London bias in the geography of these groups.

Ethnic minority access to good quality housing has also been affected by the changing role of housing associations over the last fifteen years. Since 1980, housing association activities have shifted away from rehabilitation to new construction and from building for special needs to providing lifetime rental housing for families. However, their existing housing is still skewed towards pre-1919 rehabilitated terraces, and purpose-built and converted flats. This presents problems for arranging transfers from flats to houses. According to the 1991 Census, Black Caribbean, Black African and Bangladeshi tenants are disproportionately concentrated in converted flats, the type of accommodation from which transfers are often sought, and are thus likely to be particularly affected by this problem.

The effects of the concentration of ethnic minority groups, particularly the black groups and the Bangladeshis, in some of the worst housing association and local authority housing is likely to be exacerbated by the squeeze in resources available to social landlords for the up-grading of this property. Ethnic minorities are, therefore, likely to be disproportionately caught up in the 'ghettoisation' of the poorest groups in the least attractive areas of social housing, with all the associated problems of poor schools, crime and poor employment prospects.

Monitoring of racial equality performance in the social rental sectors

In the past *local authorities* have been the subject of a large number of CRE investigations (e.g. CRE, 1984, 1988b, 1989, 1990b, 1993a) and independent research studies (e.g. Smith and Whalley, 1975; Henderson and Karn, 1987) and, not least, their own internally initiated studies (e.g. Stunnell, 1975; Parker and Dugmore, 1976; Phillips, 1984, 1986). These studies revealed 'ethnic penalties' in access, in the quality of housing allocated, in waiting times, in the treatment of homeless people, in transfers and in nominations to housing associations and the failure to provide suitable types of housing for their needs (CRE, 1993a).

Now the emphasis is upon self-monitoring of racial equality performance, but the record in this respect is very patchy and some local authorities have strongly resisted it in the teeth of CRE pressure. For instance, despite strong advice by the CRE from the early 1980s (summarised in CRE, 1991), both

Liverpool City Council and Oldham MBC resisted ethnic monitoring until they were both ultimately made the subject of formal investigations (CRE, 1989, 1993a).

Housing associations have been the subject of rather fewer investigations by the CRE (e.g. CRE, 1983, 1992) and independent studies (Niner, 1985) but they have received considerable guidance and stimulus around racial equality issues from the National Housing Federation (NHF, formerly NFHA) (e.g. NFHA, 1983, 1992a,b) and, most crucially, are subject to regulation and monitoring by the Housing Corporation, Scottish Homes and Tai Cymru, all of whom tie financial allocations to performance, including equal opportunity policies and practices. However, housing associations appear to perform better on paper than in practice. A review of practice by the CRE concluded that:

> Ethnic monitoring in many associations was a purely mechanical exercise, and no attempt had been made to use the data to improve performance in delivering a fairer housing service.
>
> (CRE, 1993b: 96)

Nevertheless, largely because of the regulatory framework,

> There is little doubt that the housing association movement, particularly in England, has generally made more progress than local authority housing departments.
>
> (ibid.: 7–8)

Ethnic minority housing associations

Ethnic minority housing associations (EMHAs) have been set up both as a response to the perceived inadequacies of mainstream housing associations and local authorities in meeting the needs of ethnic minorities and from a conviction that when ethnic minorities run their own housing services they are able to make unique contributions. Though small in terms of the numbers of homes provided, EMHAs have been a very significant and positive development. Their fundamental contribution stems from the fact that the needs of ethnic minorities are their primary concern, not just an after-thought or one duty among many, as they are for the mainstream associations.

The earliest EMHAs were founded in the 1960s and 1970s but they were very few in number and were given no special support until 1986. In that year the Housing Corporation launched its five-year 'Black and Ethnic Minority Housing Association Strategy' (B&EMHA). As a result the number of registered EMHAs rose from nineteen in 1986, to thirty-five in 1988 (Sarre *et al.*, 1989) and to fifty-eight in 1991.

This first five-year B&EMHA strategy put an emphasis on the creation of new associations but provided little advice about their continuing viability and growth, and did little for associations that were already in existence (Harrison, 1995). So in 1991, the Housing Corporation launched its second five-year strategy, 'An Independent Future', with the aim that EMHAs should own and manage 16,500 units by 1996 (HC, 1992). By March 1996, this target was exceeded since there were 17,135 units, bringing the EMHAs to a position where they can play a significant role in the provision and management of accommodation.

However, the EMHAs still have many problems. First, they are very small; in March 1994 the largest (Ujima) had just over 1,500 units. Second, they are very unevenly distributed, geographically, with poor representation in some areas of high ethnic minority population, notably the Midlands. Third, they have problems of financial viability. Two years after the first strategy was launched, the government changed the basis of housing association financing (through Part II of the 1988 Housing Act) to a more market-based approach, with private sector borrowing, market level rents, cost competition between associations for grant allocations and acceptance of greater financial risk in development costs. All these changes have penalised smaller, newer associations and particularly the EMHAs. White associations, founded in the late 1960s and early 1970s had a much longer 'lead-in' period before they had to face the harsh realities of the post-1988 regime. Most of the EMHAs had barely started before the new financial regime came into force, effectively undermining the aims of the B&EMHA strategy right from the start. On top of this have come reductions in grant rates and renewed cuts in capital allocations for rental housing. The ending of Urban Programme funding on which many EMHAs had relied provided a further financial blow.

As a result, though the second strategy aimed at creating forty viable and financially independent EMHAs by 1996, this has not been achieved. A review by the Housing Corporation in 1993 concluded that, with the changed financial regime, only a few EMHAs would achieve financial independence. A number of EMHAs have had to merge with others. And even the more securely-based ones have had to resort to partnerships, consortia and other group arrangements with mainstream associations to continue development. Many such arrangements are proving very successful but there is a risk that, because of the imbalance of resources and power, EMHAs will be co-opted into the prevailing state/market/white culture. In particular competitive financial pressures are encouraging very basic minimum standards of design, construction and management and uniformity rather than the innovation and responsiveness to community needs that the EMHAs had envisaged.

In 1996 the Housing Corporation effectively abandoned significant special help for EMHAs. This was part of government's new approach to the 'independent sector', which de-emphasised support for institutions and stressed a competitive approach to housing production. Rather than defend the EMHAs, the Housing Corporation implied that withdrawing special financial help to EMHAs did not matter because the second B&EMHA strategy period was over and, in any case, ethnic minority housing needs were being adequately met by mainstream associations (HC, 1995).

Yet an evaluation by Harrison *et al.*, (1996) concluded that the EMHAs had been 'remarkably successful'. We would agree, but also maintain that the period from 1985 to 1996 has been too short to complete the process of establishing them on a sure financial footing (Karn *et al.*, 1995). EMHAs have distinctive contributions to make, in terms of: identifying needs; bridging communications gaps with ethnic minority communities; providing a catalyst for equal opportunities initiatives by the mainstream associations; and providing professional level employment for ethnic minority staff. Perhaps most crucially, the Housing Corporation's B&EMHA strategies have constituted a unique example of British Government support for the empowerment of ethnic minority communities.

However, this is not an approach which commands widespread support or understanding and the failure of the Housing Corporation to defend its B&EMHA strategy in 1995–6 probably reflects underlying white suspicion of 'separatist' as opposed to 'integrationist' approaches to ethnic minority housing provision .

THE DECLINE OF THE PRIVATE RENTED SECTOR

In the twenty years between 1971 and 1991, the private rented sector declined from housing nearly a quarter of all households to 9 per cent. In 1971, ethnic minority groups were very heavily dependent on the private rented sector; 30 per cent of Black Caribbean and 35 per cent of Indian households were in private renting at that time. By 1991, both of these groups had largely moved out of private renting; only about 6 per cent, less than the national average, remained in this sector (Table 8.1). However, private renting still plays an important role for Black Africans (18 per cent), who are concentrated in the London housing market, for the Chinese (17 per cent) and for groups defined in the Census as 'Other Asians' (25 per cent) and 'Black other' (14 per cent). In London in particular, these groups include large numbers of students, refugees and asylum seekers (Carey-Wood *et al.*, 1994).

The quality of private rented accommodation is often very poor. According to the 1991 English House Condition Survey the private rented sector has by far the highest level of disrepair, 85 per cent higher than the owner-occupied sector, which is itself 28 per cent higher than the council rented sector (DoE, 1993: 50). There are also large numbers of relatively low quality furnished rooms and flat conversions. The 1991 census shows that 9 per cent of privately let property was not self-contained and 14 per cent consisted of converted flats, compared with 1 per cent and 4 per cent for all tenures (Howes and Mullins, 1997). The situation was far worse for ethnic minority private tenants; Black African tenants were ten times as likely as whites to live in non-self-contained property and all the other groups were more than three times as likely. They were also five times as likely as white private tenants to live in converted flats and all other groups were more than twice as likely. The particularly bad situation of Black Africans is probably the result of the large proportions of both students and refugees in this group.

Despite the poor quality of much private rental housing, rents are high because of the shortage of rental housing, not just in London or even metropolitan areas, and it has become common for deposits to be required. Many landlords are also unwilling to accept prospective tenants dependent on income support. There is also little security of tenure; assured shorthold tenancies for six months have become the norm for new private lettings.

Apart from the problems faced in common with low income white households, it is clear that ethnic minorities additionally suffer from widespread racial discrimination in the private rented sector. In 1990, a CRE investigation, using actor-testing, found that, nationally, one in five accommodation agencies were discriminating, in Ealing nearly half and in Bristol one-third (CRE, 1990c). The scarcity of private rental housing makes discrimination more likely.

THE GROWTH OF HOMELESSNESS

There has been a dramatic increase in homelessness over the last fifteen years. Even the official DoE statistics indicated nearly a threefold increase in households accepted as homeless by British local authorities between 1977 and 1992. The causes of the overall rise in homelessness have been a combination of council house sales, very low rates of rental housing production, high levels of unemployment, changing demographic patterns, notably marital breakup, and cuts in the value of benefits, particularly for young single people. Underlying all this has been a growth in socio-economic inequalities, which have particularly affected the most vulnerable groups (Murie, 1988).

The disproportionate effect of homelessness on ethnic minority groups is clear. A survey of London boroughs in 1989 found that black households were up to four times more likely than white households to become homeless and that 40 per cent of London's homeless acceptances were either 'African', 'Caribbean', 'Asian' or 'Black UK' (Friedman and LHU/LRC, 1989). In 1996, a survey of emergency homeless hostels found that one in two of the residents were from ethnic minority groups, compared with one in three in 1992 (Resource Information Service, 1996). Refugees and asylum seekers accounted for 12 per cent of the residents. Since February 1996, the plight of asylum seekers has deteriorated even further following the government's ruling that people failing to apply for refugee status at the port of entry would lose all benefit entitlements. This has led to instances of councils refusing to provide temporary accommodation for homeless and destitute asylum seekers (*Guardian*, 29 June 1996) and brought predictions from the Refugee Council of rising levels of street homelessness.

Youth homelessness is another area of growing concern (Anderson *et al.*, 1993; Randall and Brown, 1993; Davies *et al.*, 1996), again disproportionately affecting ethnic minority groups. Anderson *et al.*, (1993) report that while 26 per cent of all hostel and bed and breakfast residents are from ethnic minorities, this proportion rises to 44 per cent of 16–17 year olds and 38 per cent of those under 25. Davies *et al.*, (1996) argue that the causes of homelessness are much the same for young people in all ethnic groups; namely, family breakdown, abuse, failure of the care system and more recently, the withdrawal of benefits from 16–17 year olds. There is also a very close association between youth homelessness and unemployment, which, given the vulnerable position of ethnic minorities in the job market, has particular resonance for black and Asian youngsters. However, although the causes of homelessness are similar, Davies *et al.*, (1996) contend that the experience of homelessness is different. Their study showed that whites were more likely to have slept rough than Asians and Black Caribbeans, but that the needs of black and, in particular, the Asian homeless are not well recognised by the statutory and voluntary services. This study found that ethnic minority youngsters would prefer to be put up in hostels run by staff from their own communities, but that this sort of accommodation was very scarce.

The variable ways in which local authorities interpret their statutory duty to rehouse the homeless and, in particular, their practices in relation to 'priority need', 'intentionality' and 'local connection' disproportionately affect ethnic minority groups. The CRE found evidence that Tower Hamlets LB (CRE, 1988b) used these criteria to discriminate against ethnic minority homeless and evade their statutory obligations. This had a serious impact on the Bangladeshi community nationally, 20 per cent of whom lived in Tower Hamlets. The council argued that the wives and children of sixty Bangladeshi tenants had rendered themselves intentionally homeless by leaving Bangladesh. The CRE made it clear that councils had no right to refuse accommodation on the grounds of immigration status, but the Tower Hamlets council's stance sent a clear signal of 'ineligibility' to Bangladeshis in the locality.

The Formal Investigation into Tower Hamlets LB also found that the council had *directly* discriminated against Bangladeshi homeless families in respect of waiting times and the quality of estates to which they were allocated. Many more councils have *indirectly* discriminated against their ethnic minority applicants through their approach to homeless allocations. Driven by the need to fill their poorer voids, many local authorities have given their homeless applicants a single offer of their harder-to-let accommodation. Desperate households have been forced to accept, with the carrot that they could transfer later. In the London boroughs in particular, where there are high levels of ethnic minority homelessness, this policy has disproportionately disadvantaged ethnic minorities. Subsequent sales of the best council properties have reduced transfer options, serving to fossilise the pattern of ethnic minority concentration on hard-to-let estates.

The position for homeless families may now become much worse if the terms of the Housing Act 1996 are not repealed. Under this legislation, local authorities and housing associations are allowed to provide only temporary accommodation for up to twenty-four months for homeless people who do not already qualify through the waiting list. This will inevitably create further disruption in the lives of homeless families, particularly those with children, who need stable homes and school arrangements.

REFLECTING ON CHANGE

The foregoing discussion has documented the housing experiences and outcomes for ethnic minority groups in Britain, with particular reference to the changing conditions in the housing market over the last two decades. The picture is necessarily incomplete; we are left with many questions. For instance, to what extent is the high rate of ethnic minority homelessness the product of, say, discrimination or poverty? And to what extent is it a result of ethnic minority groups' greater exposure to new housing market forces, notably the growing shortage of social rented housing? Or, to take another example, which features of white housing are a product of 'residual' patterns in the white housing market? This is clearly the case, for instance, in the dominance of elderly white people in private renting but is it also the reason for the higher class profile of white than ethnic minority council tenants? And to what extent has the ability of Asians to purchase inner city terraced housing been a product of slum clearance ending?

These questions aside, some clear issues emerge from our review which merit further discussion, notably, first, the importance of ethnic diversity;

second, the problems in defining the concept of 'racial inequality' in housing; third, the role of racial harassment and violence in producing and sustaining patterns of inequality, and finally, the impact of racial discrimination, harassment and disadvantage on spatial concentration, segregation and dispersal of ethnic minority groups.

Ethnic diversity

An appreciation of the diversity of experience, both within and between ethnic groups, is fundamental to our understanding of the current position and future prospects for ethnic minorities in the housing market. It is a diversity which cross-cuts age, generation, gender and country of origin, and varies between locations.

Tariq Modood shows in chapter 4 that the ethnic minority experience within the labour market is becoming increasingly differentiated. This pattern of economic advantage and disadvantage is closely correlated with housing conditions. In particular, the socio-economic mobility among Indians has been clearly associated with increasing levels of suburban home-ownership (Phillips and Sarre, 1995). It is no longer valid, if it ever was, to talk about the 'South Asians' as a group. Length of settlement, levels of education and employment status, housing outcomes, religion and cultural factors serve to differentiate the Indians, Pakistanis and Bangladeshis. Modood (1992) has vehemently opposed the tendency for academics and policy makers to lapse into 'racial dualism'.

However, ethnic minority groups are also highly differentiated internally. For instance, there is a striking polarisation between suburban middle class Indians and the larger number of poorer Indians remaining in overcrowded, often substandard accommodation in the inner cities.

An acknowledgment of ethnic diversity has clear policy implications; housing strategies and racial equality targets need to take account of ethnic and class differentiation in housing need, tenure preferences, locational requirements and housing market behaviour. For instance, the diversity of experience among homeless youth, in terms of gender, age, location and ethnic group, has important implications for statutory and voluntary service provision for this group (Davies *et al.*, 1996). But equally, new housing demands will emerge with the demographic maturity of the ethnic minority groups, for instance, the growing need for more varied housing options for ethnic minority elders (Age Concern, 1991).

The number and diversity of household types within and between the ethnic groups is likely to increase significantly. Recent projections suggest that by 2011, the number of households headed by someone of ethnic minority origin will increase by 39 per cent compared with 18 per cent for white heads of households (*Roof*, July/August 1996). This reflects the age structure of the ethnic minority population. Recent qualitative research with five ethnic minority groups in Leeds explored issues related to family formation (Law *et al.*, 1996). This revealed a complexity of social processes, bound up with financial pressures and changing family life, that pointed to the potential for the formation of smaller households among the Black Caribbeans, Indians, Chinese, Pakistanis and Bangladeshis. The greatest potential for new household formation lies with the two latter groups, given their youthful age structure, relatively high fertility rates, household sizes and levels of overcrowding. However, as was previously noted, these groups also currently occupy the weakest position in the housing and employment markets, and may thus encounter difficulties in securing decent, affordable, and large enough accommodation in their preferred locations.

Conceptualising inequality

While 'racial equality' has been seen as a generally worthy goal, it is often conceptualised in a very abstract way (Smith, 1989). Law (1996) goes even further, arguing that the concept of racial equality in housing and social policy has been used in a highly contestable and contradictory way. We therefore have to ask what exactly should we be striving towards when we talk of racial equality in housing? Most problematically, how do we interpret tenure differences, notably different levels of home-ownership, in relation to racial equality? These are clearly a reflection of ethnic, class and (increasingly) generational preferences as well as ability to pay. To ignore tenure differences risks underestimating the systematic constraints faced by particular groups, while to over-stress them as symptoms of inequality devalues and oversimplifies household choices.

These dilemmas come to the fore when housing organisations attempt to put race equality policies into practice. Practitioners, faced with ethnic diversity, have often been unable to decide what constitutes 'racial equality', and hence to interpret ethnic monitoring data. Councils have tended to place great emphasis upon achieving *equality of opportunity* in terms of their rental housing allocations, but less attention has been given to the thornier issue of the way in which racial harassment or unemployment disproportionately affect ethnic groups' housing choices, particularly entry to home-ownership (Law, 1996). Those pursuing the goal of *equality of outcome* also have challenging issues to resolve. This is an almost impossible goal if considered *across* tenures. Even *within* tenures, the ability to implement this grand concept of racial equality is fraught with problems in terms of cost, practicalities, political will and public support. All too often, the quest for racial equality in the most deprived areas of local authority housing comes down to an exercise in 'sharing out the misery', choosing between poor whites and poor blacks. The result has been to escalate racial tensions, often manifest in racial harassment, when the real issues of inadequate housing investment and management resources remain unresolved (Phillips, 1984; Mullings, 1991). The concept of 'housing need' also has to be carefully scrutinised when evaluating equality of outcome; the white norm may well be an inappropriate yardstick, particularly as far as location is concerned (Henderson and Karn, 1987). This is particularly relevant in the construction of race equality targets.

Despite these difficulties of interpretation and implementation, there has nevertheless been a remarkable level of acceptance, by social landlords, of the existence of racial inequalities in housing condition. After many battles, there has also been some preparedness to act both to improve their own practice and to support the growing ethnic minority housing movement.

Racial harassment and violence

The House of Commons Home Affairs Committee, reporting on racial attacks and harassment in 1986, declared that the incidence of attacks was 'the most shameful and dispiriting aspect of race relations in Britain'. In the five years up to 1993, the number of 'racial incidents' recorded by the police nearly doubled. While an increase in recording may have played some part in this, there is a strong feeling in many communities that racist violence is rising. According to the *British Crime Survey*, in 1992, 89,000 crimes involving some racial elements were committed against Asians and 41,000 against Black Caribbeans.

The effects of racial harassment and violence and the fear of them have to be particularly stressed in explaining housing patterns. Ethnic minority groups have limited safe choices of locations, reinforcing the positive attractions of core settlement areas and restricting movement beyond them. Fear of racial harassment, and the 'managerial problems' associated with it, also prompt housing managers to make allocation decisions which minimise the potential for ethnic group conflict and violence. Racial equality of outcome cannot be attained while the fear of racial harassment pervades people's lives and housing decisions.

The experience and fear of racial harassment affect all tenures, although attention has tended to focus on the level of violence in the local authority sector because of its public accountability and greater potential for effective policy implementation. Home Office analysis of police statistics in 1989 revealed that about a quarter of all reported racially motivated incidents took place on council estates. The level of violence in some areas produces virtual 'no-go' areas (Phillips, 1984; Sheffield City Council, 1989). A recent report revealed that, despite the exhortations from the DoE and CRE, less than half of the English local authority housing departments have written policies and procedures on racial harassment (Dhooge and Barelli, 1996). A fifth of all ethnic minority tenants are renting from councils with no harassment policies, let alone the political will to tackle this problem. The larger housing associations have a better record on paper than the local authorities, with nine out of ten having written harassment policies. However, in both social rented sectors, even where harassment policies are in place, the procedures for dealing with perpetrators are highly variable and the outcome for the harassed tenant uncertain.

The record for dealing with racial harassment in the private sector is even worse. Good practice guides extend local authorities' obligations to provide support and advice to owner occupiers and private rental tenants. Leicester City Council is notable for having set up an innovative scheme providing emergency support for victims of racial harassment in all tenures, but such schemes are rare. In the private rental sector, landlord harassment is also an issue, with ethnic minority tenants (especially young blacks) being twice as likely as white tenants to experience this (GLC, 1986). Such experiences have reinforced the tendency for market segmentation in the private rental sector (see below).

Ethnic minority concentration and segregation

The development of avoidance strategies based on fear and experience of discrimination and/or racial harassment has promoted what some have referred to as market segmentation or a 'dual housing market' (Smith, 1989). This results from ethnic minorities restricting their search for accommodation to a spatially limited and usually inferior section of the housing market.

Market segmentation has found its clearest expression in the private rental sector, where there has been a long tradition of renting from a landlord of a similar ethnic origin. Similar processes have also been at work in the owner-occupied sector. In the past, reliance on word of mouth exchanges of information and private funding arrangements limited the range and price of properties considered to the poorer, cheaper end of the market (Sarre *et al.*, 1989). The entry of ethnic minority estate agents into the market, specialising in inner city properties, only served to reinforce the segregated pattern (Phillips, 1981). Now, the use of mainstream housing exchange institutions by ethnic minorities is widespread and the ethnic purchaser's housing options have widened. However, institutional discrimination, including racial steering, and fear of racial harassment still restrict housing and locational choices. The newly emerging network of black-led housing associations, while providing black people with access to better quality housing than in the past, also reinforces the pattern of segmentation in the social rented sector. Blacks are more likely to apply to black-led rather than white-led associations, which narrows their range of housing options (Law *et al.*, 1996) and often involves higher rents levels than for the equivalent mainstream housing association or council properties.

There is evidence of increasing levels of separation between whites and ethnic minority groups over the 1981–91 period, and a growing concentration of ethnic minority groups in metropolitan areas and in the poorer quality residential areas, as defined by the DoE's Index of Local Conditions (DoE, 1994). In Bradford, the proportion of the local population living in 'areas of stress' within the city, in 1992, ranged from 14 per cent of the white population to 81 per cent of the Bangladeshi population (BMBC, 1993). These areas of stress mostly coincided with the inner city. We thus again return to the crucial role of urban renewal for improving ethnic minority housing conditions.

But during the same ten-year period, there appears also to have been a modest decentralisation of ethnic minority groups within urban areas, particularly associated with the Indian population and with the second generation (Phillips and Sarre, 1995). Indians now exhibit the most widely dispersed distribution within cities, a pattern which is associated with, on the one hand, high status suburban living and, on the other, residence within the more deprived areas of the inner city. But, suburbanisation is not always easily achieved, even for those with the financial capacity to make the move. Virdee (1995), for example, has revealed the extraordinary lengths to which some ethnic minority households have gone to adapt their lifestyles to cope with the everyday risk of harassment. Furthermore, the suburbanisation process does not necessarily eradicate racial inequalities in housing condition.

Continuing segregation of ethnic minority groups in the worst housing areas of both the public and the private sectors is significant not only for the housing conditions experienced by these families, but for the other disadvantages commonly associated with residence in deprived neighbourhoods, such as poor education, health and leisure facilities, high crime and environmental incivilities.

Peach (1996) has recently made use of 1991 Census data to examine patterns of ethnic concentration and segregation in Britain. He highlights a diversity of segregation experience among different ethnic minority groups. Black Caribbeans, he argues, have experienced decreasing segregation levels over the period from 1961–91, which may be partly explained by the movement of some of these households into the council sector in the 1970s.

Bangladeshis stand out as the most concentrated and segregated of all groups, reflecting their cultural and religious needs, socio-economic status, length of residence in Britain and the impact of racial harassment, especially in the East End of London.

In discussing segregation it is vital therefore to emphasise both the positive attractions of ethnic clusters as well as the constraints experienced by many wishing to move away, such as the fear of racial harassment, low economic status and internal cultural pressures to stay.

CONCLUSION

Ethnic minority disadvantage has persisted into the 1990s, serving to marginalise and segregate ethnic minority groups. It is a disadvantage which is bound up with the persistence of barriers to ethnic minority advancement in other spheres such as education and employment as well as with broad issues relating to welfare access. As such, it is clear that we cannot understand the current housing position of ethnic minorities by looking at the housing market alone.

Continuities with the past are evident, but the last two decades have brought new and more varied housing outcomes and experiences for ethnic minorities. Ethnic minority progress within the housing market reflects the different housing demands and strategies of more settled populations and their subsequent generations, the improved financial capacity of some to meet those demands, broad societal changes which have removed some of the housing market barriers to ethnic minority progress, and the capabilities of ethnic minority groups themselves to resist discrimination and marginal- isation and to press for their housing entitlements. The emergence of the EMHA housing movement is significant in this respect, but so too are the individual strategies employed by households in resisting, for example, the discrimination and harassment that has confined so many to the poorer inner city areas or in organising to protect their interests in areas of urban renewal. It is important to stress that ethnic minority groups should not be seen as passive victims; their ethnicity is a resource to be utilised, not just a target of discrimination.

As recent analysis has shown, however, there are still 'ethnic penalties' suffered by ethnic minority groups when competing with whites in the housing and employment markets (Karn, 1997). There are two necessary strands to addressing this problem. The first is to tackle policies which are not specific to ethnic minorities but which impinge disproportionately upon them. In housing, for instance they would disproportionately benefit from increased investment in new social rental housing production and in the up-grading of run-down housing estates, from greater financial help to home-owners in renewal areas and from changing the housing benefit system to reduce the poverty trap. But since entry to the larger part of the housing market, the private sector, depends on ability to pay, they would also benefit from policies which promoted their employment opportunities, such as improved education and programmes to promote youth and adult training and employment, especially in inner city areas.

The second strand of policy is to address those problems which are specific to ethnic minority groups, such as racial discrimination, racial harassment and racial violence. Without this type of initiative, ethnic minority groups will not be able to benefit from more redistributive social policies, remaining last in the queue for education, jobs and housing.

In relation to these two types of policy approach, the housing situation of ethnic minority groups suffers from a double handicap; first, the very low priority currently being accorded to housing issues by all three main political parties, and second, the low priority given to racial equality again by all three parties. In addition, municipal 'race' politics have lost their vigour. The radical era of head-line 'anti-racism' has passed and we have entered what Law (1996) refers to as a period of 'liberal equal opportunities management'. Gilroy (1992) has called it 'the end of anti-racism'. Hence, in the 1990s, equal opportunities issues appear on the housing agenda and are enshrined in policy, but are all too often effectively reduced to bureaucratic discussions about monitoring and ethnic record keeping.

We have stressed, throughout this chapter, the salience of ethnic diversity for interpretation of ethnic minority housing experiences and outcomes, for understanding preferences and aspirations and for policy formulation. However, there is a danger that concern with ethnic diversity and 'equal opportunities management' takes precedence over 'race' issues. Despite growing minority empowerment, white institutions retain over-whelming power in the allocation of housing and employment resources. There is also broader neglect of Britain's deepening social, economic and spatial inequalities, which are indissolubly intertwined with racial in-equalities.

REFERENCES

Age Concern (1991) *Time for Action: Consultation Document on the Needs of Asian Elders*. (Age Concern, Rochdale).

Anderson, I., Kemp, P. and Quilgars, D. (1993) *Single Homeless People*. (London: HMSO).

BMBC (1993) *Areas of Stress*. (Bradford: Bradford Metropolitan Borough Council).

Brown, C. (1984) *Black and White Britain*. (London: Heinemann).

Carey-Wood, J., Duke, K., Karn, V. and Marshall, T. (1994) *The Settlement of Refugees in Britain*. (London: Home Office).

CHAS (1994) *All in One Place: The British Housing Story, 1973–1993*. (London: Catholic Housing Aid Society).

Commission for Racial Equality (1983) *Collingwood Housing Association Ltd.: Report of a Formal Investigation*. (London: CRE).

Commission for Racial Equality (1984) *Race and Council Housing in Hackney*. (London: CRE).

Commission for Racial Equality (1985) *Race and Mortgage Lending*. (London: CRE).

Commission for Racial Equality (1988a) *Racial Discrimination in a London Estate Agency: Report of a Formal Investigation into Richard Barclay and Co*. (London: CRE).

Commission for Racial Equality (1988b) *Homelessness and Discrimination: Report into the London Borough of Tower Hamlets*. (London: CRE).

Commission for Racial Equality (1989) *Racial Discrimination in Liverpool City Council: Report of a Formal Investigation into the Housing Department*. (London: CRE).

Commission for Racial Equality (1990a) *Racial Discrimination in an Oldham Estate Agency: Report of a Formal Investigation into Norman Lester and Co*. (London: CRE).

Commission for Racial Equality (1990b) *Out of Order: Report of a Formal Investigation into the London Borough of Southwark*. (London: CRE).

Commission for Racial Equality (1990c) *'Sorry It's Gone': Testing for Racial Discrimination in the Private Rental Sector*. (London: CRE).

Commission for Racial Equality (1991) *Code of Practice in Rented Housing for the Elimination of Racial Discrimination and the Promotion of Equal Opportunities*. (London: CRE).

Commission for Racial Equality (1992) *Racial Discrimination in Hostel Accommodation: Report of a Formal Investigation of Refugee Housing Association Ltd*. (London: CRE).

Commission for Racial Equality (1993a) *Housing Allocations in Oldham: Report of a Formal Investigation*. (London: CRE).

Commission for Racial Equality (1993b) *Housing Associations and Racial Equality: Report of a Formal Investigation into Housing Associations in Wales, Scotland and England*. (London: (CRE).

Cross, M. (1991) Editorial *New Community*, 17 (3), p. 311.

Davies, J. *et al.* (1996) *Discounted Voices: Homelessness among Young Black and Minority Ethnic People in England*. (Sociology and Social Policy Working Paper 15, University of Leeds).

Department of the Environment (1988) *English House Condition Survey 1986*. (London: HMSO).

Department of the Environment (1993) *English House Condition Survey 1991*. (London: HMSO).

Department of the Environment (1994) *Index of Local Conditions*. (London: HMSO).

Dhooge, Y. and Barelli, J. (1996) *Racial Attacks and Harassment: the Response of Social Landlords*. (London: HMSO).

Dorling, D. (1997) 'Regional and local differences in the housing tenure of ethnic minorities', chapter 8 in V. Karn (ed.) *Ethnic Differences in Employment, Education and Housing in Britain: Ethnicity in the 1991 Census, Volume 4*. (London: ONS).

Gilroy, P. (1992) 'The end of anti-racism', in J. Donald and A. Rattansi (eds) *'Race', Culture and Difference*. (London: Sage).

Greater London Council (GLC) (1986) *Private Tenants in London*. (GLC Housing Research and Policy Report no. 5).

Harrison, M. L. (1995) *Housing, 'Race', Social Policy and Empowerment*. (Aldershot: Avebury).

Harrison, M. L., Karmani, A., Law, I., Phillips, D. and Ravetz, A. (1996) *Black and Minority Ethnic Housing Associations: An Evaluation of the Housing Corporation's Black and Minority Ethnic Housing Association Strategy*. (London: Housing Corporation).

Henderson, J. and Karn, V. (1987) *Race, Class and State Housing: Inequality and the Allocation of Public Housing in Britain*. (Aldershot: Gower).

The Housing Corporation (1992) *An Independent Future; the Second Black and Ethnic Minority Housing Association Strategy, 1992–96*. (London: Housing Corporation).

The Housing Corporation (1995) *Black and Minority Ethnic Housing Needs: An Enabling Framework*. Consultation Paper. (London: Housing Corporation).

Howes, E. and Mullins, D. (1997) 'Ethnic minority tenants', chapter 10 in V. Karn (ed.) *Ethnic Differences in Employment, Education and Housing in Britain: Ethnicity in the 1991 Census, Volume 4*. (London: ONS).

Karn, V. (1983) *Race and Housing in Britain: The Role of the Major Institutions*. (London: Heinemann).

Karn, V. (1997) '"Ethnic penalties" and racial discrimination in education, employment and housing: conclusions and policy implications', chapter 13 in V. Karn (ed.) *Employment, Education and Housing Among Ethnic Minorities in Britain: Ethnicity in the 1991 Census, Volume 4*. (London: ONS).

Karn, V., Kemeny, J. and Williams, P. (1986) *Home-ownership in the Inner City: Salvation or Despair*. (Aldershot: Gower).

Karn, V., LaTourelle, D., Symes, M. and Todd, M. (1995) *Housing Design and Management for Ethnic Minorities: Do Housing Associations Meet their Needs?* Working Paper: School of Social Policy and Department of Architecture (Manchester: University of Manchester).

Karn, V. and Lucas, J. (1996) *Home-Owners and Clearance: An Evaluation of Rebuilding Grants*. (London: HMSO).

Lambert, C. (1976) *Building Societies, Surveyors and the Older Areas of Birmingham*. Working Paper no. 38. Centre for Urban and Regional Studies. (Birmingham: University of Birmingham).

Law, I. (1996) *Racism, Ethnicity and Social Policy*. (London: Prentice Hall).

Law, I. *et al.*, (1996) *Equity and Difference: Racial and Ethnic Inequalities in Housing Needs and Housing Investment in Leeds*. (University of Leeds, School of Sociology and Social Policy Research Report).

London Housing Unit and London Research Centre (1989) *One in Every Hundred: A Study of Households accepted as Homeless in London*. (London: LHU/LRC).

McIntosh, N. and Smith, D.J. (1974) *The Extent of Racial Discrimination*. (London: PEP).

Modood, T. (1992) *Not Easy Being British: Colour, Culture and Citizenship*. (London: Runnymede Trust and Trentham Books).

Mullings, B. (1991) *The Colour of Money: the Impact of Housing Investment Decision Making on Black Housing Outcomes in London*. (London: London Race and Housing Research Unit).

Murie, A. (1988) 'The new homeless in Britain', in G. Bramley *et al.*, (ed.) *Homeless and the London Housing Market*. (Bristol: School of Advanced Urban Studies).

National Federation of Housing Associations (1983) *Race and Housing: Still a Cause for Concern*. (London: NFHA).

National Federation of Housing Associations (1992a) *Equal Opportunities in Housing Associations: Are You Doing Enough?* (London: NFHA).

National Federation of Housing Associations (1992b) *Racial Equality Strategy: Promoting Good Practice and Positive Action*. (London: NFHA).

Niner, P. (1985) *Housing Association Allocations: Achieving Racial Equality*. (London: Runnymede Trust).

Page (1993) *Building for Communities: A Study of New Housing Association Estates*. (York: Joseph Rowntree Foundation).

Parker, J. and Dugmore, K. (1976) *Colour and the Allocation of GLC Housing*, Research Report 21. (London: Greater London Council).

Peach, C. (1996) 'Does Britain have ghettos?' *Transactions, Institute of British Geographers* 21 (1), pp. 216–35.

Peach, C. and Byron, M. (1993) 'Caribbean tenants in council housing: "race", class and gender', *New Community*, 19 (3), p. 407.

Phillips, D. (1981) 'The social and spatial segregation of Asians in Leicester', in P. Jackson and S. Smith (eds.) *Social Interaction and Ethnic Segregation*, IBG Special Publication 12. (London: Academic Press).

Phillips, D. (1984) *Monitoring of the Experimental Allocation Scheme for GLC Properties in Tower Hamlets*. (London: GLC Report no. TH173A).

Phillips, D. (1986) *What Price Equality? A Report on the Allocation of GLC Housing in Tower Hamlets*, GLC Housing Research and Policy Report, 9. (London: GLC).

Phillips, D. (1997) 'The housing position of ethnic minority home owners', chapter 9 in V. Karn (ed.) *Employment, Education and Housing Among Ethnic Minorities in Britain: Ethnicity in the 1991 Census, Volume 4*. (London: ONS).

Phillips, D. and Sarre, P. (1995) 'Black middle class formation in contemporary Britain', in T. Butler and M. Savage (eds) *Social Change and the Middle Classes*. (London: UCL Press).

Randall, G. and Brown, S. (1993) *The Rough Sleepers Initiative: An Evaluation*. (London: HMSO).

Ratcliffe, P. (1992) 'Renewal, regeneration and "race": issues in urban policy', *New Community*, 18 (3), pp. 387–400.

Ratcliffe, P. (1996) 'Methodological refinement, policy formulation and the future research agenda: some brief reflections', in P. Ratcliffe (ed.) *Social Geography and Ethnicity in Britain: Ethnicity in the 1991 Census, Volume 3*. (London: OPCS).

Resource Information Service (1996) *Emergency Hostels: Direct Access Accommodation in London 1996*. (London: London Boroughs Grants Committee and Single Homelessness in London).

Rex, J. and Moore, R. (1967) *Race, Community and Conflict: A Study of Sparkbrook*. (London: OUP).

Sarre, P., Phillips, D. and Skellington, R. (1989) *Ethnic Minority Housing: Explanations and Policies*. (Aldershot: Avebury).

Sheffield City Council (1989) *Because the Skin is Black*. (Sheffield: Sheffield City Council).

Smith, D. and Whalley, A. (1975) *Racial Minorities and Council Housing*. (London: Political and Economic Planning).

Smith, S. (1989) *The Politics of 'Race' and Residence*. (Cambridge: Polity Press).

Stevens, L., Karn, V., Davidson, E. and Stanley, T. (1982) *Race and Building Society Lending in Leeds*. (Leeds: Leeds Community Relations Council).

Stunnell, J. G. (1975) *An Examination of Racial Equity in Points Scheme Housing Allocations*. Research and Information Report (London: London Borough of Lewisham).

Virdee, S. (1995) *Racial Violence and Harassment*. (London: Policy Studies Institute).

9 'Race' and the criminal justice system

Marian FitzGerald

It is nearly thirty years since the authors of one of the earliest, major studies of British race relations urged:

> that the methods of collecting and presenting data be improved to allow accurate assessment of the rates of crime and delinquency among ethnic and other minority groups.

(Rose, 1969: 726)

Only recently has a system of ethnic monitoring been imposed on all police forces in England and Wales, although ethnic data have been generated at the other end of the criminal justice system, as prison statistics, since the mid-1980s. These have shown a fairly consistent pattern; but the debate about how that pattern should be interpreted has generated more heat than light.

Meanwhile, in an almost parallel development, the issue of the victimisation of ethnic minorities has entered the policy agenda, but the focus here has been the question of racial harassment (FitzGerald, forthcoming); and, although police figures for 'racial incidents' have been available since the mid-1980s, by contrast with the prison statistics they are provided at a very crude level of aggregation and lack the detail to 'explain' the considerable fluctuation they have shown over that time.

In part for reasons of space and in part because of the disparity in the available statistics, the main focus of this chapter is the treatment of ethnic minorities in the criminal justice process as suspects and offenders. Two health warnings, though, should be issued at the outset. One is that it is an error (albeit a conventional one) to assume that suspects and offenders constitute a separate category from victims of crime; for this implies that groups which appear to be disproportionately involved in crime cannot also suffer at the hands of criminals. The second is that it is unsafe to take at face value patterns of apparent 'ethnic' difference in statistical data. Rather, one needs fully to explore *all* possible explanatory variables in addition to ethnicity and the interactions between them. Additionally, the statistics cannot safely be interpreted in a vacuum; they need to be understood in both their organisational and historical context.

The concluding section of this chapter returns to these points and draws out some of their implications; but the chapter begins with some background before exploring the evidence which is currently available on the levels and patterns of offending by different ethnic groups in Britain and the response of the criminal justice system.

BACKGROUND

The historical, socio-economic and demographic context will be familiar to many readers and aspects of it are referred to by other authors in this volume. It is, though, essential to set out some of the main facts which are relevant to interpreting the currently available data on 'race'[1] and crime, including the key stages in the development of post-war British race relations.

The main primary immigration of the post-war period from former colonies in the 'New' Commonwealth took place in the 1950s, 1960s and 1970s; but the timing both of primary immigration and of immigration for family reunion took place at different times and different stages for different groups. The result of this is, broadly speaking, that groups with origins in the Caribbean are the longest established of the ethnic minorities from the New Commonwealth. They are now into their third British-born generation, while the Bangladeshis are the most recent and there is still some family formation continuing among this group. It also means that there are considerable differences between the groups both in the proportion who were actually born in the United Kingdom and in their age structures.

Two other related points are worth recalling. First, although all of these groups settled mainly in urban areas and the broad patterns of initial settlement remain, their distribution across those areas has been uneven and it has also been uneven within the urban areas where they have settled (see Table 9.1). London has been the most important urban area for all groups (and particularly for the black groups) with the exception of the Pakistanis. Second, there are important differences between and within the minorities themselves: at the aggregate level, the socio-economic profile of the Indian population is not dissimilar to (and in some respects more privileged than) that of whites, while the Black Caribbeans are much more disadvantaged and the Pakistanis and Bangladeshis still worse off.

In the early years, discrimination was totally unchecked by legislation and racial tensions were largely ignored by politicians. What tends to be forgotten now is that the group from the West Indies, the earliest arrivals, were certainly harassed and that their harassment led to riots in the late 1950s

Table 9.1 Key characteristics of the ethnic minority population

	Black			Asian				Other		White
	Caribbean	African	Other	Indian	Pakistani	Bangladeshi	Chinese	Asian	Other	
Per cent of total	0.9	0.4	0.3	1.5	0.9	0.3	0.3	0.4	0.5	94.5
Greater London	58.2	77.1	45.2	41.3	18.4	52.7	36.1	57.1	41.7	10.3
Met non-London	28.1	11.7	28.2	34.3	59.1	31.4	28.5	21.6	28.5	29.6
Born in UK	53.7	36.4	84.4	41.9	50.5	36.6	28.4	21.9	59.8	95.8
Age 16–24	14.9	16.6	19.0	15.2	17.5	17.6	17.9	14.7	15.2	12.6
Unemployed males 16–24	37.6	41.6	35.2	27.5	36.1	20.5	15.4	29.4	29.4	17.4

Source : Census figures, 1991

in both Nottingham and Notting Hill. But the same group also began, around this time, to complain of harassment by the police, and this issue was taken up by campaigning groups and in the literature by the 1960s (Hunte, 1966).

The police, while rejecting West Indian claims of harassment, also maintained an official position for a long time that there was no problem of crime among ethnic minorities. Giving evidence in 1972 to a House of Commons Select Committee on Police Immigrant Relations, police forces acknowledged widespread concern about 'growing tensions' but concluded 'beyond doubt' that:

> Coloured immigrants are no more involved in crime than others nor are they generally more concerned in violence, prostitution, and drugs. The West Indian crime rate is much the same as that of the indigenous population, the Asian crime rate is very much lower.
>
> (Select Committee 1972, main report p. 71)

By the late 1970s, however, there had been a significant escalation, polarisation and indeed politicisation of the debate around race and crime. The police had rescinded their position of four years earlier, when the Select Committee took evidence on the situation of 'the West Indian community' more generally. In a memorandum, the Metropolitan Police concluded that, while further evidence was needed on 'this sensitive and emotive subject':

> already our experience has taught us the fallibility of the assertion that crime rates among those of West Indian origin are no higher than those of the population at large.
>
> (Select Committee 1977, vol II, p. 182)

And when they were challenged on this apparent departure from their previous position they submitted a further memorandum stating that: 'from current statistics available, our overall experience of 1971 no longer holds good' (ibid., vol. III, p. 689).

At around the same time, the Scrap Sus campaign was formed. Led largely by black people, its goal (which it ultimately achieved) was the repeal of section 24 of the 1824 Vagrancy Act under which people (and disproportionately black people) were arrested by the police on suspicion of being about to commit an offence (Demuth, 1978). The media had also discovered 'mugging' which they treated like the proverbial dog with a bone; and in 1982, the Metropolitan Police Commissioner selectively used police statistics to identify black people as being disproportionately involved in street crime in a controversial and (at that time) unprecedented press release (Scotland Yard, 10 March 1982).

Thus, the issue of 'race' and crime was first raised by minority groups and campaigning organisations in terms of police harassment of black people; and by the late 1970s concerns were also being raised nationally about the long-standing phenomenon of the harassment of Asians by their fellow citizens (Bethnal Green and Stepney Trades Council, 1978). So 'race' and crime was squarely on the political agenda by the early 1980s. However, the central question had become whether or not *black* people were disproportionately criminal, as the police figures and sections of the media suggested. Since then, the riots of 1980, 1981 and 1985 have firmly entrenched both the form of the question and its position as a standing item on the agenda. The Asian groups, on the other hand, entered the debate as a separate item lower down the agenda, as victims of an ethnically-specific form of crime.

Before moving on to look at the current research and statistical evidence on the question of the role of ethnicity in offending, it is worth recapping on the academic attention which the issue has received over time. Rose *et al.*, in their major study of 'Colour and Citizenship', in 1968 had little empirical research evidence to draw on in their coverage of 'The Police and Law Enforcement'. Apart from material provided by the police themselves, they could only cite 'an article by Bottoms and Lambert's unpublished work' (ibid., 357). Throughout the 1970s, British political and sociological literature reflected an increasing interest in these issues, with the best known and most comprehensive study of this period published exactly ten years after Rose (Hall *et al.*, 1978). The cumulative momentum within these disciplines was evident through the 1980s and continues. However, remarkably little attention was given to these issues in the mainstream of academic criminology. Indeed, it was not until the Commission for Racial Equality sponsored the Hood Report (published in 1992) that there was really a major empirical breakthrough undertaken by a criminologist – although that in itself was limited because it was confined to decisions in the Crown Court in one area of the country.

If the issues of 'race' and crime were slow to reach the agenda of academic criminologists, their policy implications could not be ignored. It is, therefore, probably no coincidence that much, if not most, of the empirical research in this area from the late 1970s was undertaken by the Home Office Research and Planning Unit. Academic criminologists, meanwhile, inasmuch as they addressed the issue, seem to have tied themselves in quite a number of knots. In particular, those who have sought to prove racial discrimination in the criminal justice system have been confronted with dilemmas because of the apparently contrasting experience of the Caribbean and Asian groups. Seeking illumination in the extensive American literature, they have often identified superficial parallels between black groups in both countries which, however unwittingly, have risked compounding pathologised notions of black 'criminality'. Attempts to 'explain' the apparent differences between the different ethnic groups are often based on such sweeping generalisations that they have come dangerously close to stereotyping, as the folllowing example illustrates:

> The question arises of the differences between Asian and West Indian youth. As a result of discrimination, the unemployment rate for ethnic minority youth in general has risen at a much faster rate than for their white counterparts, but between youth of West Indian and Asian parentage there are two differences which have the effect of comparatively insulating the latter from the process of relative deprivation. Firstly by comparison with West Indian youth, Asians have a more substantive opportunity structure within their own community; this is due to the larger size of the professional and business class in the Asian community. Secondly, the distance between Asian culture and indigenous British culture is greater than that between the latter and West Indian culture. Assimilation to indigenous British standards and aspirations has thus probably been a more rapid process for youth of West Indian parentage and hence relative deprivation is felt more acutely with the consequent fostering of a counter-culture.
>
> (Lea and Young, 1982, p. 8)

THE EMPIRICAL EVIDENCE

Despite the rapid developments of the last ten to fifteen years, the statistical sources and empirical research on ethnic minorities as suspects and offenders are mostly confined to England and Wales and remain patchy. So the inferences we can draw at present are necessarily tentative, although the data are accumulating and the 1996 extension of police ethnic monitoring, along with a number of current empirical research projects, are likely to catalyse understandings considerably within the next few years.

The scene for the discussion is set by the prison statistics since they are the longest-established and most detailed source available. Since 1985, they have consistently shown over-representation of black people in British prisons.

The form of ethnic classifications used by the Prison Service changed in 1992, so the 1985 figures must be regarded as only approximating to those for 1995. The previous system used the categories: White; West Indian/Guyanese/African; Indian/Pakistani/Bangladeshi; Chinese/Arab/Mixed; Other/Not recorded including refusals. Of these, the first three are broadly comparable with the current classification system and Table 9.2 has been constructed to facilitate this comparability and show trends over the ten-year-period. However, this masks some of the finer detail available in the more recent data, aspects of which are worth drawing out here.

Table 9.2 Ethnic composition of the prison population, England and Wales, June 1985 to June 1996

	White	Black	Asian	Chinese/Other/ Not recorded
Males %				
1985	83	8	2	7
1995	83	11	3	3
Females %				
1985	78	12	2	8
1995	76	20	1	4

Source: Prison statistics, 1995

For purposes of comparison, Table 9.2 groups together the Chinese and Others with the Not recorded group; yet the 'Other/Not recorded' group had dropped from about 5 per cent in 1985 to 1 per cent for males and 3 per cent for females by 1992 and the subsequent 'Unrecorded' group was down to less than 1 per cent in 1995. Further, many of the 'Mixed' group who were classified with the Chinese in 1985 may now be captured within the 1995 black group, thereby inflating it relative to its 1985 'West Indian' counterpart. This, together with the redistribution of the 5 per cent who, in 1985, were classed as 'Other' or 'Not recorded', will partially account for the apparent 3 per cent increase in the black male group over the ten years. The rise in black female prisoners, on the other hand, is dramatic; but it should be pointed out that this does not represent a gradual increase. Rather, there was a sudden leap in the early years, with the percentage already standing at 20 per cent by 1989. Finally, it is also worth noting that it is now possible

Table 9.3 Adult sentenced prisoners 1995: offence group by ethnic origin and gender (percentages)

	White (%)		Black (%)		Asian (%)
	Males	*Females*	*Males*	*Females*	*Males*
Violence against the person	23	21	20	8	24
Rape	5	—	6	—	5
Other sexual offences	6	1	1	—	3
Burglary	17	5	10	1	6
Robbery	13	8	23	5	12
Theft/handling	10	23	5	7	6
Fraud and forgery	3	7	2	7	7
Drug offences	8	20	20	61	16
Other offences	12	10	6	7	16
N	31,555	1,111	3,975	276	1,044

Source: Prison statistics, 1995

to subdivide the 'Asian' group into Indians and Pakistanis/Bangladeshis. In 1995, they accounted for 1.2 and 1.7 per cent respectively of the male prison population – an apparent under-representation of Indians and a slight over-representation of Pakistanis and Bangladeshis.

As Table 9.3 illustrates, the prison statistics also show apparently different patterns of offending by ethnic groups. (Figures for Asian females are not included since they numbered only twenty-two.)
Particularly of note here are:

* the relatively high proportion of white males and females imprisoned for offences of violence compared to the black groups (although the proportion for Asian males is actually slightly higher than for whites);
* the relatively high proportion of white male prisoners in the burglary category;
* the relatively high proportion of black male prisoners convicted of robbery;
* a higher proportion of white female prisoners convicted of theft/handling offences; and
* very strikingly higher proportions of the minorities imprisoned for drugs offences – which accounted for well over half of all black female prisoners.

There are two main limitations to the prisons data given above as a starting point for the debate: (1) they do not differentiate between British ethnic minorities and those normally resident abroad; and (2) they relate to the end point of the criminal justice system and refer, therefore, only to a very small (and probably atypical) proportion of all offenders.[2]

The data collected since 1992 have again helped considerably in overcoming the first of these problems by providing a further breakdown of ethnic minority prisoners by nationality. Place of residence, of course, cannot necessarily be inferred from nationality; but it certainly provides us with a better approximation than was previously available and a very much sounder basis for comparisons with the general population. The figures in Table 9.4 show small differences from Table 9.2 for men from ethnic minorities. Once foreign nationals are discounted, though, there is a striking drop for black women – from 20 per cent of the total population to 11 per cent. This figure is nearly identical to that for black males and suggests, very crudely, that the presence of black people in the prison population is about nine times higher than their presence in the population at large would predict. Not shown here are figures for ethnic differences in offending. These remain broadly in line with the picture in Table 9.3, except for drugs offences. Black people are still over-represented in drugs offences but the figure for British nationals reduces to 14 per cent for men and 44 per cent

Table 9.4 Prison population at 1995 (British nationals only)

| | White | | Black | | Asian | | Chinese and Other | |
	Male	Female	Male	Female	Male	Female	Male	Female
Prisoners	87.1	86.1	9.7	11.0	1.9	0.9	1.3	2.0
General population*	95.4	95.3	1.2	1.5	2.7	2.4	0.7	0.7

Source: Prison statistics, 1995
* Figures for the male population aged 15–64 and females aged 15–64 (British nationals only).

for women (by contrast with 41 and 76 per cent respectively for black foreign nationals).

The prison statistics, however, can tell us little about what has happened at the key points in the criminal justice process before this stage shown in Figure 9.1. The evidence we have to date varies in both quantity and quality at each of these previous, critical stages. I have described the main sources at length elsewhere (FitzGerald, 1993); for present purposes, it may be summarised as follows. At the beginning of the process we have two major unknowns. One is that we know little or nothing about actual rates of offending by different ethnic groups as reported by themselves in self-report surveys – although a recent Home Office study (Graham and Bowling, 1995) suggests that black young people report no more offending than whites while the rates for the Asian groups are much lower. Also, we know very little about whether crimes committed by different ethnic groups are more or less likely to be reported. The most recent British research on this issue (FitzGerald and Hale, 1996) tends to confirm that whites are slightly more likely to report crimes they believe were committed by ethnic minorities (44 per cent) than those committed by whites (40 per cent). Some caution is needed, however, since reporting rates vary for different types of crime and it is already apparent that the pattern of crimes committed by minorities may be different from those committed by whites; so this might explain the apparent difference in reporting rates.

However, only a small proportion of crimes reported result in a suspect being apprehended (see note 2) and in that sense it is more important to know whether there are any ethnic differences in apprehension rates. Certainly, evidence has been accumulating that black people are disproportionately brought into the system through pro-active policing. The most robust data come from various studies of stops by the police. In particular, Wesley Skogan's analysis of the British Crime Survey in 1988 (Skogan, 1990) has again been confirmed using the data from the 1994 survey (Bucke, 1996; FitzGerald and Hale, 1997). The survey consistently shows that, even when other relevant factors are taken into account, black

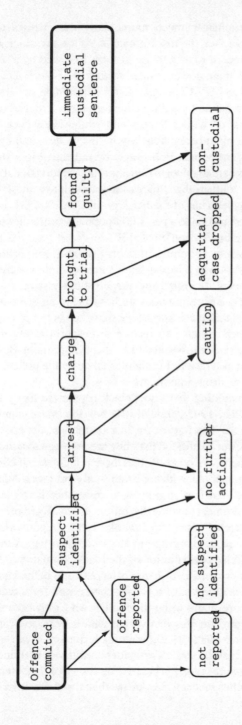

Figure 9.1 Criminal justice process from offence to imprisonment

Source: Marian FitzGerald, 1997

people remain disproportionately much more likely than whites to be stopped by the police. Moreover, the Inspectorate of Police has, since April 1993, required an ethnic record to be kept of all stops followed by a search made by the police using their powers under section 1 of the Police and Criminal Evidence Act 1984 (PACE stop/search). These data are limited because they provide no breakdown within ethnic minority groups but are simply presented in terms of whites versus non-whites. However, considerable local variation is already apparent within this picture; and figures already released by the Metropolitan Police may be indicative in showing that these local differences extend down to divisional and subdivisional level within forces. They also confirm that figures for 'non-whites' mask very much higher levels of stop/searches of the black groups. In 1994, 31 whites were stopped and searched in London per 1,000 population; the figure for Asians was 36; but that for black people was 137.

It is, however, important to remember that only a small proportion of stops actually result in arrest. Much less is known about ethnic differences in the more common routes of entry into the criminal justice system, although the Hood Report confirms previous studies (including Stevens and Willis, 1979) in suggesting that black people are more subject to pro-active policing. That is – whether or not they feature disproportionately in the crime reports to which the police respond – black people are more likely to be brought into the system as a result of initiatives taken by the police, such as targeted street robbery or drugs operations.

Certainly evidence is mounting that fewer black people are likely to be cautioned than whites (CRE, 1992), though it is possible that Asians are more likely to be cautioned. The figures for blacks, though, appear to be largely explained by the lower likelihood that they are prepared to admit the charges brought against them. We do know that there is a greater likelihood that black people will be charged with indictable-only offences (Walker, 1988, 1989; Hood, 1992); and it is important to remember here that the charge which is brought is subject to some discretion, especially in offences of medium seriousness (Blom-Cooper and Drabble, 1982). In particular the impact of variations by area in charging practices needs to be taken into account, given the very skewed distribution of the black population.

Not only does a higher proportion of black offenders and defendants go to the Crown Court because they have a higher charge rate for indictable offences, they are also more likely to be tried at Crown Court because in triable-either-way cases they are less likely than whites to be tried in the magistrates' court (Walker, 1988, 1989; Walker, Jefferson *et al.*, 1989; Brown and Hullin, 1992; Hood, 1992). The evidence still leaves it unclear, however, whether the reason for this is primarily the choice of the defendant or the choice of magistrates. Again, we know that there are important differences by area in magistrates' patterns of committal for Crown Court trial, though the implications of this for minorities have not systematically been explored. And the effect of remands should also be borne in mind. Hood showed that, taking everything else into account, black defendants were far more likely than whites to be remanded in custody; and one of the consequences of this was that they were disproportionately brought to trial *from* custody. This in turn increased the probability that if they were found guilty they would be given a custodial sentence. Certainly we do know that black people tend disproportionately to plead not guilty to the charges against them, and this may be part of the reason why they have a higher acquittal rate; but, of course, if they are found guilty this too results in more severe and longer sentences (Home Office, 1994; Hood, 1992).

The evidence consistently shows that black defendants who are found guilty are less likely to receive non-custodial sentences (Home Office, 1989; Brown and Hullin, 1992; Moxon, 1988; Voakes and Fowler, 1989); and this point takes us back directly to the prison statistics which show that both black and Asian defendants receive longer prison sentences than whites. A statistical bulletin produced by the Home Office in 1994 looked more closely at this and shows that when account is taken of age, type of offence and court of sentence, the difference in sentence length – although reduced – still remains (see Table 9.5).

Table 9.5 Males received into prisons in 1990: average sentence length in days

	Actual length	Excess	Normalised length	Excess
Under 21				
White	372	−11	380	−3
Black	501	+118	419	+36
Asian	491	+108	427	+44
All	383			
21 and over				
White	544	−27	553	−18
Black	776	+206	669	+98
Asian	642	+71	618	+47
All	571			

Source: HOSB 21/94

This calculation does not take into account other important factors – in particular, seriousness within offence category, plea and previous convictions. Hood, however, takes a wide range of relevant variables into account, and still finds an unexplained excess in the proportion of adult male black offenders sentenced to prison, though the rate of imprisonment for Asians was, if anything, slightly lower than for comparable whites. For both minorities, sentence lengths were significantly longer than for whites, even when other relevant factors were taken into account.

So the overall picture is that, for various reasons – not all of them clearly identified as yet or fully understood – black suspects and offenders seem disproportionately likely to be brought into the criminal justice process in the first place and disproportionately less likely to be filtered out of it at each of the key stages before the end-point of imprisonment. The picture for Asians is much less clear but, inasmuch as any tendency is discernible, it is in the opposite direction *up* to the point of sentencing.

DISCUSSION

Three main explanations have been advanced for the ethnic differences in the statistics and research findings presented in the previous section. They have variously been ascribed to:

1 socio-economic factors;
2 discrimination by the criminal justice system; and
3 ethnic specific differences (including differences in rates and patterns of offending, regardless of socio-economic factors).

It has also been suggested that all three are at work and that they interact in complex ways (Reiner, 1989; Jefferson, 1988). This possibility is explored more fully below; but it is best to begin by looking separately at the evidence for each of these 'explanations' in turn.

Socio-economic factors are undoubtedly relevant. Since they tend generally to be so highly correlated with offending (that is, offending as represented by criminal justice data) it would be unbelievable if the most disadvantaged ethnic groups were not disproportionately involved in offending. Analysis of the National Prison Survey of 1992 (FitzGerald and Marshall, 1996) comes up with the blindingly obvious finding that black and white prisoners are far more similar in socio-economic terms than are black and white people in the population at large. More tangentially – and in some ways more illuminating for that reason – the British Crime Survey shows that ethnic minorities are disproportionately victimised relative to whites but that once these differences are explored with rigour they are largely explained by socio-economic factors rather than by ethnicity (Mayhew, Dowds and Elliott, 1989; FitzGerald and Hale, 1996a).

Socio-economic factors are almost certainly not sufficient, though, to explain away completely the difference between black and white people in both levels and patterns of offending. A further objection raised to the socio-economic explanation should, however, be treated with caution. The argument that the 'Asian' groups are also deprived but are even less involved in crime than whites tends to ignore the important fact that the 'Asian' group is very diverse.[3] It is dominated numerically by the Indians whose socio-economic profile is similar to that of whites and, in some respects, better.[4] Yet it contains two groups who are still more disadvantaged in socio-economic terms than the Black Caribbeans. However, as has already been pointed out, an important difference between these groups is in their age structure: the Pakistanis and Bangladeshis are much younger than the black groups and larger numbers than previously are just about now hitting the peak period for offending. In conjunction with the figures for 16–24-year-olds shown in Table 9.1, the figures for 0–15-year-olds should also be cited. This age group constituted 19 per cent of whites in 1991, compared with 22 per cent of Black Caribbeans and 29 per cent of Indians. The figures for Pakistanis and Bangladeshis were 43 and 47 per cent respectively. We are, therefore, likely to see an upsurge in rates of criminal activity among these groups for several years to come – although it will continue to be masked as long as it is subsumed within an omnibus 'Asian' category. A critical issue for the future is the way in which both the media and the criminal justice system respond to this development; for there is a clear danger that what is essentially a demographic and socio-economic phenomenon will become racialised, with the danger that this will fuel prejudice and generate moral panics, labelling and self-fulfilling prophecies.[5] One pointer to the future here may be the events in Bradford in June 1995. By contrast with Meadowell, Blackbird Leys, Luton and other symbolic locations in recent summer disturbances largely involving white youths, Bradford was treated as a re-run of the disorders of the previous decade – but played out this time with an 'Asian' cast.

Moving on to the second possible 'explanation', our understanding of *discrimination* needs to be sufficiently refined to encompass indirect as well as direct discrimination and to appreciate the specific ways in which the criminal justice process may allow the former. Studies which have controlled for socio-economic factors (Hood, 1992; FitzGerald and Marshall, 1996) tend to find that *most* of any remaining ethnic differences can be explained in terms of apparently race-neutral legal factors such as charge, plea, prior remand in custody and court of trial. My 1993 Royal Commission report, however, shows how many of these apparently neutral factors are themselves variously:

- open to discretion (and, therefore, the possibility of bias); and
- influenced by socio-economic considerations in ways which inevitably have an adverse impact on minority suspects and which – if they cannot be shown to be strictly necessary – raise the possibility of indirect discrimination.

(ibid., 1993)

More research attention needs to be focused on these areas, rather than on trying to unearth what Robert Reiner refers to as 'the will o' the wisp of "pure" discrimination' (Reiner, 1993). This is not to deny that direct discrimination occurs; but Hood – who has produced the most authoritative empirical evidence of direct discrimination to date – has two very relevant findings on this point which have tended to be ignored. One is that direct discrimination accounts for only a very small part of the ethnic difference in sentencing. The other is that direct discrimination is not endemic in the system: of the Crown Court centres in his study, the largest handled over half the cases he sampled and produced equitable outcomes for defendants from all ethnic groups.

On the other hand, it is spurious to argue that there is *no* discrimination in the system because Black Caribbeans appear to be treated differently from the 'Asian' group.[6] This argument is flawed on three grounds. One is that different stereotypes are held for different groups (Jefferson, 1993: 37) and, as the background section to this chapter has illustrated, stereotypes of the black criminal and the 'Asian' victim have become embedded over twenty years or more.[7] The second objection is, again, that the category of 'Asian' is of very limited use in this context; but we currently lack information on the different experiences of Indians, Pakistanis and Bangladeshis (though FitzGerald and Hale (1997) offer some new insights). Thirdly, echoing the black groups thirty to forty years ago, the 'Asian' groups have themselves begun to allege police discrimination, as was shown in media coverage of incidents in Bradford in summer 1995 and in evidence to the enquiries held subsequently.[8]

Finally there remains the thorny question of whether there are, in fact, real *ethnic differences* in levels and patterns of offending which have nothing to do with socio-economic factors or discrimination. Thus far, we have seen both direct and circumstantial evidence that the first of these factors has a powerful influence and that discrimination plays a subtle but possibly important role, although its precise nature and scale remains to be explored. Yet, even if these factors together could explain most of the ethnic differences we have observed, some outstanding questions would still remain. The two most obvious examples are: why there are such striking differences in the offence patterns of different groups; and why the Black Caribbean groups disproportionately plead not guilty and elect for crown court trial, thereby increasing their chance of being sentenced to custody (and for longer than would otherwise have been the case.)

It is very difficult to explore these questions without falling into the danger of stereotyping on the basis of crude group averages. Individual members of ethnic minorities are as different – and every bit as likely *not* to conform to some ethnically-based statistical norm – as individual whites.

However, ethnic differences throughout the criminal justice process may not fully be explained until some account is taken of ethnic differences in: (a) lifestyle; (b) opportunity structures; (c) the experience of the criminal justice system; and, importantly, (d) the extent to which these differences in opportunity structures and differences in the experience of the criminal justice system are *collectively* perceived; as well as (e) the ways groups have adapted – and continue to *adapt* – to these differences in opportunity structures and their experience of the criminal justice system.

With regard to lifestyle factors, a range of survey data have provided evidence of ethnic differences – for example, in the number of evenings people spend out per week (controlling for age and gender) in preferred forms of leisure activity, access to a car, etc. Such material is the bread and butter of commercial organisations looking to expand their market among different groups of consumers in the population; but these dif-ferences also have obvious implications for the extent to which different groups may be exposed to the attention of the police (see FitzGerald and Sibbitt, 1997).

Differences in opportunity structures are only dimly reflected in socio-economic snapshots, although they have been documented in a number of studies going back many years and most recently in four volumes of detailed analyses of the 1991 Census (ONS, 1996).

This chapter has, in outline, tried to document the differences in ethnic groups' experience of the criminal justice system. Such an account, though, cannot adequately convey how the *cycle* of this experience, over decades and generations, has developed its own dynamic. Perennially adding new data to the collective memory, it will constantly shape and reinforce both individual and groups perceptions. These, in turn, will come into play in interactions with the criminal justice system; and they will have their counterpart among the agents of that system (a point returned to in the conclusions). A systematic study of this process and its implications would be challenging (not to say daunting, since it is not possible to re-write history and wipe the slate clean). But evidence that the process is at work has been accumulating for many years, particularly in terms of minorities' per-ceptions of the police.

The study by Gaskell and Smith in 1981 was by no means the earliest, but it was particularly telling. It showed that the attitudes of a very tightly matched group of unemployed young men were very similar with regard to a range of British 'institutions'. The outstanding exception was the police. All the young men displayed negative attitudes towards the police, but those of the black group were very significantly more so. More recently, the British Crime Survey and other sources have consistently continued to reproduce the same picture; but they have begun to add detail concerning the Asian groups. Levels of dissatisfaction with the police are, overall, higher among Pakistanis than any other ethnic group; and, although mistrust of the police is most acute among black people, a significant minority of young people in the Asian groups appears to be losing faith in them also. Nor should it simply be assumed that these perceptions result from people's experience of the police as suspects and offenders. In 1991, exactly the same proportion of BCS respondents overall had reported crimes to the police as had been stopped in vehicles (Skogan, 1994); and dissatisfaction with the police response is much higher among ethnic minority victims of crime than whites. It rises to half of all Pakistani victims (compared to a third of whites) and is even more pronounced in the case of racially motivated victimisation (see Table 9.6).

Table 9.6 Perceptions of the police by different ethnic groups (per cent)

	White	Afro-Caribbean	Indian	Pakistani
Police locally do a fairly/very poor job				
(all)	18	20	19	26
16–24	22	32	26	23
Police don't treat everyone fairly				
(all)*	42	69	45	47
16–24	51	81	51	51
Fairly/very dissatisfied with police response to recorded crime				
(victims only)	33	40	46	45
Fairly/very dissatisfied with police response to racially motivated crime				
(victims only)	—	62	54	54

Source: British Crime Surveys, 1992 and 1988 combined
* 1988 data only.

Space – and the dearth of available research – do not lend themselves to any sensible exploration of points (d) and (e) above. All that can usefully be said here are two things. One is that we shall not begin to come to terms with the issues until we have begun to understand these collective perceptions in their historic dimension and the practical implications of these. Of immediate concern to this chapter are their implications on the streets, in police custody suites, in courtrooms, in alternatives to custody and in prisons; but they also go wider, to the provision of family support and education, the operation of labour markets and many other areas of social and economic policy. The second point to bear in mind is that models do exist for this type of research. In Britain the best examples are the longitudinal studies[9] and some of the best ethnographic work in criminology (for example, Foster, 1990), although, to date, these have tended to ignore the dimension of ethnicity. But examples exist elsewhere, such as Mercer Sullivan's 'Getting Paid' (Sullivan, 1989). In an urban American context, he powerfully describes the real-world experiences of white, black and Hispanic youngsters who are comparable in socio-economic terms but whose expectations and opportunities are differentially structured by their immediate physical, political, economic, familial and communal environments.

CONCLUSIONS

We have made rapid progress in recent years to fill major gaps in the statistics available on 'race' and crime in the United Kingdom. Our understanding of the issues, however, has not necessarily kept pace; yet we are moving inexorably to generate more and more data, which will need rigorous interpretation and appropriate responses at the level of both policy and practice. This chapter suggests two sets of preconditions for achieving this. One concerns the concepts and methodologies we need to develop in order to explore ethnic 'facts' in a more sophisticated way. The second concerns the historical and philosophical understandings which need to underpin that exploration.

First, it is obvious that none of the three 'explanations' which I have rehearsed here is sufficient on its own to explain the problem of 'race' and crime: all are likely to be at work. We are not in a position to draw firm conclusions about the balance between them; but a greater challenge still is to understand the ways in which they *interact*.

The extensive ethnic data now available from the Census, the Labour Force Survey (LFS) and other sources open up the possibility of looking far more rigorously at the socio-economic dimension than has even been considered so far. While recognising the pitfalls of this approach, it seems important to have some idea of the extent to which one would *predict* that different groups would show up in the criminal justice statistics. That done, it should be possible to focus with more precision on the other two areas of possible 'explanation' for any *remaining* ethnic differences.

In terms of identifying any discrimination, the argument here has been that the emphasis needs to shift *away* from notions of conscious, direct and systemic discrimination. But I would also suggest that we need to develop far more sophisticated understandings of the ways in which *discretion* is exercised throughout the criminal justice process. It is entirely possible that the power of discretion is more often than not exercised in the direction of lenience – in favour, that is, of mitigation and of giving suspects a second chance – rather than being used to its most punitive limit.[10] The scope for discretion is by no means undesirable; but it might be necessary to examine whether discretion is extended with equal beneficence to all those who are legitimately suspected of crime – bearing in mind that even if some groups were treated less leniently this would (a) not constitute discrimination in the technical sense since it would come entirely within the bounds of legitimate discretion; and (b) would not of itself prove that prejudice was at work in every case where the treatment could be shown to be inequitable. For example, if criminal justice practitioners were simply more self-conscious about their exercise of discretion in dealing with certain groups, they might unwittingly be more inclined to 'play it by the book' – failing to recognise that 'playing it by the book' may in effect treat these groups more disadvantageously. The cumulative effect of such decisions could produce markedly more serious outcomes for those individuals than comparable whites; and the sum total of such decisions would be reflected in significant differences in the statistical averages for different groups.

Second, the role and inter-relationship of these 'explanations' cannot be captured in a snapshot picture, even one which is far more detailed than is likely to develop from the initial returns of police ethnic monitoring. For there is an important *time* dimension to all of this; and the issues have to be seen in terms of a dynamic relationship, forged (and constantly re-forming) within that time dimension. That is, we are not dealing simply with objective facts which can be reduced to and understood in statistical terms. We are dealing with mutual perceptions, sometimes with folklore and certainly with collective memories; with often bitter experience at both the individual and the group level; with peer group norms – and with the attitudinal and behavioural consequences of these. Moreover, there are two parties to this relationship – the criminal justice agencies on the one hand and the different ethnic minorities on the other; and different perceptions, memories, etc. will come into play on both sides.[11] It is now nearly thirty years since the Commissioner of Police for the Metropolis wrote:

> Complaints of police 'brutality', of West Indians afraid to complain at police stations for fear of being 'beaten up', and protest marches and deputations in support of these allegations, have all been part of the deteriorating background to the pattern of police and immigrant relations during the last six months.
>
> (Sir Joseph Simpson, quoted in Rose *et al.*, 1969: 349)

We need to bear in mind that there are major difficulties in turning around any relationship which has developed unhealthy patterns and been accumulating baggage for so long. To do that, both parties need to see each other differently, to listen and, above all, to be willing to change. In that sense, it would be worse than ironic were the publication of the new police monitoring data to be used to fuel a further outbreak of hostilities. Rather, if they are interpreted with adequate rigour, underpinned by a constructive understanding of their context and its history, they may help in raising the right questions. They will not, of themselves, though, provide the answers.

NOTES

1 The term race is used here and throughout in inverted commas to indicate that it is used only as a shorthand term, borrowed from popular discourse, and implies no support for a biological concept of race which has behavioural implications. It might be noted, though, that this popular usage reflects the terms of the British legislation which itself reflected acceptable American usage of twenty years ago.

2 Only about 47 per cent of crimes committed are reported to the police and only about 27 per cent are actually recorded in police statistics while only about 2 per cent result in a conviction of any sort.

3 The argument is rarely posed quite so starkly but is implicit in the convoluted arguments some authors advance to smooth over the difficulties this apparently presents. One example is the quotation from the New Left Criminologists given earlier; Smith, quoted at note 6 below is another.

4 According to the 1991 Census, 41 per cent of Indian men who were economically active were in jobs classified as 'Professional/managerial' compared to 36 per cent of whites.

5 When I raised this point at the British Criminology Conference in 1995, sections of the media obliged by illustrating it, reporting my presentation under headlines like 'Research warns of Asian "time bomb"' (*Independent*, 22 July 1995) and 'Criminals: Fury as Home Office warns of threat from Asian youngsters' (*Eastern Eye*, 1 August 1995).

6 The argument was put thus by David Smith:

> The theory that Afro-Caribbeans but not South Asians are singled out for discriminatory treatment by crime victims and the police does not fit with the wider picture of racial discrimination and disadvantage in Britain.
>
> (Smith, 1995: 444)

7 Indeed, it should be remembered that the evidence of the British Crime Survey is that black people are disproportionately more likely than whites also to be *victims* of crime and that their levels of victimisation are comparable with those of 'Asians' (FitzGerald and Hale, 1996).

8 By 1988 the British Crime Survey already showed that a quarter of Pakistanis and Indians aged 16 to 24 believed that the police did not treat Asians equally (FitzGerald and Hale, 1996: 29).

9 For a review, see Graham, 1988.

10 Moxon in his study of sentencing at the Crown Court (Moxon, 1988) identified a much longer list of factors which disposed courts in favour of lenience than pushed them towards the more punitive end of the sentencing tariff. Walker (1988 and 1989), found a higher use of custody for black adult males but not for juveniles; and Hood (1992) similarly found that the ethnic penalty in sentence

178   *Marian FitzGerald*

length applied only to black adult males and was more marked in offences of
medium seriousness. At least part of the reason for these findings may be that
courts have less discretion in the sentencing of juveniles and that the discretion
they do have is greatest for offences of medium seriousness.

11 Thus Jefferson on contact between the police and black youth:

> At this point the self-fulfilling prophecy, the vicious circle, the amplification
> of deviance (both police and youth deviance) is set in motion. Police enter
> encounters expecting trouble and act aggressively to pre-empt it. Black youth
> similarly expect trouble and create the necessary ('disrespectful') mind set to
> cope. The resulting 'trouble' demonstrates well . . . a deadly dynamic of
> mutual distrust.
>
> (Jefferson, 1988: 537)

REFERENCES

Bethnal Green and Stepney Trades Council (1978), *Blood on the Streets*.
Blom-Cooper, L. and Drabble, R. (1982) 'Police perceptions of crime: Brixton and
the operational response', *British Journal of Criminology* 22: 184–7.
Brown, I. and Hullin, R. (1992), 'A study of sentencing in the Leeds magistrates
courts. The treatment of ethnic minority and white offenders', *British Journal of
Criminology* 32: 41–53.
Bucke, T. (1996) *Ethnicity and Contacts with the Police: Findings from the British
Crime Survey*. Research Findings no. 42. Home Office.
Commission for Racial Equality (1992) *Juvenile Cautioning – Ethnic Monitoring in
Practice*.
Demuth, C. (1978) *'Sus': A Report on the Vagrancy Act 1824*. Runnymede Trust.
FitzGerald, M. (1993) *Ethnic Minorities and the Criminal Justice System*. Research
Study no. 20. The Royal Commission on Criminal Justice. HMSO.
FitzGerald, M. (forthcoming) 'Racial harassment: issues of measurement and
comparison', in Layton-Henry, Z. and Wilpert, C. (eds) *Challenging Racism and
Discrimination in Britain and Germany*. Francis Pinter.
FitzGerald, M. and Ellis, T. (1992) 'Racial harassment: the evidence', in Kemp,
C. (ed.) *Current Issues in Criminological Research*, vol. 2. Bristol and Bath Centre
for Criminal Justice.
FitzGerald, M. and Hale, C. (1996) *Ethnic Minorities: Victimisation and Racial
Harassment. Findings from the 1988 and 1994 British Crime Surveys*. Home
Office Research Study no. 154. HMSO.
FitzGerald, M. and Hale, C. (1997) *Ethnic Minorities and Police Stop/Searches
in London and Elsewhere: A British Crime Survey Analysis*. Home Office.
FitzGerald, M. and Marshall, P. (1996) 'Ethnic minorities in British prisons', in
Matthews, R. and Francis, P. (eds) *Prisons 2000*. Sage.
FitzGerald, M. and Sibbitt, S. (1997) *Ethnic Monitoring by Police Forces in
England and Wales: A Beginning*. Home Office.
Foster, J. (1990) *Villains: Crime and Community in the Inner City*. Routledge.
Gaskell, G. and Smith, P. 'Are young blacks really alienated?', *New Society*, 14 May
1981.
Graham, J. (1988) *Schools, Disruptive Behaviour and Delinquency: A Review of
Research*. Home Office Research Study no. 96. HMSO.

Graham, J. and Bowling, B. (1995) *Young People and Crime*. Home Office Research Study no. 145. HMSO.

Hall, S., Critcher, C., Clarke, J., Jefferson, T. and Roberts, B. (1978) *Policing the Crisis*. Macmillan.

Home Office Prison Statistics England and Wales (Annual). HMSO.

Home Office (1989) Statistical Bulletin 5/89 *Crime Statistics for the Metropolitan Police District by Ethnic Group, 1987: Victims, Suspects and Those Arrested.*

Home Office (1994) Statistical Bulletin 21/94 *The Ethnic Origins of Prisoners: Ethnic Composition of Prison Population 1985 to 1993; Study of Population on 30 June 1990 and Persons Received in 1990.*

Hood, R. (1992) *Race and Sentencing*. Oxford University Press.

House of Commons Select Committee on Race Relations and Immigration (1972) *Police/Immigrant Relations*. HMSO.

House of Commons Select Committee on Race Relations and Immigration (1977) *The West Indian Community*. HMSO.

Hunte, J. A. (1966) *Nigger-Hunting in England?* West Indian Standing Conference.

Jefferson, T. (1988) 'Race, crime and policing', *International Journal of the Sociology of Law* 16: 521–39.

Jefferson, T. (1993) 'The racism of criminalization: police and the production of the criminal other,' in Gelsthorpe, L. *Minority Ethnic Groups in the Criminal Justice System*. Cropwood Conference Series no. 21. Cambridge.

Lea, J. and Young, J. (1982) 'The riots in Britain in 1981: urban violence and political marginalisation', in Cowell, D., Jones, T. and Young, T. (eds) *Policing The Riots*. Junction.

Mayhew, P., Dowds, L. and Elliott, D. (1989) *The 1988 British Crime Survey*. Home Office Research Study no. 111. HMSO.

Mayhew, P., Aye Maung, N. and Mirrlees-Black, C. (1993) *The 1992 British Crime Survey*. Home Office Research Study no. 132. HMSO.

Moxon, D. (1988) *Sentencing Practice in the Crown Court*. Home Office Research Study no. 103. HMSO.

Office of National Statistics (1996) *Ethnicity in the 1991 Census*. HMSO.

Reiner, R. (1989) 'Race and criminal justice', *New Community* 16/1: 5–21.

Reiner, R. (1993) 'Race, crime and justice: models of interpretation' in Gelsthorpe, L. (ed.) *Minority Ethnic Groups in the Criminal Justice System*. Cropwood Conference Series no. 21. Cambridge.

Rose, E. J. B., Deakin, N., Abrams, M., Jackson, V., Preston, M., Vonage, A. H., Cohen, B., Gaitskell, J. and Ward, P. (1969) *Colour and Citizenship*. Institute of Race Relations/Oxford University Press.

Scarman Lord (1981) *The Brixton Disorders: Report of an Inquiry by the Rt. Hon. Lord Scarman* OBE. HMSO.

Skogan, W. (1994) *Contacts between Police and Public: Findings from the 1992 British Crime Survey*. Home Office Research Study no. 134. HMSO.

Smith, D. (1995) 'Youth crime and conduct disorders' in Rutter, M. and Smith, D. (eds) *Psychosocial Disorders in Young People: Time Trends and their Causes*. Wiley.

Stevens, P. and Willis, C. (1979) *Race, Crime and Arrests*. Home Office Research Study no. 58. HMSO.

Sullivan, M. (1989) *'Getting Paid': Youth, Crime and Work in the Inner City*. Cornell University Press.

Voakes, R. and Fowler, Q. (1989) *Sentencing, Race and Social Enquiry Reports*. West Yorkshire Probation Service.

Walker, M. (1988) 'The court disposal of young males by race in London in 1983', *British Journal of Criminology* 28: 441–60.

Walker, M. (1989) 'The court disposal and remands of white, Afro-Caribbean and Asian men (London 83)', *British Journal of Criminology* 29: 353–67.

Walker, M., Jefferson, T. and Seneviratne, M. (1989) *Race and Criminal Justice in a Provincial City*. Paper presented at British Criminology Conference, Bristol.

Willis, C. (1983) *The Use, Effectiveness and Impact of Police Stop and Search Powers*. Research and Planning Unit Paper 15. Home Office.

10 The participation of new minority ethnic groups in British politics

Harry Goulbourne

INTRODUCTION

This chapter discusses spontaneous protest, organised representation, and participation within the party and electoral systems by African Caribbeans and Asians who are the two largest and most salient new minority ethnic groups in Britain. No account is taken of the activities of new white minority ethnic groups (Cypriots, Greeks, Italians, Maltese, Poles, Turks, Ukrainians and others), nor of the Chinese and Vietnamese Asian communities. Individuals from new white groups, such as Michael Portillo or Michael Howard, have been able to participate in national politics with little or no attention to their ethnic origins. But this is an option that is unavailable to individuals from nearly all African Caribbean and Asian groups. The Chinese and Vietnamese communities may become more visible particularly if sizeable migration from Hong Kong occurs after the island reverts to China in 1997, but for the moment while they do participate in politics their participation is less visible than is the case with African Caribbean and Asian communities. Indeed, political participation in these communities may be understood in terms of Milbrath's (1965) distinctions between *gladiatorial activities* (holding public or party office, becoming a candidate for such office, seeking funds for the party, taking part in strategy meetings and spending time on campaigning), *transitional activities* (attendance at public meetings or rallies, contributing money and getting in touch with an official or party leader), and *spectator activities* (wearing a button or sticker, trying to influence others to vote in a particular way, starting a political discussion, voting, exposing oneself to political stimuli). But dramatic and promising as the active participation of individuals from these two sets of communities in the nation's political life has been, there is still some way to go before participation assumes the regular presence of black and brown Britons in the corridors of power at Whitehall and Westminster. If, however, the notion of Britain as a multicultural society is to be taken seriously, then the active political participation of people from all segments of society must become as much a reality as their participation has been in other areas of national life such as sports, entertainment and business.

SPONTANEOUS PROTEST

Some of the most dramatic moments in the participation of Caribbean and Asian minorities in British social and political life have been through spontaneous action bred of frustrations with the relevant authorities. Large-scale public disruptions, in particular riots and mass demonstrations, have been used by loosely organised groups to express the bitter feelings of their communities about the introduction or implementation of specific policies. In their account of different types of group behaviour, Almond and Powell described these forms of political participation, as well as assassinations, as being 'anomic', suggesting, by the use of this key concept from Emile Durkheim (1970), that such participation is disorganised and uncoordinated. They described 'anomic' interventions as being 'more or less spontaneous penetrations into the political system' (Almond and Powell, 1966, p. 75–6), and they were of the view that such interventions were limited in the scope of issues they espoused. While it may be true that such events are not the result of much deliberation and organisation, it must be noted that it is actually through such mass demonstrations and riots that some far-reaching public policy initiatives came to be placed on the public agenda for what David Easton (1953) called 'authoritative' resolution. Two dramatic events or sets of events will illustrate the importance of this kind of participation in British politics by minority ethnic groups.

The first of these was the disturbances in Brixton, South London, during the weekend of 10–12 April 1981. As Lord Scarman, who was asked to investigate the disturbances, reported in November of the same year:

> the British people watched with horror and incredulity an instant audio-visual presentation on their television sets of scenes of violence and disorder in their capital city, the like of which had not previously been seen in this century in Britain ... demonstrating to millions of their fellow citizens the fragile basis of the Queen's peace.
>
> (Scarman, 1981, p. 1)

These disturbances had an international impact, and hinted that the British political system was less capable than many had been led to believe when it came to managing change and integrating new social groups into its civic culture and polity. The disturbances triggered similar activities in other parts of the country in subsequent months. In July, following an attack by the right-wing skinheads on young Asians in Southall, a confrontation developed between Asian youths and the police who had arrived ostensibly to mediate and maintain the peace. Confrontations between black youths and the police occurred in Toxteth in Liverpool, Moss Side in Manchester, Handsworth in Birmingham, and in Wolverhampton and Smethwick. The events served to highlight a number of problems that Caribbean and Asian communities had long faced in the decaying inner cities. These included severe tension between the Caribbean communities and the police in the inner cities, where community spokespersons had long blamed the police for harassment and brutality particularly against young men. In the Asian communities the problem with the police was the opposite: community leaders accused the police of inactivity, particularly in relation to racist attacks on individuals in their communities (see, for example, Scarman, 1981, pp. 12–13; also, Solomos, 1988, chap. 3).

The Brixton disturbances became the catalyst for change, however limited these may now appear to be. The nation's attention was drawn to the manifold social and economic problems Caribbean and Asian communities faced in the decaying inner cities, problems which had been well documented by academic researchers, journalists and others over several years (see, for example, Humphry, 1972; Daniel, 1968). But it took large-scale public disturbances to alert policy makers and implementers to the need for appropriate action to be taken. Scarman could not fail to find that other underlying problems needed to be addressed by local and national authorities and a range of statutory bodies such as the police and the criminal justice system. These problems included disproportionately high unemployment, poor housing in Caribbean and Asian communities, and other forms of disadvantages resulting from widespread racial discrimination.

But riots and spontaneous activities do not always have the desired effects on the political process. Such appears to have been the case when, in 1985, Caribbean youths rioted in Handsworth and parts of London in demand of reform and better treatment by local and central government. When PC Keith Blakelock was killed on the depressed Broadwater Farm housing estate in Tottenham, North London, the response from the general public was unsympathetic to the rioters. The authorities were able to ride out what appeared to be temporary and localised crises. In the mid-1990s Asian youths also rioted in cities such as Bradford in demand of better treatment from the police in their communities and against high unemployment. But here again, the instrument of relatively unorganised spontaneous intervention in the political process was less effective than it had been a decade earlier. This does not, however, detract from the occasional effectiveness of rude intervention as one form of participation in politics. At the very least, these interventions introduce new variables for politicians and other decision-makers to take into account, and such interventions thereby disturb the system from its sometimes strong and comforting complacency.

The second example of spontaneous intervention into the overall socio-political process, which acted as a powerful catalyst unlocking latent tension in society, was the response to the publication towards the end of 1988 of Salman Rushdie's *The Satanic Verses*. Overnight the Rushdie affair became one of the most dramatic events of our time. Increasing murmurs about the offence of the novel to the Moslem faith and community were given an added force in February 1989 when the Ayatollah Khomeini of Iran called on the faithful anywhere in the world to punish Rushdie by death for the novel's alleged blasphemy against Islam. These developments captured the nation's attention and have remained an important, if no longer a major, factor in international affairs. The Ayatollah's *fatwa* became the focus around which many British Moslems, particularly in Bradford, mobilised to express their feelings about the perceived status of Islam in society. Their organisations led mass demonstrations against the author, the book and its publishers, and the intensity of the furore was such that there were public burnings of the book. For a while, lives and public order in the realm appeared to be under an irrational and incomprehensible threat. Salman Rushdie went into hiding and has led a unique life of a forced recluse – a life which seems a worse punishment than ever the Tsars or Stalin could devise in banishing their critics to Siberia or the gulag archipelago. The Rushdie affair has continued well into the 1990s, long after the death of the Ayatollah himself, causing much pain and suffering for devout Moslems, but particularly to Salman Rushdie himself.

Such sufferings apart, the continuing importance of this long played out drama is the large question it raises about some cultural and political certainties in British society. The Rushdie affair brought back onto the public agenda the question of the relationship or the balance between religious faith and the faith in a rational secularism that informs general public values in the modern state and the comity of nation-states. For better or for worse, the Rushdie affair has raised the important question of the traditional liberal freedom of the individual to write and publish when the exercise of this freedom conflicts with the collective right of groups to the protection of the law against abuse. This revisitation or reconsideration appears to be particularly relevant in a society in which a not insignificant part of public philosophy is multiculturalism, that is, a socio-political order in which each culture, including religion, is mutually honoured and respected (see Jenkins, 1967; Swann, 1985). For some, however, the nature of the opposition to Rushdie seemed an unnecessary and retrogressive step into a past in which religious prejudice and dogma arbitrarily and cruelly dominated society (see, for example, Appignanesi and Maitland, 1989).

This contention continues to reverberate in British society, with the CRE and other bodies calling for toleration. For example, one view is that the law of blasphemy – which provides state protection with respect to blasphemy against the official Church of England's teachings – should be so extended that it protects all faiths. An alternative view is that the state should abolish this exclusive provision in the law, and instead allow all denominations and faiths to contend with the profanities of the secular world – as in the United States where Thomas Jefferson's legacy of distancing the state and a person's religion still obtains. In this situation, the CRE has called for a national debate on problems of religious pluralism and toleration that face the nation (CRE, 1995, 1991, 1990a, 1990b).

Spontaneous interventions into the political system, such as riots and large-scale demonstrations, are not to be seen as factors external to a political system; they are sometimes the invigorating elements which provide the opportunity for necessary reform and change. They are disturbing because they occur unexpectedly and threaten the apparently stable and smooth running of affairs, but we do not need to be adherents of George Sorel's syndicalist teachings to recognise the utility of spontaneous interventions for an established socio-political system such as Britain's. This creative feature of spontaneity may be one aspect of popular action that escaped Vladimir Ilyich Ulyanov (Lenin) in his critique of political spontaneity, but then his concern was with the Tsarist socio-political order which had long passed the point of redemption through the steady change brought about by consent, compromise and reform that was greatly admired by thoughtful political sociologists such as the French aristocrat de Tocqueville (1955).

ORGANISED PRESSURE ACTIVITIES

There is a wide range of groups that seek to apply pressure or influence on the political process of decision-making and implementation. Finer defined such groups to be those which are 'occupied at any point in trying to influence the policy of government in their own chosen direction' (Finer, 1966, p. 3). For some theorists, however, the absence of overt pressure does not mean that there is an absence of such groups and their activities. This is the conclusion to a long discussion over the distribution and exercise of power in Anglo-American societies (see for example, Backrach and Baratz, 1963; Crenson, 1971; Lukes, 1976). But from Arthur Bentley (1967) at the beginning of the century, to more sceptical analysts in the 1960s, advocates of group theory argued that pressure or interest groups were vital parts of a healthy and functioning democracy, because they mediate between government and public in ways that are indispensable for a democratic society. In a restatement of his position, Finer later suggested that there are four preconditions for the effective participation of individuals through pressure groups in a democratic order. These include the existence of unlimited freedom of speech, association and access to government; unlimited freedom of individuals to join and quit groups; a perfect leader/member responsiveness inside groups; and a perfect membership of groups. This last precondition is a little strange for a democratic theorist because, in a democratic order, the individual must be able to exercise the freedom not to join organised groups, or quit them, as Finer's second precondition takes account of. Be that as it may, Finer correctly concluded that not only must individuals feel that they are participants, they must also see themselves as participants. He also correctly concluded that even in the most favourable situations – long thought by democratic theorists to be Britain and the United States – the possibility of the conditions he identified being met are low.

Indeed, these stiff conditions cannot be met by groups in minority ethnic communities any more than they can be met in the wider society. For example, Asian associational groups tend to be organised around kinship (see John, 1969; Ballard, 1994), but even here, where considerable pressure to conform may be presumed to exist it would be unrealistic to expect a perfect coincidence of membership. In Caribbean groups this coincidence of perfect membership would be an impossibility because of the high incidence of individuality[1] that obtains. These communities and the groups which have emerged within them might meet some of the conditions detailed by Finer, but to fail in one is to fail in all, and none could meet them because they are also contradictory. The suggestion, therefore, that arises from this is that representation of interests through associational groups is not particularly effective even in the most open democratic socio-political system. Moreover, to achieve a degree of success, groups seeking to exert pressure on authorities must learn the styles and acceptable procedures of these authorities, or these groups' efforts may be ignored because of the inappropriateness of the mode of their representation (Dearlove, 1973). This is not, however, to suggest that these kinds of groups are irrelevant to the process of political participation. Pressure groups do have significant functions in democratic theory and practice (see Goulbourne, 1975), and this approach to understanding political participation may be sensibly applied to understand the forms of participation that have been used by minority ethnic groups. These groups play important roles in the political system by articulating community needs as interpreted by some key community figures who occupy gatekeeping positions. Through membership of such groups and the activities they engage in, individuals are integrated into the wider political system in so far as members become involved, however marginally or minimally, in discussions about public affairs.

Additionally, such groups are of considerable importance to political authorities and other providers of services in helping in the implementation, if not formulation, of policy. For example, under the 1976 Race Relations Act local and education authorities as well as other bodies are to provide service fairly to all irrespective of race; the newer de-centralised health trusts are also expected to provide fair and equal services to all. In such circumstances, organisations that were structured to provide services and support for a hitherto relatively homogeneous, mono-cultural, white society, need the help of community-based groups to improve delivery of services to minority ethnic communities. Sometimes, authorities aid the establishment of such groups, and since authorities control funds and other resources, they can sometimes destroy what autonomy groups may have. After all, decision-making authorities are not themselves neutral bodies simply responding to extraneous pressure. They have their own interests and agendas as well as wider constituencies to take into account, and they are themselves competing players in a wider and unpredictable or uncertain political environment.

There are different kinds of groups in the African Caribbean and Asian communities that have sought to exert influence on the decision-making process at national and local levels. Probably the best known of these which aimed to unite indigenous whites, African Caribbeans and Asians at national level, was the Campaign Against Racial Discrimination (CARD). In the mid-1960s CARD, involving a number of outstanding individuals such as its founder Marian Glean (later O'Callaghan), Richard Small, Dipak Nandy, Joe Hunte, Jeff Crawford, Hamza Alavi, Rattan Singh, Jagmohan Joshi, David Pitt – all of whom were later to become important figures in different areas of work – failed to unite the wide range of community groups which sprang up in Asian and Caribbean communities in the early years of entry and settlement. Not surprisingly, therefore, as Heinemann's detailed study of the group revealed, key individuals such as Anthony (now Lord) Lester, and his strategically placed friends such as Ian McDonald, Michael Zander, Jeffrey Jewell and Richard Small had far more influence on the 1965 Race Relations Act than did CARD as an organisation (Heinemann, 1972, chap. 4).

Again, in 1976 when there was no national multiracial body like CARD, individual influence was perhaps more important than collective action on the part of organised community interests. None the less, as Sobeen has pointed out, the Act originated within the context of mass union activity by Asian workers at the Mansfield Hosiery Mills in 1972, the dramatic disputes at Imperial Typewriters in Leicester in 1974, and the growing militancy among Caribbean youths in the inner cities (Sobeen, 1990, chap. 6). It took individual effort, however, to convert this social material into actual political capital to be used in bringing about change. The relative distance of African Caribbeans and Asians from the corridors of power at Whitehall and Westminster has meant that the individuals who played these key gate-keepers' roles were from the majority indigenous population. It is appropriate to ask whether today, as new minorities become more integrated into the political system, these gatekeepers will continue to be almost exclusively from the majority population.

Over the last ten or so years a number of semi-professional bodies have been active in attempting to apply pressure within occupations, perhaps reflecting a shift in collective action away from multiple to single occupations. For example, concerned teachers from all communities have organised around issues about education, and some of the points they raised informed the Swann Committee report of 1985. Issues about the low academic attainments in schools by pupils of Caribbean backgrounds, mother tongue teaching for children of Asian backgrounds, and the educational needs of a society that have been increasingly described as multicultural, have featured in debates about education over the past two decades or more, and they have formed the basis for organised group behaviour. In the late 1980s and into the 1990s a range of issues surfaced about social care provisions for groups with specific needs in both African Caribbean and Asian communities. These included issues about the desirability of black children being adopted by white families (Arnold and James, 1989), the care of the elderly (Blakemore and Boneham, 1994), problems of health care for people from different cultural backgrounds and questions of mental health, sickle cell anaemia and thallasemia (Ahmad, 1994; Ahmad and Atkin, 1996). Relatively non-contentious matters such as food preference and life-styles have become important items on the agenda of some groups, and should be seen as aspects of the politics of cultural identity which are now relevant for groups in both the majority and minority ethnic communities.

Another example of pressure being brought to bear on the establishment are the activities of African Caribbean and Asian lawyers in their own profession. From colonial times the Bar has been attractive to upwardly mobile members of these communities (S. Goulbourne, 1989a). By the 1980s this was being reflected in the incidence of a high proportion of British Asian and Caribbean students graduating with law degrees and opting predominantly for careers at the Bar, law centres and local authorities.[2] On qualifying, however, this new generation found their paths to the profession as effectively blocked as they had been for their parents (S. Goulbourne, 1989b). The radical Society of Black Lawyers, founded by Rudy Narayan and Sigbhat Kadri, soon brought on board the younger generation, including individuals such as Peter Herbert, Makbool Javaid and Chris Boothman. The Society's main aim has been to improve access to justice in Britain, but in practice perhaps their main achievement has been to convince first the Bar Council, and the more reluctant Law Society, to examine their exclusionary practices and introduce new and fair codes of conduct in relation to recruitment and the provision of services to the public. Through vociferous and militant protest, these lawyers managed slowly to bring about a recognisable degree of change in the profession. For example, there is now a handful of Queen's Counsels and judges, and a number of firms and chambers have been encouraged to develop professional codes of conduct regarding recruitment and management so that applicants from minority ethnic groups can now have the expectation that they will be considered. This story has been, on a lesser scale, replicated in some of the other traditional professions, such as the church, where black and Asian Christians have organised to combat racism and exclusion (see, for example, Johnson, 1991; Charman, 1979; Howard, 1987).

Such pressure group activities have not, however, been limited to groups from the communities under discussion. Various bodies, such as the former community relations councils and the present Racial Equality Councils, have been important in local activities to promote good race relations (Gay and Young, 1988). It is properly widely acknowledged that the Commission for Racial Equality have played an important part in tackling racial discrimination in these and other areas of national life. For example, in April 1996 the army entered into an agreement with the Commission to ensure applications from minority ethnic groups were treated seriously and fairly. Some years earlier, the Commission alerted an unsuspecting public and diligent groups to the unjust practices of selection of students for medicine at St George's Hospital in London (see, for example, CRE, 1988; also, Johnson and Songster, 1995; Johnson, *et al.*, 1996). To be sure, some institutions and professions put up a tough fight in defence of the *status quo ante*. But perhaps the institutions most resistant to change for a fairer and more just society, where new minority ethnic groups are concerned, have been the universities, particularly the older ones in which minority ethnic groups are represented mainly through the registration of students, but are unashamedly exploited for pecuniary and reputational purposes by these institutions' promotion brochures. Where minority ethnic groups are concerned the employment of academic staff has gone with little or no scrutiny and comment, and this is in sharp contrast to the proper, regular and frequent scrutiny of employment profiles of women in these universities.

In general, however, it is difficult to assess the impact or influence of minority ethnic associational or secondary groups on the decision-making processes in occupations or in national and local governments. The impression given is that these groups serve multiple functions, introducing individuals to participate, however minimally, in the process through which decisions affecting their lives and the well-being of the whole society are made. These organisations also help the authorities by providing contact points for discussions and sometimes act as buffer zones between the authorities and communities. The officers of many of these organisations are also more highly trained and formally educated than in the past, and there is a far greater sophistication in how they go about their business, such as forming local, national and sometimes international networks for mutual assistance and sharing common and comparative experience.

THE POLITICAL PARTIES AND THE ELECTORAL PROCESS

The participation of African Caribbean and Asian minorities in the party political and electoral systems has been more dramatic and visible, and therefore apparently more successful than in the sphere of outside pressure group activity. The political party is, of course, the body that has most effectively organised voters in modern societies, and while actual memberships of parties may be relatively low, leaders usually try to make effective use of members' resources and loyalty at times of local and national elections. Since the mid-1970s, the votes of minority ethnic communities have been sought by politicians from the three major parties, and the forthcoming national elections will not be an exception. Indeed, it appears that these voters may be crucial in marginal seats, and in 1996 not even the Labour Party would take their support for granted (see, for example, *Birmingham Post*, 17 July 1996).

There have, of course, been attempts by individuals in the minority ethnic communities to run as independent candidates in local and parliamentary elections, as well as attempts to form parties, which generally espouse single issues. Such action is usually because an aspiring politician has a grievance against one of the main political parties. Rudy Narayan's stand as an independent black candidate against the national leadership's choice Kate Hoey in the Vauxhall by-election in June 1989 is a case in point (*Daily Telegraph*, 25 May 1989; *Observer*, 21 May 1989). The founding of a Moslem party in the late 1980s, and the establishment of an organisation calling itself the Moslem Parliament of Great Britain, are examples of members from a distinctive minority group wanting to find what they consider to be a more appropriate voice for their grievances outside the established parties. In June 1996 it was reported that the leader of the latter group, Dr Muhammad Ghayasuddin, called on Moslems to boycott the general elections, and thereby jettison Labour's chances of victory in about forty seats where Moslem leaders believed voters in their community held the electoral balance between the parties (*Daily Star*, 25 June 1996). In the late 1960s and first part of the 1970s, many groups in the African Caribbean communities voiced a similar disillusionment with the established parties, but by the late 1970s this had changed to active participation by the politically active within the parties (see FitzGerald, 1988, 1984; Egbuna, 1971; Goulbourne, 1991b). In the run-up to the 1997 general elections there is again much concern about the intention of young black men not to vote, but this may be a reflection of a generalised disillusionment with electoral politics.

Overwhelmingly, however, aspirant politicians from both African Caribbean and Asian communities have sought to participate within the established political and electoral systems. Multiculturalism, embracing pluralism in the cultural sphere, has little meaning in the political sphere where unitary tradition and structures remain intact. Nor has there been any pressure for, or hint of, the kind of political pluralism known as consociational representation where, as in Belgium, different ethnic groups enjoy representation in the legislature or the executive. Political pluralism in Britain means what group theorists have meant by pluralism, namely, the existence and participation in the political process by a variety of associational groups organised around conflicting economic, political, professional and institutional interests – not overt ethnic interests. Participation in politics by minority ethnic groups has remained within the acceptable framework of traditional politics – Bernie Grant's sporting of a colourful African dress at the opening of Parliament in 1987, notwithstanding. Being a first past the post, single, non-transferable, voting system, the electoral and party political systems may also have what Maurice Duverger (1967) saw as an in-built protection against the temptation to fragment and, therefore, open the gate for all political factions to be represented in the Commons as political parties.

For more than two decades, a number of psephologists and other observers of the local and national electoral processes have been providing much useful data about the levels of party political participation of African Caribbeans and Asians in Britain. The location and relevance of minority ethnic voters, their intention and actual patterns of voting, the attitudes of candidates, and the responses of the parties to the presence and participation of voters and politicians from these communities have received much attention from academics and journalists since the two general elections of 1974 (see, for example, Anwar, 1994; Sewell, 1993; Saggar, 1992; Layton-Henry, 1992; Messina, 1989). There is no need here to go over what is now familiar ground, because it has been these aspects of political participation by Asians and African Caribbeans, rather than the wider contributions of political sociology, that have interested most commentators. However, it may be worth mentioning a few salient points about these formal or structured forms of political participation by these groups.

Drawing on data provided by polling organisations such as Harris, the OPCS, the 1991 National Census of Population and more specifically focused surveys conducted by academics, commentators interested in the electoral process have been able to highlight a number of important features in minority ethnic participation. Anwar suggests that in 1991 there were seventy-eight parliamentary constituencies with an excess of 15 per cent minority ethnic votes, and thirty constituencies in which the percentages of ethnic minority populations are a majority, close to a majority or a large single whole (Anwar, 1994, chap. 2). In the same year there were fifty-five wards throughout the country in which the minority ethnic groups accounted for more than 50 per cent of the population. The new minority ethnic groups are concentrated in clearly identifiable parts of the country: Caribbean communities in the South East, particularly London, and in the West Midlands, principally Birmingham, and Leeds, Manchester, and Bristol; African groups in the port cities of Cardiff, Liverpool and Manchester as well as the university cities of Oxford and Cambridge; and South Asians in west and north-east London, Slough, the Thames estuary, Kent, the East and West Midlands, particularly Birmingham and Leicester, West Yorkshire, Blackburn and Greater Manchester (Owen, 1996). It is not surprising, therefore, that it is mainly in constituencies located in areas such as Birmingham, Leicester, Manchester outside London and Lambeth, Vaux-hall, Southall, Brent, Tottenham and so forth that ambitious politicians from minority ethnic communities have challenged, and are challenging, politicians from the majority ethnic community for seats in Parliament.

The age profile of Asian and African Caribbean communities may also be favourable to greater electoral participation and representation in the future. Owen describes the age profiles in all these communities to be pyramidic, with the elderly forming an apex and younger generations broadening farther down the structure (Owen, 1996, 1993). In general, however, this is true only for all minority ethnic groups taken together; disaggregated according to age they reveal significant variations. For Caribbean groups the pyramid bulges widest at the 25–29 age group, followed by 20–24 and 30–34; compared to Africans and mixed black groups the base (aged 0–19) is fairly narrow. South Asian groups, on the other hand, are significantly widest at the 0–19 age bands, and this is fairly consistent for Bangladeshis, Indians and Pakistanis. There are, of course, slight gender variations in these communities, but psephologists have not been particularly interested in the gender distribution of minority ethnic voters, other than to say that in the Asian communities men tend to be overwhelmingly the players in the public arena and in Caribbean communities there is significant participation by women alongside men. In general, the youthful profile of minority ethnic communities would suggest that in future we may expect to see greater participation or representation. The study of voting intentions, however, suggests that those 18–34 were relatively less likely to vote than those over 34 years of age (Anwar, 1994, p. 39).

In a democracy people who are eligible to vote need to register in order to realise their civic responsibilities as members of the franchise. In 1964 it was found that less than half of Commonwealth immigrants were on the electoral roll. This is somewhat surprising, at least for Caribbean voters, given the high turnouts recorded in the Caribbean (see, for example, Emmanuel, 1993; Stone, 1974), but it may be best to see this in light of the expectations of the immigrant generation to return within a relatively short time span (Goulbourne, 1980; Western, 1992; Thomas-Hope, 1992; Chamberlain, 1997). The same may have been true for migrants from the Indian sub-continent, who also had aspirations of an early return (see Anwar, 1979). In 1974, whereas only 6 per cent of whites were off the electoral roll, 24 per cent of minority ethnic voters were unregistered. In 1979, a survey in 24 parliamentary constituencies of 1,115 whites, 595 Asians, 152 African Caribbeans and 65 members from other communities, revealed that whereas only 7 per cent of whites were not registered, 23 per cent of the other groups were not on the electoral roll. Drawing on OPCS and CRE surveys, Anwar found that in London in 1981 Asians and African Caribbeans had double the non-registration rates when compared to whites. A CRE survey in the inner cities in 1983 – a time of heightened political awareness of black and Asian politicians in the Labour Party – showed that while white registration had declined from 93 per cent to 81 per cent, and African Caribbeans had also fallen from 81 per cent in 1979 to 76 per cent, there was a marginal improvement in the Asian communities from 77 per cent to 79 per cent (Anwar, 1994). Mich LeLohe, who has spent many years studying Asian voters in Bradford, has described them as model European citizens because of their higher than average turn-out at European and other elections in the city (LeLohe, 1990).

Of all the political parties Labour has benefited most from minority ethnic participation in elections. An overall 70 per cent of African Caribbean and Asian votes went to Labour in the 1983 general elections; in the next elections in 1987, when there was a shift to the Conservatives, 61 per cent of Asian voters and 92 per cent African Caribbean voters, compared to 31 per cent of white voters, went to Labour (Anwar, 1994, p. 37). There may be several reasons for this strong support for the Labour Party.

First, Labour has long been positively associated with issues that have concerned people from Britain's former colonies. Under the influence of Lord Passfield, the Fabian leader Sydney Webb, the Labour Party from the late 1920s took an interest in the emerging labour movement in the colonies and with de-colonisation the party supported the cause of nationalists for independence long before the Conservative prime minister, Harold Macmillan, in 1959 recognised that there was an irresistible 'wind of change' in Britain's empire in Africa. Second, the Labour Party has managed to maintain a positive image of being sympathetic to the concerns of immigrants and their descendants. In this regard, Labour's objection, while in opposition, to the 1962 Commonwealth Immigration Act appears to have compensated for their claim in 1965 that as the government of the day they had done better than the Conservatives in keeping black and brown immigrants out of the country (see Goulbourne, 1991a, p. 110). It is sometimes suggested that the (almost Pavlovian) tendency of the Conservative Party since 1964 to use immigration as an election issue, continues to encourage Asians to vote Labour, because while primary immigration has long been effectively stopped, the reunion of families, particularly from the Indian sub-continent, remains an issue.

Perhaps the third factor which explains overwhelming black and brown electoral support for Labour is that it was under a Labour government in 1965 that the first legislation against racial discrimination was introduced. The law was strengthened under Labour in 1968, and again in 1976. Supporters of the legislation and the work of the CRE still argue that the present law fails to go far enough in combating racial discrimination in housing, employment and education, and with the Rushdie affair it has been suggested that the law of blasphemy should be extended to protect all groups against religious discrimination. But there is a recognition that at least Labour has demonstrated a willingness to take action, where even after nearly two decades in office the Conservatives have consistently refused to take necessary action in any area of national life when recommendations have been made by the CRE under the provision of the 1976 Act (CRE, 1991; also, Bindman, 1996; Lester, 1994).

Given the overwhelming support Labour enjoys in both Asian and African Caribbean communities, it is not surprising that from time to time the party is advised not to take such support for granted, but this is usually to warn the leadership of the potential danger involved in keeping individuals from these groups at the margins. For example, during the 1992 general election campaign the question of Asian support for Labour featured much in the media, especially after a suggestion that the strong support given in 1987 could drop to half. Mihir Bose, commenting on this in the *Daily Telegraph* (2 April 1992) stressed that it would be a mistake for the two main parties to see Asian voters as a unified bloc of voters. He pointed to the obvious distinctions between Moslems and Hindus and between Indians, Pakistanis and Bangladeshis, and identified conflicting interests of Indians and Pakistanis over India's and Pakistan's opposing claims over Kashmir. India itself featured in the elections as Gerald Kaufman, Labour's shadow foreign secretary, and Douglas Hurd the foreign secretary visited New Delhi. Earlier in January, Douglas Hurd had made a policy statement about Kashmir at a meeting in Luton which has a large Asian population, reportedly to the amusement of the Indian High Commission in London (*Independent*, 17 January 1992). Class differential within the large and varied Asian communities may also be having an impact on party political support, and it has been suggested that Asians may shift their majority allegiance from Labour to Conservatives in the way that the Jewish community have done since large-scale migration from East and Central Europe from the turn of the century. As Bose noted in 1992, the Durbar Club of Asian businessmen was a useful source of funding for the Tories, who enjoyed: 'intimate dinner parties where ministers can feel like representatives of the viceroy at the court of some Indian maharajah. The only difference from the raj is the absence of a tiger shoot' (*Independent*, 2 April 1992, p. 5).

Not surprisingly, like voters from their communities, African Caribbean and Asian aspirant politicians have shown a marked preference for seeking careers within the Labour Party. But all parties, including the SDP and fringe parties such as the Greens, are seen as legitimate avenues for black and brown politicians to seek active participation. Between 1950 and 1979 thirteen candidates from these communities were put forward by the three main parties, but none succeeded at the polls, because only in one instance was a candidate in a winning position (Anwar, 1994, pp. 43–4). The numbers increased dramatically in 1983, when there were eighteen candidates, but again only one had a sporting chance of winning. The next few years witnessed a dramatic increase in militancy among African, Caribbean and Asian politicians and the clear demand by Black Sections in the Labour Party for minority candidates to be nominated for winnable seats (see, Shukra, 1990). While the Conservatives gave formal recognition to the Anglo-Asian Conservative Association and the Anglo-West Indian Association in the 1980s and the subsequent One Nation Forum, Labour's leadership fought against recognition of Black Sections, and Bill Morris' Society of Black Socialists was a compromise. But it was Black Sections that had the more visible success in gaining national and local party support for winnable seats to be allocated to credible black and brown politicians.

The election of Diane Abbot, Paul Boateng, Bernie Grant and Keith Vaz in 1987 from a field of twenty-seven candidates from minority ethnic backgrounds marked a dramatic step forward in the active participation of minority ethnic groups in British politics. In a by-election in November 1991

Dr Ashok Kumar won Langbaurgh in Yorkshire for Labour, and in the 1992 general elections Piara Khabra was also elected, although on this occasion Kumar lost to his Conservative opponent. In the 1992 general elections, the parties fielded twenty-three candidates who were members of minority ethnic communities: nine by Labour, eight by the Conservatives, and six by the Liberal Democrats. The Conservatives for the first time in the post-war years returned a minority ethnic candidate, Nirj Joseph Deva (for Brentford and Isleworth), but the controversial candidacy of John Taylor for the safe Conservative seat of Cheltenham resulted in him being beaten by the SDP candidate in a swing of 5.2 per cent away from the Conservatives (Layton-Henry, 1992, p. 120). The victorious SDLP candidate had taken a message from the Tory rebels (who had opposed Taylor's candidacy on the basis of colour) when the SDLP stressed that theirs was a local man, thereby implying that John Taylor, who was a Solihull man, was not local. This, however, was hardly the point; what focused attention was the black and white colours of the candidates. For the 1996 general election, the three main political parties again selected a number of candidates from minority ethnic communities, for example, nine by Labour, a similar number by the Conservatives and fifteen by the Liberal Democrats. The breakdown into groups of the Liberal Democrats' candidates is interesting because they reveal the wider participation by minority ethnic groups: four were of African Caribbean origins; two of Chinese origins; one of Iraqi origin; and eight of South Asian backgrounds.

While the 1987 and 1992 elections were important events, there was a general consciousness in both communities that these politicians were building on a tradition established before there were sizeable African Caribbean or Asian communities in the country (see, for example, *Independent*, 25 July 1992). Three Asians – Dadabhai Naoroji, Sir Mancherjee Bhownagree, and Shapuriji Saklatvala – had earlier in the late nineteenth century and first two decades of the present century been members of the House of Commons for the Conservatives, Labour and the Communist Party, and Lord Sinha of Raipur had sat in the Lords. In the post-Second World War years there have also been Lords Constantine, Pitt, Chitnis, and Desai, and Baroness Flather, the first female minority ethnic member of the Upper House, and in late 1996 John Taylor's elevation to the Upper House as Lord Warwick give the Conservatives, for the first time in the post-Second World War era, a majority of members from minority ethnic communities.

Minority ethnic candidates had gained access to the world of local politics before the breakthrough in Parliament, but the pattern of strong Labour and relatively weaker Conservative support also obtained at the local level. For example, in 1974 there were twelve minority ethnic councillors in the

London boroughs (ten Labour, two Conservatives), increasing in 1978 to seventy-nine out of a total of 1,914, that is, 4 per cent of the total when the minority ethnic population accounted for over 12 per cent of the city (Anwar, 1994, p. 49). By 1986 the situation had progressively changed again, with a total of 142 London councillors from minority ethnic communities. From the Asian communities there were sixty-eight councillors, sixty-four of them in the Labour Party, and two each in the Conservative and Liberal/SDP parties; of the sixty African Caribbeans, fifty-five were Labour, four Conservatives and one Liberal/SDP, demonstrating the strength of the Labour Party in these communities (Anwar, 1994, p. 49). Such representation increased in 1993 to 179 Asians and African Caribbeans, but Anwar has pointed out that the overall share in the numbers of seats remained under 10 per cent in London (ibid., p. 51). In the second city, Birmingham, which became the single largest local authority following the demise of large metropolitan boroughs in the mid 1980s, in 1982 only twenty-three of 375 candidates for the city council were from African Caribbean and Asian communities, and only five were elected. In contrast, in 1991 twenty-one councillors in the city came from the two main minority ethnic communities, all within the Labour Party. A similar story of steady increase in the election of candidates from these communities is told by Anwar with respect to country and district elections. In general, he found that Asian men constitute a majority of minority ethnic councillors, with very few Asian women being elected; in the African Caribbean communities women tend to actively participate.[3]

Before the 1987 elections there were other notable successes in local government by politicians from minority ethnic backgrounds. Bernie Grant had become leader of Haringey Council, Merle Emory leader of Brent, and Linda Bellos leader of Lambeth. In a number of cities, Asians and African Caribbeans were becoming mayors, and, in general, although there were far too many small cities in which black and brown Britons were not always standing nor being elected to councils and statutory authorities, the picture was changing. Cities with high concentrations of Asians and Africa Caribbeans experienced increased local participation, particularly in the Asian communities such as Leicester and Bradford (see, for example, LeLohe, 1990). In Coventry there was no African Caribbean person on the city council until the election of Eric Linton in 1994; the same was true for the substantially larger Asian community until the late 1980s.

No doubt, as Anwar (1994) argues, a fairer representation of politicians from minority ethnic backgrounds would mean that considerably more of them would be present at Westminster and in town halls up and down the country. It may be noted, however, that perhaps fewer rather than more politicians from minority ethnic backgrounds would be elected if they depended exclusively on minority ethnic votes. After all, on demographic grounds such as numbers and distribution of minority population, and within a first past the post electoral system with a tenacious two party arrangement, the support of voters from the majority population is important for candidates from minority ethnic groups. The parties which enjoy traditional loyalty have an important part to play here, as John Taylor's experience in Cheltenham demonstrated. It is unlikely that in the near future there will be far reaching constitutional changes, which could strengthen political participation by minority ethnic groups. African Caribbean and Asian politicians do not therefore have any choice but to continue to combine protest with compromise within the two main parties.

Given the impressive party political loyalty of minority ethnic voters and politicians, questions may be asked about what steps political parties are taking to enhance the participation of individuals from minority ethnic communities within the parties' structures. For example, how many individuals are there from these communities who are employed by the parties as agents and research officers, and how many sit on their most senior committees? As an employer the Labour Party, like many employers, requests each applicant for a job to state their ethnic origin. This ethnic monitoring commenced only in autumn 1995, and the information is confidential, so that the party cannot say how many of their employees are from minority ethnic backgrounds. This may also be the case with respect to the Liberal Democrats, who made the additional point that while there is one person from a minority ethnic community employed at party headquarters in London, they do not know how many may be employed by individual constituency offices. In 1966 Diane Abbot was the only member from a minority ethnic group sitting on the Labour Party's National Executive Committee. The Liberal Democrats have one person from the Asian community on their Federal Executive Committee, and one African Caribbean person on their Federal Policy Committee; these two persons and a third party member from a minority ethnic community were expected in autumn 1996 to participate in election contests for membership to these committees. While the parties had been actively seeking support from the minority ethnic communities during elections, it appears that the active participation within these organisations is less actively pursued, or if pursued, not monitored as a potential area of change. Nor have the parties so far taken active steps to encourage the proper participation of individuals from minority ethnic groups in the civil service and the foreign service.

Finally, it might be noted that many, if not all, the battles by politicians from minority ethnic communities to integrate their communities into the body politic have taken and are taking place within the Labour Party. In the 1980s Labour experienced the emergence, rise and decline of Black Sections (see Shukra, 1990), and the party continues to be carefully watched by activists from black, brown and white communities to see whether local and national leaders are fair to minorities. For example, when Tony Blair's New Labour launched a party manifesto document in July 1996, a member of the Society of Black Socialists within the party attacked it for showing too few black and brown faces, and likened the pictures to that of the car company Ford, which had earlier whitened black workers' faces in a brochure for distribution in East Europe. It was said that of 230 faces only six could be recognised as black in the party's brochure, and although the party denied any intention of excluding African Caribbeans and Asians, the Society feared that Blair's New Labour was keen to show the party to be representative of white middle class Britain (see *Sunday Express*, 7 July 1996).

The most dramatic challenge, however, that Labour faced in the mid-1990s from minority ethnic politicians and as the party prepared for election and government after seventeen years in opposition was what David Blunkett, Party Chairman and Shadow Education and Employment Secretary, called Asian entryism. The concept seems to embody the notion of conspiracy on the part of shadowy Asian bosses directing their clients within the party in the style of Boss Tweed in an earlier era in American pork barrel politics. The coverage in the press tells of attempts by groups of Asians joining the party *en bloc* rather than individually. Such 'godfather' politics have been talked about for some time since the late 1980s (see Jeffers, 1991), but it is in the second half of the 1990s that these kinds of politics have come into prominent public view. The phenomenon has affected a number of constituencies in Birmingham, Glasgow Govan, Manchester Gorton, Bow and Poplar in London, and there have been serious charges of malpractice in Keith Vaz's constituency, Leicester East. In each of these cases the situation is slightly different, but they amount to accusations of Asian vote-rigging and counter accusations by Asians that the Labour leadership is deliberately blocking the aspirations of Asians to become members of Parliament.

These experiences[4] marked a significant shift away from the kinds of pressure Black Sections sought to bring to bear on the party to ensure selection for winnable seats by politicians from minority ethnic communities. What is seen as Asian block votes in the party is another means to secure selection for Asian politicians in those areas where significant numbers of Asian voters live. Competent leadership, as Blunkett appeared to suggest, is called for so that the kinds of activities Asian politicians are accused of do not become the norm in a number of constituencies. At the same time greater sensitivity to the aspirations of Asian politicians must be shown by the party that has benefited most from the votes of minority ethnic communities. As one Asian party member in Manchester stated, Asians 'joined the Labour Party to support it, not to damage it' (*Guardian*, 30 August 1994).

CONCLUSION

Participation by minority ethnic groups in British national politics has not yet reached a point where black and brown ministers, as a matter of course, sit at cabinet meetings and appear on our television sets and radio and in the newspapers strenuously defending and explaining government policy. Nor are they familiar, unremarkable, faces in the corridors of Whitehall. It seems today that we are still a long way from seeing black, brown as well as white faces as neighbours in Downing Street. None the less, there has been a transition from what Milbrath called *spectator* participation (such as voting) to *gladiatorial* participation (such as running for public office). A wide range of intermediary activities are being engaged in through secondary or associational groups at the heart of the nation as well as in some provincial centres. These organisations are vital for the proper working of a democratic socio-political order, and African Caribbeans and Asians have been ardent participant citizens in this collective endeavour. The entry, settlement and reproduction of African Caribbean and Asian communities in Britain have helped to further develop and expand the capacity of the political system through the active participation of new citizens in the discussion and deliberation of public matters. This dynamic process continues and will almost certainly have important implications for Britain's role in an integrating Europe.

NOTES

1 Such individuality or individualism is, of course, a vital aspect of democratic theory and practice, although, as with Caribbean groups in Britain, this democratic virtue works against effective organisation and action.
2 It was not until the 1990s that young people from the minority ethnic communities began to look to the other branch of the law to become solicitors.
3 Muhammad Anwar estimates that there are presently about 400 Asian and African Caribbean councillors in Britain. I am grateful to Anwar for discussing his work in this area with me.
4 For a detailed discussion of these developments, see Goulbourne (forthcoming).

REFERENCES

Ahmad, W. (ed.) (1994) *'Race' and Health in Contemporary Britain*, Milton Keynes: Open University Press.
Ahmad, W. and Atkin, K. (eds) (1996) *'Race' and Community Care*, Milton Keynes: Open University Press.
Almond, G. C. and Powell, G. B. (1966) *Comparative Politics: A Developmental Approach*, Boston and Toronto: Little, Brown.
Anwar, M. (1979) *The Myth of Return*, London: Heinemann.
Anwar, M. (1994) *Race and Elections: The Participation of Ethnic Minorities in*

Politics, Monographs in ethnic relations, no. 9, Coventry: ESRC Centre for Research in Ethnic Relations (CRER), University of Warwick.

Appignanesi, L. and Maitland, S. (eds) (1989) *The Rushdie File*, London: Fourth Estate Ltd.

Arnold, E. and James, M. (1989) 'Finding black families for black children in care: a case study', *New Community*, vol. 15, no. 3.

Bachrach P. and Baratz M. (1963) 'The two faces of power', *American Political Science Review*, 56, pp. 947–52.

Ballard, R. (ed) (1994) *Desh Pardesh: the South Asian Presence in Britain*, London: Hurst & Company.

Bentley, A. (1908) (1967) *The Process of Government*, Massachussetts: The Belnap Press of Harvard University Press.

Bindman, G. (1996) 'When will Europe act against racism?', *New Law Journal*, 9 February.

Birmingham Post, *passim*.

Blakemore, K. and Boneham, M. (1994) *Age, Race and Ethnicity: A Comparative Approach*, Milton Keynes: Open University Press.

Chamberlain, M. (1997) *Narratives of Exile and Return*, London: Macmillan.

Charman, P. (1979) *Reflections: Black and White Christians in the City*, London: Zebra Project.

Commission for Racial Equality (1988) *Medical School Admissions: Report of a Formal Investigation into St George's Hospital Medical School*, London: CRE.

—— (1990a) *Britain: A Plural Society, Report of a Seminar*, Discussion papers, no. 3, London: CRE.

—— (1990b) *Law, Blasphemy and the Multi-faith Society, Report of a Seminar*, Discussion papers, no. 1, London: CRE.

—— (1991) *Second Review of the Race Relations Act 1976: A Consultative Paper*, London: CRE.

—— (1995) *Annual Report 1994*, London: CRE.

Crenson, M. A. (1971) *The Un-Politics of Air Pollution: A Study of Non-Decision-making in the Cities*, Baltimore and London: Allen & Unwin.

Daniel, W. (1968) *Racial Discrimination in Britain*, Harmondsworth: Penguin.

Dearlove, J. (1973) *The Politics of Policy in Local Government*, Cambridge: Cambridge University Press.

Durkheim, E. (1970) *Suicide: A Study in Sociology*, London: Routledge & Kegan Paul.

Duverger, M. (1967) *Political Parties: Their Organisation and Activity in the Modern State*, London: Methuen.

Easton, D. (1953) *The Political System*, New York: Knopf.

Egbuna, O. (1971) *Destroy this Temple: The Voice of Black Power in Britain*, London: Macgibbon and Kee.

Emmanuel, P. (1993) *Governance and Democracy in the Commonwealth Caribbean: An Introduction*, Cave Hill: Institute of Social & Economic Research.

Finer, S. E. (1966) *Anonymous Empire: A Study of the Lobby in Great Britain*, 2nd edn, London: Pall Mall Press.

Finer, S. E. (1972) 'Groups and political participation', in G. Parry (ed.) *Participation in Politics*, Manchester University Press.

FitzGerald, M. (1984) *Political Parties and Black People*, London: Runnymede Trust.

—— (1988) 'Afro-Caribbean involvement in British politics', in M. Cross and H.

Entzinger (eds), *Lost Illusions: Caribbean Minorities in Britain and the Netherlands*, London: Routledge.

Gay, P. and Young, K. (1988) *Community Relations Councils: Roles and Objectives*, London: Public Studies Institute / CRE.

Goulbourne, H. (1975) 'Teachers and pressure group activity in Jamaica, 1894–1967', DPhil Thesis, School of Social Sciences, University of Sussex.

—— (1980) 'Oral history and black labour: an overview', *Oral History*, vol. 8, no. 1.

—— (ed.) (1990) *Black Politics in Britain*, Aldershot: Avebury.

—— (1991a) 'Varieties of pluralism: the notion of a pluralist post-imperial Britain', *New Community*, vol. 17, no. 2, January.

—— (1991b) 'The offence of the West Indian: political leadership and the communal option', in M. Anwar and P. Werbner (eds), *Black and Ethnic Leaderships: The Cultural Dimensions of Political Action*, London: Routledge.

—— (forthcoming) *Race Relations in Britain*, London: Macmillan.

Goulbourne, S. (1989a) 'Access to legal education and the legal profession in Jamaica', in W. Twining (ed.), *Access to Legal Education and the Legal Profession*, London: Butterworths.

—— (1989b) 'Minority entry to the legal profession: a discussion paper', *Policy Papers in Ethnic Relations*, Coventry: CRER.

Heinemann, B. W. (1972) *The Politics of the Powerless: A Study of the Campaign Against Racial Discrimination*, London: Institute of Race Relations/Oxford University Press.

Howard, V. (1987) *A Report of Afro-Caribbean Christianity in Britain*, Department of Theology and Religious Studies, University of Leeds.

Humphry, D. (1972) *Police Power and Black People*, London: Panther.

Jeffers, S. (1990) 'Black sections in the Labour Party: the end of ethnicity and "godfather" politics?', in P. Werbner and M. Anwar (eds), *Black and Ethnic Leaderships: The Cultural Dimensions of Political Action*, London: Routledge.

Jenkins, Roy (1967) 'Racial equality in Britain', in Anthony Lester (ed.), *Essays and Speeches by Roy Jenkins*, London: Collins.

John, DeWitt (1969) *Indian Workers Associations in Britain*, London: Oxford University Press / Institute of Race Relations.

Johnson, M. R. D. (1991) 'The churches, leadership, and ethnic minorities', in P. Werbner and M. Anwar (eds), *Black and Ethnic Leaderships: The Cultural Dimensions of Political Action*, London: Routledge.

Johnson, M. R. D. and Songster, D. (1995) *A Measure of Equity*, Coventry: CRER.

Johnson, M. R. D., Wright, A., Jeffcoat, M. and Petherick, R. (1996) 'Local authority occupational therapy services and ethnic minority clients', *British Journal of Occupational Therapy*, vol. 59, no. 3.

Lasswell, H. (1936) (1958) *Politics: Who Gets What, When, How*, Cleveland/New York: Meridian Books.

Layton-Henry, Z. (1992) *The Politics of Immigration*, Oxford: Blackwell.

LeLohe, M. (1990) 'The Asian vote in a northern city', in H. Goulbourne (ed.) *Black Politics in Britain*, Aldershot, Avebury.

Lester, Lord Anthony (1994) 'Discrimination: what can lawyers learn from history?', *Public Law*, summer, pp. 224–37.

Lukes, S. (1976) *Power: A Radical View*, London: Macmillan.

Messina, A. M. (1989) *Race and Party Competition in Britain*, Oxford: The Clarendon Press.

Milbrath, L. (1965) *Political Participation*, Chicago: Rand McNally.
Owen, D. (1993) *Ethnic Minorities in Great Britain: Age and Gender Structure*, National Ethnic Minority Data Archive: 1991 Census Statistical Paper no. 2, Coventry: CRER.
—— (1996) 'Size, structure and growth of the ethnic minority populations', in D. Coleman and J. Salt (eds) *Ethnicity in the 1991 Census*, vol. 1, London: HMSO.
Saggar, S. (1992) *Race and Politics in Britain*, London: Harvester Wheatsheaf.
Scarman, Lord (1982) *The Brixton Disorders 10–12 April 1981: Report of an Inquiry by the Rt Hon the Lord Scarman, OBE*, Cmnd. 8427, London: HMSO.
Sewell, T. (1993) *Black Tribunes: Black Political Participation in Britain*, London: Lawrence and Wishart.
Shukra, K. (1990) 'Black sections in the Labour Party', in H. Goulbourne (ed.), *Black Politics in Britain*, Aldershot: Avebury.
Sobeen, P. N. (1990) *The Origins of the Race Relations Act*, Research paper in ethnic relations no. 12, Coventry: CRER.
Solomos, J. (1988) *Black Youth, Racism and the State: The Politics of Ideology and Policy*, Cambridge: Cambridge University Press.
Stone, C. (1974) *Electoral Behaviour and Public Behaviour in Jamaica*, Mona: Institute of Social and Economic Research.
Swann, Michael Lord (1985) *Education for All: Report of the Committee of Inquiry into the Education of Children from Ethnic Minority Groups*, Cmnd. 9453, London: HMSO.
Daily Star, passim.
Daily Telegraph, passim.
Guardian, passim.
Independent, passim.
Observer, passim.
Sunday Express, passim.
Thomas-Hope, E. (1992) *Explanation in Caribbean Migration: Perception and the Image*, London: Macmillan.
Tocqueville, Alexis de (1856) (1955) *The Old Regime and the French Revolution*, New York: Doubleday.
Western, J. (1992) *A Passage to England: Barbadian Londoners Speak of Home*, London: UCL Press.

11 British race relations in a European context

Ann Dummett

The prefatory framework of dates set out opposite is selective, and the following chapter is not a full historical account of British race relations in a European context, but an introduction to current questions.

I

At each stage in the twentieth century British race relations have been influenced by Britain's relations with other parts of the world. In the great imperial age up to the end of the Second World War the fate and aspirations of the small number of black, South Asian, Chinese and other non-white residents were linked to movements for colonial freedom. In the post-war era they were affected by the new ideal of the multiracial Commonwealth in opposition to the old ideal of the white Dominions forming the Commonwealth while other peoples were relegated to a lower status. With Britain's heavy dependence upon the United States, and the increase of US influence on many aspects of British life in the cold war period, anti-racists in Britain looked to the example of American civil rights from the 1960s onwards, while US styles of racism became more familiar, through films and documentaries, than before. Now, as the century draws to its close, Britain's position in the world has changed again. Since 1973 she has been – sometimes uneasily – a member of the EC. People concerned with race relations have begun to see our own situation in a European context.

Recognition of this new context has been slow to arrive. For one thing, British habits of mind and political attitudes are always resistant to foreign notions. English was the language of the empire, the Commonwealth and the United States, and debates about race relations, encircled by this English-speaking world, could move freely from place to place. The EU is multi-lingual, and its styles of thought, its legal language and its assumptions about cultures belong to a continental, not an Anglo-Saxon, model.

1957 Treaty of Rome, now officially known as the Community Treaty, founds the European Community (EC), its institutions and methods being defined.

1973 United Kingdom becomes a member state.

1986 Single European Act: a set of amendments to the original Treaty, signed by Mrs Thatcher and ratified by Parliament.
European Parliament's Evrigenis report on racism and fascism.
Solemn Declaration against Racism and Xenophobia.

1990 European Parliament's Ford report on racism and xenophobia.

1991 New set of amendments to the original Treaty signed at Maastricht. These set up a European Union (EU) with the same membership as the EC but legally distinct. The Union has three 'pillars': the EC itself for social and economic policy; the Western European Union for cooperation on defence and foreign policy; and committees of ministers and officials to deal with police and judicial cooperation and with immigration from outside the Union.

1993 Maastricht Treaty comes into force.

1994 In June the European Council (or 'summit') meeting of heads of government sets up the Kahn Commission to devise, as a matter of urgency, a European strategy against racism and xenophobia.
European Commission White Paper urges Treaty amendment on race.

1995 The Kahn Commission reports but most of its recommendations are put aside.
Schengen arrangements for border-free travel begin to come into effect.
The European Commission issues its first ever Communication on racism, xenophobia and anti-Semitism, and proposes European Year Against Racism.
The ETUC and UNICE (Europe-wide equivalents of the TUC and CBI) produce a joint code of practice on racial discrimination in employment.
The Reflection Group (Foreign Ministers) prepares agenda for the Inter-Governmental Conferences and considers a race amendment in principle.

1996 Inter-Governmental Conferences begin to prepare new Treaty amendments for 1997.
July: Council of Ministers resolves to make 1997 a European Year against racism, xenophobia and anti-Semitism.

Furthermore, latent British suspicion and hostility towards 'the Continent', and some countries in particular, have been fanned in recent years by certain politicians and tabloid newspapers.

At the beginning, there was also opposition to joining the Community because of a belief that this was a betrayal of the Commonwealth. Britain, some held, was shifting away from the ideal of multiracial equality and an international network spread through every continent to membership of an all-white rich man's club, designed to benefit capitalists. This view is not as important now as it was in the 1960s and 1970s. Few people now dare call capitalism a dirty word and, besides, the British Government's immigration and nationality policies (whichever party has been in power) since 1962 have arguably done more damage to the Commonwealth ideal than any other policy.

Though geographically more distant the Commonwealth used to feel closer to us than the rest of Europe. The growth of tourism has done little to increase British understanding of other European countries. The besetting problem is a widespread British belief that our situation is utterly different from that of all other European countries and that we are much better at dealing with ours than they are with theirs. This belief makes a bad basis for cooperation, and stands firmly in the way of understanding.

Language is a problem, not just because only a small minority of British people is completely at ease in any European language other than English, but because the terms used in discussions of race relations cannot be directly translated and are not understandable without some awareness of the situation in each country. In the English language itself there are heavy overtones of meaning in the terms used. These have been created by political events. Fifty years ago, the word 'immigrant' meant just what it said: one who entered a country from outside and lived there for a shorter or longer period. The anti-immigrant propaganda which entered politics in the 1950s was not directed against all immigrants but only against those who were not white, and thus 'immigrant' became a racist word in debate. The word 'coloured' for those who were not white was objected to by some countries, but a universally acceptable, alternative term has been a matter of controversy. For some 'Black' was the correct description for all non-whites; the rather clumsy 'black and ethnic minorities' made an acceptable compromise for others. The way one uses 'immigrant', 'migrant', 'Black', 'black', 'ethnic minority' and other terms is a signal, in Britain, of a particular set of political and racial attitudes – just as, in discussing northern Ireland, the words 'Ulster' and 'the six counties' send radically different political messages. In continental countries the debate uses the same terms, directly translated but with different meanings. Again, there is controversy; some may object to 'migrant' and 'immigrant' but for the most part these words are acceptable. 'Ethnic minority' usually means something quite different from our usage: it refers to minorities within the citizen population who are of European origin. Danish-speakers in Schleswig-Holstein, German-speakers in the Alto Adige region of Italy, Hungarians in Romania – these are 'ethnic minorities'.

Unfortunately the British reaction has often been that these foreigners have got it wrong. They must be politically naive if they talk about 'migrants' and if they do not realise that you have to be black to suffer from racism. Moreover, they do not have our Race Relations Act. They are twenty years behind us. They need our instruction on what to do. Some British anti-racists, who fiercely denounce the Act's shortcomings when they are in Britain, cross the Channel and begin to tell people in other countries that Britain alone has got the right legislation and they should all copy us. All this is uncomfortably reminiscent of Mrs Thatcher's remarks at the French celebrations of the 1789 revolution, when she told the French that Britain had invented freedom.

Although the symptoms of racism are much the same everywhere – violent attacks, daily discrimination, unequal treatment – there is no uniform pattern of perception or remedy across the continent. The French think it is racist to define anyone as a member of an ethnic group; the Dutch rely on such definition for a positive action programme. In northern Italy, there is often as much hostility to south Italians and Sicilians as to Africans. In Germany, Poles and Italians are at risk from neo-Nazis, but everyday discrimination is worse for the Turks than for them.

How then do British race relations fit into this complicated picture? British citizens of any origin can now live or work in any EC member state. EC law forbids discrimination on grounds of nationality between different EC nationals, but has no separate provision on race or ethnic origin or to deal with discrimination against third-country nationals from outside the EC. To reach another EC country, however, British people must still pass through border controls. Ironically, this is a matter of concern to minorities here largely because of the fear of discriminatory treatment on return to Britain by the immigration authorities. The Schengen agreement, which was concluded separately from the EC framework, was aimed at lifting border controls and is now in effect between most EC countries. British people, therefore, moving between Germany and Italy or Holland and Belgium will not be checked there. They must face checks on returning to Britain, whose government has strongly resisted any lifting of border controls.

Neither the Schengen agreement nor Article 7a of the Union Treaty forbids internal checks on migration status in member countries. Minorities in Britain have been fearful of increased internal surveillance here as a result. It is the responsibility of each member state to decide what internal checks to carry out.

Another minority worry has been about harmonisation of visa policy. Agreement on which nationals from outside the EC will need a visa has been reached in principle: it was intended that from 1997 such nationals, once admitted to any EC country for a three-month visit, would be able to move between EC states on the one visa. Most Commonwealth countries would be visa countries. This is not entirely the fault of the EC institutions. The British Government failed to oppose the listings in meetings of the Council of Ministers: by contrast, the Spanish Government successfully opposed including most Latin American countries on the visa list. Implementation has been delayed.

Matters connected with migration, internal surveillance, and the fear of racial violence in other EC countries have been the chief worries among minorities here. There is widespread ignorance, shared with the white majority, of positive aspects of European Community membership. But the importance of the European Court of Justice to minority rights is considerable, as the *Singh* judgment demonstrated in 1992, providing a way round the 'primary purpose' rule in UK immigration law.

In 1986 the European Parliament brought racism openly on to the European agenda by publishing the Evrigenis report on the growth of racism and fascism in Europe. In the years 1984–89 the Parliament included for the first time some elected representatives of extreme-Right parties, and this fact had greatly alarmed most of the members. Publication of the Evrigenis report (PE 97.547) was followed by a Solemn Declaration in June 1986, made by the Parliament, Commission and Council of Ministers together with representatives of all the member states, condemning racism and xenophobia. Unfortunately, none of the Evrigenis proposals for action were put into effect. It is the Council of Ministers of the EC which has decisive powers on action, but political will to tackle racism and xenophobia was lacking. However, from then on the pressure for action mounted.

The Ford report, conducted for the European Parliament in 1990, repeated and added to the Evrigenis recommendations, and the Commission acted on one of them: the establishment of the Migrants Forum, a body intended to represent minorities throughout EC territory and to play an advisory role.

Also in 1990, Geoffrey Harris, then a senior adviser to the President of the European Parliament, published his book *The Dark Side of Europe* (1990)[1], describing the activities of the extreme Right since 1945. In his view, the extreme Right had never disappeared but merely lost respectability after the Second World War. Its adherents were never effectively purged from official positions in the countries which had been Nazi or Fascist, and its views continued to be held by a significant number of people besides the small number of uniformed street demonstrators who appeared sporadically. In the 1970s an intellectual New Right came on the scene in several countries, reviving old myths of European superiority, claiming the need to protect European culture, and indulging in anti-Semitism. At the same time the oil crisis had dealt a sudden and disorienting blow to the economic growth and full employment which much of Europe had enjoyed for twenty years, and faith in centrist political parties was everywhere shaken.

Since the 1970s there have been periodic surges of electoral support for the extreme Right, for example in British local elections in 1976, French local elections in 1983 and parts of Germany in 1989. It was these *electoral* successes which especially alarmed mainstream politicians. But the main cause for alarm for vulnerable minorities has been the increase in racial violence, partly directly committed and partly encouraged by extreme-Right supporters, in Europe over the last two decades. It is impossible to quantify this increase accurately, as different countries keep their statistics on different bases and also because most racist crime is never reported or prosecuted. But the testimony of anti-racist groups at local level shows that this increase has certainly happened. Another problem is to define exactly what one means by 'extreme Right'. At one end is an international Nazi terrorist network. This overlaps with young 'Right-radical' networks of 'naziskins', whose message is spread through 'oi' music with hate lyrics encouraging the killing of blacks, foreigners and Jews: these are the foot-soldiers of street attacks. At a more 'respectable' level there is some overlap between membership of frankly extremist groups and membership of mainstream Right-wing parties. During the 1980s there was a perceptible swing to the Right (in a general, not extremist, sense) in many countries, with Reaganism in the United States, Thatcherism in Britain, a change of direction in Mitterand's France, and so on. Governments backed away from former Centre-Left policies and at the same time sought to appease extreme-Rightists and prevent a growth in electoral support for them by becoming tougher on immigration and asylum and less generous to minorities already in their midst.

Meanwhile, extreme-Right groups had their own international links and it was becoming clear that tackling them might require international action. International conferences, bringing together anti-racists from EC countries, began to increase. One notable example in 1987 was a conference jointly organised by the British-based International Alert and the Netherlands-based Institute of Human Rights, where an attempt was made to set up a central point for exchanging information regularly between non-governmental organisations. This attempt, like many others in the next few years to establish a pan-European anti-racist network, proved difficult to realise. No such network could operate without considerable funds for travel, translation and a staff large enough to deal with contacts in all the countries concerned. This was beyond the resources of voluntary groups whose primary concern was, in any case, work at local or national level: besides, there was a problem of management and control. In 1990, a British-based organisation, Standing Conference on Equality in Europe (SCORE UK) was formed and funded by the Commission for Racial Equality. It established some international contacts but could not overcome all the problems of establishing a large network. Its importance within Britain has been to stimulate interest in race relations in the rest of Europe and show that British race relations are part of a larger pattern.

Other organisations in Britain, since the late 1980s, have performed this function too: the Local Government Information Bureau has laid great stress on work against racism and conveyed this concern to the EC's Committee of the Regions, formed after the Maastricht Treaty was agreed. The Law Society, which has a permanent office in Brussels, has cooperated with the Bar Council in promoting the idea of European Community legislation against racial discrimination. A few local Racial Equality Councils have shown special interest in European affairs and established links with organisations on the continent. All such separate developments have gradually transformed British concern with racism on the continent from the widespread ignorance and indifference of the period up to the mid-1980s. It is now common for speakers from other EC countries to be present at British conferences on race. Such participation was almost unknown ten years ago.

The Commission for Racial Equality had done some work intermittently on the European Community in the 1970s, but its chief concern had been the possible effects of EC legislation on the law in Britain, in so far as these might be indirectly racially discriminatory. In 1989 the CRE set up an internal working group to consider what its responsibilities might be in the context of the coming single market. Already, British citizens had the right to move to other EC countries for employment. These rights were now to be added to. But settled Commonwealth-country citizens had no rights in the single market. The gap between them and British citizens would widen. What could be done?

Freedom of movement across borders was meant to abolish frontier checks on everyone, EC nationals and third-country nationals alike. This abolition would in turn require some kind of agreement and coordination between member states in controlling the external border between the European Community and the outside world: anyone allowed to cross this external border would be able to move freely between the member states. Since the mid-1980s, member governments had been involved in secret meetings of officials and ministers outside the framework of the main

Community institutions to discuss joint action on immigration policy. The Joint Council for the Welfare of Immigrants therefore had begun to take a special interest in European developments.

The Institute of Race Relations predicted in 1988 that 'the problem for an open Europe' would be 'how to close it – against immigrants and refugees from the Third World'. In 1991 a special issue of the IRR's journal, *Race and Class*, entitled 'Europe: variations on a theme of racism', warned of 'institutionalised racism' and 'the drift towards an authoritarian European state'. A. Sivanandan's editorial also included the potent term 'Fortress Europe', which he has used repeatedly in other articles (including a highly influential one in the *New Statesman*) and which has been taken up by many of those among Britain's minorities who are suspicious and fearful of the European Community.

While the CRE and JCWI were concerned with practical problems and specific legal changes, IRR's approach was more ideological. It associated 'Europe' in general with old imperialisms, cultural agressiveness and a threat from the extreme Right. IRR publishes periodically a 'European Race Audit' which is devoted almost entirely to bad news – of which, in truth, there is plenty – from other European countries about racist incidents, violence, oppression of immigrants and asylum-seekers, fascist successes and racist statements by prominent people. As a source of information and ideas, IRR has much to offer. But its focus is very narrow. The assumption seems to be that Europe is inevitably and unchangeably racist, and there is nothing much that anyone can do about this. Unfortunately this approach does not lead its followers into much action beyond denunciation.

The great difficulty for British people involved in race relations, when they attempt work at European level, is that they are plunged into an unfamiliar world, where they do not know their way about. In domestic politics, they know what an Act of Parliament is and how it is prepared and passed; they have some idea of the legal system and the courts' ways of working; they know in general what minorities live in Britain and how they are faring, and altogether have a lot of knowledge which they take for granted. They do not realise how little they know of institutions elsewhere. In the early 1990s, one often heard 'Schengen and Trevi' mentioned jointly as a threat when the subject of 'Europe' came up. But very few of those who denounced Schengen and Trevi could tell you precisely what these names referred to, what these groups did, what their legal status was, or just why they were so worrying. The groundwork for understanding just was not there.

Those who try to discover and understand more may find that the British assumptions they quite naturally have get in the way of such discovery. How many black people are there in France? Well, nobody counts them. How many racist crimes in Germany? These are not counted in the same way as they are in Britain. Does any other country have a Race Relations Act? Well, the laws are framed in a different manner, with separate civil and criminal codes: you need to understand this framework a little before going on to ask about the race provisions – and so on. There is a lot of informaton to be gained, but it is not easy to find until one knows the right questions to ask. And finding the right questions depends upon *general* knowledge of other countries and of the Community institutions.

Why should we bother? What do workers in British race relations stand to gain from understanding, and working in, a European context? There are three answers. First, we cannot ignore the European context because British law is increasingly determined at European level, not only by Community law but by joint action agreed between governments outside the Community framework. Harsh new measures on asylum and immigration in 1996 are part of such agreed action. Second, the increasing mobility of people around the continent results in problems for minority members from Britain who go to countries where they do not get the same legal protection as in Britain. These problems can affect workers, students, trainees and tourists. Third, real new benefits are possible for British race relations if European Community law is changed so as to deal with racism. Even without the rapid movement to federalism which some people in Britain abhor, we are *already* bound into European law and institutions to an extent which makes it essential for us to understand and work with European developments. Even if Britain were to leave the European Community, Britain could not ignore the Community. Also, her membership of the larger, looser Council of Europe would continue. And if even this were to go, and Britain was left an offshore island outside a large continental bloc, our relative powerlessness and insignificance would force some accommodation with the great European power across the narrow Channel.

II

There is often confusion in Britain about the names and functions of institutions across the Channel. For example, the terms 'European Community' and 'European Union' are often used as though they were interchangeable, which they are not. The Community's highest Court, the European Court of Justice, is often confused with the Court of Human Rights at Strasbourg. It is important to be clear about such distinctions, because any Treaty amendment which deals with race will depend for its effectiveness upon which institutions it empowers.

The drive towards European unity which began after the Second World War found its first expression in the Council of Europe, an organisation which at first consisted of NATO countries. There are now thirty-nine member states. The Council of Europe adopts conventions and treaties which do bind members. The best known of these is the European Convention on Human Rights and Fundamental Freedoms, whose Court of Human Rights is based, with other Council institutions, at Strasbourg, a city frequently fought over in past centuries and thus a symbol of commitment to peace.

This desire for peace underlay the foundation of the original European Economic Community in 1957: its six members already looked to closer political union, freedom of movement and equality between the people of its member states to achieve this end. Anyone joining the Community must accept all the provisions of the Treaty of Rome 1957, together with subsequent amendments to the Treaty. Once a state has joined, it takes part in all Community legislation and in further amendments to the Treaty. Its population joins the electorate for the European Parliament and its nationals acquire important rights usable in all member states. They are also eligible to work in Community institutions, which always include nationals from each state. The impression often conveyed by the British media that the Community consists of a lot of foreigners imposing their will on Britain is not accurate. Britain is in there, legislating for foreigners just as much as they are taking part in legislating for us.

There is nothing in the original Community Treaty about race. One might have expected that British governments, proud of our Race Relations Act, would have urged from the outset that the Community should produce similar legislation to bind all member states. But British governments have, ever since we joined, tended to see the Community in a different light from the way its founders saw it and its other members see it. The whole purpose of joining was to help British trade and the British economy: this, though not the opinion of Euro-enthusiasts like Edward Heath, who played the vital role in negotiating our entry, or Roy Jenkins, who became President of the European Commission, was clearly the view of Harold Wilson and Margaret Thatcher, and of the civil servants and business people who had favoured joining, and it is a view which still comes through many public statements. Membership is all about advantage for Britain. In this atmosphere, the idea of legislating for racial equality throughout the Community, even if such legislation were to benefit minorities from Britain while they were in other member countries, could not arise.

Even now that the idea is favoured by most other EC governments, the Major Government consistently resisted the call to support EC legislation on race. From 1991 to 1994 the Chairman of the Commission for Racial Equality corresponded with the Prime Minister, urging the cause of a Treaty amendment and a directive against racial discrimination. The reason for the government refusal is simple and is consistent with general policy towards the EC. No new powers must be given to the Community at the expense of the government at Westminster. In particular, no new jurisdiction is to be allowed to the European Court of Justice, the Community's Court at Luxembourg whose decisions are superior to those of national courts on any matter where Community law applies.

This British hostility to increased powers for the Community is long-standing, and did much to shape the Treaty on European Union agreed at Maastricht in 1991. That Treaty established a new European Union, based on three 'pillars'. The first pillar is the Community, and its responsibilities include economic and social affairs. The second pillar is foreign and defence policy, and is entrusted not to the Community but to the Western European Union, an independent inter-governmental group. The third pillar concerns immigration (from outside the member states' territories) and also police and judicial cooperation. It is operated by national governments negotiating with each other in committees of officials and ministers, including the old (but now renamed) Trevi and Ad Hoc committees. In practice third-pillar procedures have been secretive and have paid little attention to the representatives of the European Parliament and Commission who are entitled to attend. The third pillar process cannot legislate: it produces Joint Actions and Resolutions on which member states' executive organs agree to act on broadly the same lines, using the powers they have in their own states to implement policies. These policies are not subject to the jurisdiction of the European Court of Justice.

Many people are unhappy with the second and third pillars, and would like to see them abolished and their functions redistributed. As 'immigration', in the third pillar, is understood to include matters to do with integration of third-country nationals in the Union territory, there are on the other hand some who would like the new Treaty to place responsibility for dealing with racism with the third pillar. But the European Commission, together with many NGOs, is insistent that dealing with racism should be part of social policy, in the first pillar, which would mean dealing with *citizens* in danger of discrimination as well as with resident foreigners. Placing responsibility for race issues with the third pillar would greatly reduce the coverage and effectiveness of any action.

Meanwhile, responsibility for dealing with racial discrimination varies widely between the member states. In Germany, there is no specific legislation. There are provisions in the Basic Law to protect human rights and outlaw anti-Semitism, but it is exceedingly difficult for an individual to find a remedy under these provisions and it is not unlawful for a bar to refuse a customer or an employer to refuse a job applicant on racial grounds. France has a large body of law against racism, but it has been very little implemented. Prohibition of discrimination in employment, for example, gives rise to perhaps a dozen cases a year – a ludicrously small number. The process in France is a criminal one, and public prosecutors may be unwilling to take action. There have been examples of discrimination at high level: the National Employment Agency (ANPE) has several times been prosecuted for using ethnic statistics: in fact it has used these to assist in acts of discrimination, but it is an offence under French data protection law to keep ethnic records. French law emphasises prohibition of racist utterance in speech or writing, but has not been used successfully against the French National Front. In Italy, the Mancino Law of 1992 concentrates on racist violence and propaganda rather than on everyday discrimination. Extra sentences can be imposed for violent acts where there is shown to be a racist motive. Here again, however, the law has been very little applied, and numerous acts of blatant racist violence have gone unpunished. The two countries closest to Britain in their approach are the Netherlands, which has now a well-developed case-law in race cases, and procedures based in both the civil and criminal codes, and Belgium, which has established a body similar to the CRE under a comparatively recent anti-racist law.

Variations in national legislation do not tell the whole story. In France, the situation is rather worse than the letter of the law would lead one to expect. In Germany, on the other hand, enormous efforts are being made in some regions (notably the Länder of Berlin and Hesse) to provide protection and practical help to minorities. Passing national legislation is not the only key to successful action, although it is essential to an effective mechanism for the whole jurisdiction.

The British Government is happy to see the CRE, or any other body, encourage national governments to pass their own race legislation. It is happy to cooperate in the programmes on racism run by the Council of Europe, whose work is advisory only. It will not oppose any Community activities concerned to overcome racism, so long as these do not require new powers. But when power is at stake, the answer is 'No'. National sovereignty is invoked.

A sovereign state has power within its own jurisdiction, but this power is always limited by those international agreements into which the state has voluntarily entered. The use of broadcasting channels and of air lanes for aircraft, the extent of territorial waters, and dozens of other matters are regulated by international agreements: Britain cannot break these agreements by claiming sovereignty, any more than a landlord can say he will do what he likes with his property when he has already contracted with someone else for its use. The argument is not really about sovereignty, it is about recognising the political obligation incurred by joining the Community in the first place.

The *legal* obligation to abide by Community law is clear, and is not denied in practice although it is repeatedly denied in rhetoric and public relations. *Political* obligation is another matter: it involves a sense of loyalty, of duty owed to others; it is a shadowy form of contract, in which the different parties are bound together for some purpose and each expects the other to observe certain moral standards in keeping the agreement. No such sense of political obligation has informed Britain's membership of the European Community. Of course other member governments are concerned with their own national interests, as Britain is, but most are accustomed to promote it through cooperation and the use of compromise in give-and-take negotiations. Such a method of working is unfamiliar to British politicians because of our electoral system, in which the winner takes all and no compromise between political parties is necessary. Where governments are always coalitions, as in many continental countries, the habit of negotiation and compromise comes naturally.

If a sense of political obligation towards the Community existed, it would be obvious that Britain had a duty not only to its own people but to the peoples of the Community as a whole to press for action against racial discrimination.

III

In Community language, racism, xenophobia and anti-Semitism are put together to describe the problem to be tackled. The emphasis on xenophobia is necessary because in many continental countries the dividing line which matters is not between blacks and whites, simply, but between citizens and foreigners. The concept of citizenship or nationality as a legal base for rights, a political base for membership of society and an emotional tie of belonging is far stronger on the continent than in Britain. The notion of rights for resident foreigners is admissible but only if these rights are established on quite a different basis from the rights and character of citizens, given as a concession to people who are still outsiders.

The European Union contains approximately 10 million third-country (non-EC) nationals, in addition to minorities of foreign or colonial descent within each citizen body. Turks form the largest group of foreign residents: 2 million of them are in Germany. Next in numbers come former Yugoslavs, Moroccans, Algerians, Poles, Americans and Tunisians. Looking at countries individually, one finds that smaller groups differ according to the country's historical associations, with Surinamese in the Netherlands, Brazilians and Cape Verdians in Portugal, and so on. But different countries' past demands for labour produce a different pattern again: Luxembourg has a large immigrant population of varied origins, including many south

Europeans from countries which are now in the EC and who are therefore not counted among third-country nationals.

These figures do not give a clear picture of the target groups of racism and xenophobia for two reasons. First, nationality laws vary. France has had a liberal nationality law until recently, with a large allowance for obtaining citizenship by birth in France, so that many French residents of North African origin are citizens. But Germany retains the principle of citizenship by descent, so that the second and third generations of Turkish families there are still counted as foreigners. Belgium comes in between, giving citizenship by birthplace to the second but not the first generation born in Belgium. Second, gypsies (Roma and Sinti, travellers) are targets but may be counted as citizens. They are numerous in southern Europe but their problems are often ignored or denied. Furthermore, there are unknown numbers of illegal residents, particularly in southern Europe coming from Africa. Harsh efforts are now being made to expel as many as possible: meanwhile, they are especially vulnerable to violence, very low-paid employment and lack of welfare rights.

As in Britain before the PEP report of 1967 appeared, a strong research backing is absent. The European Commission has produced studies, several times over, of the legislative and constitutional measures which exist in each member state to tackle racism and xenophobia, but information on these measures is of limited value when one knows neither the level of enforcement nor the details of the situation which has to be tackled.

The concern that exists in many countries has, however, found expression in the demands of the European Parliament, the efforts of the European Commission to put the matter on the agenda, and a voluntary international effort in which the CRE played a leading part: the Starting Line group.

In 1991, a small group of individuals concerned with work against racism and originating from different EC countries had the idea that demands for a European directive against racial discrimination would never get anywhere if these demands stopped short of spelling out what such a directive would say. Existing demands were too vague. Detailed provisions must be spelt out. The next step was the idea of drafting a text in the precise form of a European directive. Working out such a text would require thinking out difficult questions: what definitions to use; how wide the coverage of a law should be; what to say about enforcement mechanisms, and so on. An expert draftsman with long experience of Community institutions was invited to join the group, which then met in Brussels with the Churches' Committee for Migrants in Europe (CCME) acting as host and organiser.

The organisations involved at this early stage were the CCME itself, the Commission for Racial Equality in London, the Dutch National Bureau against Racism and the office of the Commissioner for Foreign Affairs in

Berlin. They were joined by two distinguished international lawyers from Italy, by Belgians who later were able to represent the Belgian Centre for Equal Opportunities and the Struggle against Racism, and by others who attended in their individual capacity including two French experts and some civil servants of the European Commission. Later, certain Europe-wide organisations joined in: Caritas Europa of the Catholic Church, the Migrants Forum, the European Jewish Information Centre and the European Anti-Poverty network. Individual lawyers and academics and community workers have also contributed. The group, though it had the official backing of a number of important organisations, remained informal and flexible.

Drafting the text, clause by clause, turned out to be an exceedingly useful exercise, not only because it involved discussion of specific measures for tackling discrimination but because it showed how differently the subject could be approached by people from different countries, even though their aims and principles were very similar. Much of the strength of the text derives from these working discussions. They have made it possible, eventually, for readers in many countries to accept the draft with little or no demand for amendments.

The text when ready was given a name: the Starting Line.

There is now an impressive list of supporting groups in every member state of the EC. The document's importance was recognised by the European Parliament, which voted twice, in 1993 and 1994 (Resolutions PE 177, 105 December 1993 and PE 184.353/43, October 1994) to ask the Commission to use the Starting Line as the basis for drawing up a directive.

The Starting Line dealt with both racism and xenophobia and with religious hatred and discrimination. Following the example of the Equal Opportunities Directive of February 1976, concerning equality between men and women, it was based on Article 235 of the Treaty, which says:

> If action by the Community should prove necessary to attain, in the course of the operation of the common market, one of the objectives of the Community, and this Treaty has not provided the necessary powers, the Council shall, acting unanimously on a proposal from the Commission and after consulting the Assembly [i.e. the Parliament], take the appropriate measures.

Legal opinion was divided on whether Article 235 was an adequate basis when there was no direct mention of racism or xenophobia in the Treaty. The problem was really quite as much political as legal: the basis for dealing with sex equality had been a very slender one.

However, despite widespread support, the campaign for a directive seemed unlikely to produce action unless the Treaty itself was amended. A new round of amendments being due in 1996, the Starting Line group set itself to draft a model amendment to the Treaty to deal with racism and xenophobia. This text was given the name: the Starting Point.

A series of seminars was held in every member state to gain support for the Starting Line and Starting Point. While these steps were being taken, a new initiative suddenly appeared in June 1994 from the European Council (the summit meeting of the EC) at the joint suggestion of the French and German governments. It was agreed that a body be set up to devise, as a matter of urgency, a European strategy against racism and xenophobia, this body to report within a year so that its report could be acted on in June 1995.

The body set up was the Kahn Commission. It reported in April 1995 with numerous suggestions, one of which was that the Treaty should be amended: the terms recommended were very similar to those of the Starting Point. Unfortunately the Cannes summit in June 1995 did nothing about most of the Kahn proposals.

Already in 1992 the Economic and Social Committee of the EC had called for a ban in the Treaty on discrimination on grounds of sex, colour, race, or opinions and beliefs. The Migrants Forum, created by the Commission in late 1990, has persistently called for a Treaty amendment and a directive. The European Commission urged, in its White Paper on Social Policy in July 1994, that when the Treaties were revised they should contain a specific reference to combating discrimination on grounds of race and religion. In December 1995 the Commission issued its first ever Communication on racism, xenophobia and anti-Semitism. Commissioner Flynn has repeatedly pressed for action.

IV

At the time of writing, it is impossible to discuss race relations in a European context in a way which will be useful a few months hence. Events are moving too quickly. Even the near future is too uncertain.

All governments except the British appear to favour an amendment on racial and religious discrimination. Meanwhile, however, other efforts at European level will be made. Already the ETUC and UNICE have agreed a code of practice which owes much to the CRE's Code on employment. The Council of Ministers decided in July 1996 to make 1997 a European Year against racism, xenophobia and anti-Semitism. The European Commission is setting up an Observatory on racism as an information and research centre. It is also supporting several projects run by migrants' organisations and other NGOs to combat racism and xenophobia and tackle social exclusion.

This chapter has concentrated on European Community law because it takes effect in all member states and is justiciable by the European Court of

Justice. A Community directive imposes time limits on governments for its fulfilment in domestic legislation, and the European Commission monitors its workings. European law is thus a particularly efficient instrument for overcoming doubts, delays and unequal levels of legal protection on the part of different countries. Once in force, it can serve as a safeguard against the whittling away of rights. Race legislation would provide a basic standard of protection throughout the territory. This should, incidentally, serve the purposes of the single market by making freedom of movement easier for minorities. But legislation of this kind is not the only possibility for improving race relations in the Community at large. There is already Community legislation banning racist material in television broadcasting. Commissioner Flynn wants a law to permit legally resident third-country nationals in any one EC country to have the right to move to, and work in, any other. There are many possibilities. Nor should the steady work of the Council of Europe, the minority organisations brought together in the Migrants Forum, local and regional groups, and in some cases the positive efforts of national governments themselves, be forgotten. There is now an impetus behind efforts to combat racism in Europe, from which minorities in Britain should eventually stand to benefit.

NOTE

1   Harris, G. (1990) *The Dark Side of Europe*, Edinburgh: Edinburgh University Press.

12 Immigration and ethnic relations in Britain and America[1]

John Stone and Howard Lasus

Attempts to compare and contrast the patterns of race and ethnic relations in the United States and Britain face a number of problems. Despite some shared characteristics, like language and certain traditions of democratic participation and political culture, the two societies are in many important respects quite different.[2] It is not simply an issue of relative size, although on this dimension comparisons between the European Union and the United States make more sense, but rather a question of contrasting conceptions of the nature of citizenship and national identity.[3] These in turn affect the social response and political discourse concerning racial and ethnic diversity on either side of the Atlantic.[4]

While seeking to understand the bases of ethnonationalism, Walker Connor has stressed in many of his writings (Connor, 1994) that 'immigrant societies' operate with a fundamentally different set of dynamics from 'homeland societies' that base their legitimacy on claims – albeit largely mythical ones – of common ancestry. On such a continuum, the United States joins immigrant societies like Canada, Australia and Argentina[5] as far as the dominant perception of its organising principles is concerned, while the United Kingdom is much closer to its European neighbours like France and Germany. As a result, the fact of immigration is part of the charter myth of US society, while in Britain the immigrant has a longer and more tenuous path to walk in order to arrive at a comparable level of acceptance.

This is not to deny, of course, the reality of anti-immigrant rhetoric and action in US history or in the current political situation. Throughout 1995, and particularly in the period leading up to the presidential elections of November 1996, there has been a major national debate concerning the appropriate level of immigration for contemporary US society. Both the Clinton administration and the Republican-controlled Congress have been vying with one another to propose increasingly draconian methods to eliminate illegal entry to the United States, and also to substantially reduce the availability of employment-based immigrant visas.[6] Nevertheless, it is important to stress the countervailing belief that the United States is also, to use John F. Kennedy's famous description, 'a nation of immigrants'. So while at the levels of culture and social structure considerable differences would lead us to expect fundamental contrasts between the two states, much evidence from contemporary research suggests the opposite.[7]

CONVERGENCE OR DIVERGENCE IN THE ERA OF THE 'SPECIAL RELATIONSHIP'?

Previous efforts to sort out the nature of these contrasts go back almost half a century. Writing in 1952, the US anthropologist Ruth Landes reached the following assessment of the state of race relations and racial attitudes in Britain:

> Something else was going on and it could be grasped if the right questions were asked. 'Prejudice' seemed to muddy up the approach; it did not seem a helpful assumption in Britain. In America I knew it for a sociological reality, distinct and compelling. An organized system of values and conduct ... but in Britain I see no such orientation. In this sense, therefore, I would say there is no prejudice.
>
> (Landes, 1952: 133)

Two decades later another prominent US observer of the British scene would voice a very different opinion. Thomas Pettigrew, at that time a distinguished Harvard sociologist and expert on race relations, found the similarities greater than the differences. While reviewing a major study of British race relations, *Colour and Citizenship* (1969), he wrote:

> Typical of race relations specialists and their predictions, I fervently hope I am wrong in all respects in my dour expectations for the future of British race relations. But I would be less than honest if I did not report that nothing [in this study] reassures me in this respect. On the contrary, virtually every page further convinces me against my wishes that such a fate is imminent.
>
> (Pettigrew, 1970: 347–8)

These conflicting views reflected differences that occurred as a result of increasing racial contacts in post-war Britain, but they also stemmed from two different interpretations of the nature of that contact. The influential British sociologist Michael Banton characterised these as the 'immigration perspective' and the 'racial perspective', and studies of inter-racial contacts during the 1950s often stressed the former. Banton's *The Coloured Quarter* (1955) and Sheila Patterson's *Dark Strangers* (1963) and *Immigrants in*

Industry (1968) followed this line, placing stress on the nature of the 'host' society, the peculiarities of British culture and the mysteries of the class system. From these diverse elements arose a network of unstated assumptions on which society rested and which tended to be baffling to the outsider. Such an analysis lead to a Goffmanesque exploration of complex and subtle notions of the proper way to behave – 'the unannounced rights and obligations of people in particular situations ... which constitutes the unspoken language of British social life'. Implicit in this approach was the view that the important differences between immigrant and host were cultural ones that would disappear over time. Thus, apparent cases of discrimination were interpreted as resulting as much from a lack of cultural adaptation as from the racial prejudice of the host society.

The plausibility of this interpretation was gradually undermined by the turn of events in Britain during the late 1950s and 1960s which produced some high profile comparisons with the turbulent Civil Rights decade in the United States. Migration of Afro-Caribbeans which reached a peak in the mid-1950s fell back in response to rising levels of British unemployment and then rose more rapidly as an unanticipated reaction to the demands for immigration restrictions. At the same time, immigration from South Asia – India and Pakistan – gathered pace. The first British race riots since 1919 took place in Nottingham and Notting Hill in 1958, and while these were tame by US standards (no one was killed or seriously wounded) they did elevate the issues of immigration and race relations to national prominence. Local political pressures led to the passage of the first of a series of restrictive immigration measures, the Commonwealth Immigrants Act of 1962.

This was passed by a Conservative government but was not repealed by the socialists when they returned to power two years later. The position of the Labour Party on race relations was schizophrenic, particularly as the majority of (coloured) immigrants were concentrated in urban constituencies like the one lost to an overtly racist Conservative candidate at Smethwick, Birmingham in the election of 1964.

By the middle of the decade, the Government response to racial conflict appeared to mirror the US Civil Rights legislation, although in a somewhat weaker form. In reality, there were significant differences particularly when it came to immigration policy. Anti-discrimination legislation was passed in 1965, outlawing incitement to racial hatred and discrimination in places of public resort, and in 1968 these tentative measures were extended to the provision of goods, facilities and services (including education). Whereas the Civil Rights legislation of 1964 and 1965 was complemented by an overhaul of the most blatant biases in US immigration policy, in Britain further restrictions were being placed on incoming immigrants from the New Commonwealth, representing a flagrant case of bi-partisan political support for racial discrimination on the issue of entry into the United Kingdom.

Both major political parties were reacting to the emergence of Enoch Powell as a racial demagogue following his notorious 'rivers of blood' speech in April 1968. In that speech, Powell pointed to the racial turmoil in the United States as a warning of what to expect in Britain if immigration from the New Commonwealth was not stopped and measures taken to encourage the repatriation of immigrants already settled in the country.[8] While the US strategy emphasised the need for greater consistency between anti-discrimination policies and immigration; the British Government argued that restrictions on immigration were the *sine qua non* for a successful equal opportunity campaign at home. The rationale behind this strategy was best captured in Roy Hattersley's much quoted claim that 'integration without control is impossible, but control without integration is indefensible'.[9]

The strengthening of British anti-discrimination legislation in the 1976 Race Relations Act belatedly recognised the importance of indirect forms of discrimination. It also highlighted the key issue of enforcement that depended as much on political leadership and commitment as on the legislative framework. This was to prove crucial in the conservative swing of the 1980s with the Reagan–Bush and Thatcher–Major administrations being less than enthusiastic about these measures, adopting at best a strategy of benign neglect and at worse actively trying to limit or impede the enforcement of equal opportunity legislation.

Pettigrew's predictions, written in 1970, that British race relations were heading in the same direction as those in the United States were based on a series of factors. It was not only that the profile of racial attitudes revealed remarkable parallels but so too did the evidence on discrimination. In Pettigrew's words:

> The pattern of discrimination against non-whites in housing, education, and employment, carefully described in *Colour and Citizenship*, differ only in detail and magnitude from those in the United States. Immigrant–police tensions, the difficulties facing social workers, the undue reliance upon volunteer efforts at remedy, a rising sense of relative deprivation among both non-whites and working class whites, the strident extremist organizations opposing integration, the withdrawal tendencies of the oppressed groups, even the well-intended mistakes of Roy Jenkins as Home Secretary comparable to those of John Kennedy as President, and the critical role of racism in the 1968 and 1970 political swings to the right in the United States and the United Kingdom – the list constitutes a chilling catalogue of the symptoms of a pending and profound national crisis in race relations.
>
> (Pettigrew, 1970: 346)

Against this gloomy vision of the British future, some observers pointed to at least three major elements that might result in a more optimistic outcome:

1 the recent nature of immigration in the British situation;
2 the time lag between US and British race relations; and
3 the smaller numbers and percentages of minorities in Britain.

However, each of these factors was subject to a variety of interpretations. Some commentators regarded the fact that racial diversity in Britain was the result of recent patterns of immigration from ex-colonial territories as a positive factor, far removed from the entrenched history of slavery and segregation that characterised the African-American experience in the United States. However, the logic of this position breaks down if one remembers the 'salt water fallacy', a tendency to ascribe far too much importance to the differences between the 'internal colonialism' of the United States and the legacy of exploitation and prejudice that permeated British and other European imperial regimes. It could be argued that the one crucial claim that blacks in America had which did not easily apply to the Black British was their 'indigenous' status, an issue on which only the native Americans could make a more powerful case. It is true that many of the post-war migrants were British passport-holders which gave them the right of abode in the former 'mother country', but gradually this shared Common-wealth citizenship was diluted or rendered meaningless as different classes of British passport-holders were created for those not born in the country or related by direct kinship to those that had been. Just as America was abandoning the racial biases implicit in its immigration policy, so British immigration regulations were being re-written to effectively discriminate against non-white British passport holders.

A second argument suggested that the United Kingdom was following much the same trajectory as US race relations but was in many respects approximately two decades behind. If this were correct, the optimists suggested that Britain could learn from US mistakes in the area of Civil Rights and other forms of public policy relevant to race relations. In a certain sense the citizens of the United States could act as a living laboratory for social engineering, allowing their transatlantic cousins the luxury of selecting those strategies that had been shown by experience to be successful. However, there is little evidence that such cross-national learning took place and, as Rose and his collaborators clearly documented, the 1968 Race Relations Bill 'contained the same inadequate enforcement provisions which US Civil Rights Acts have amply demonstrated to be doomed to failure'[10] (Pettigrew, 1970: 347). If anything, the impatience of Britain's racial minorities was exacerbated by the North American example of riots and mass mobilisation allowing less time to resolve racial conflicts and to develop tested mechanisms that would enable the country to move towards racial justice in a constructive and peaceful manner.

A third argument stressed the smaller numbers and percentages of minorities in Britain which might, in theory at least, facilitate the full integration of immigrants of colour into the economic, social and political institutions of the society. However, crude numbers have always been a deceptive issue in immigration and ethnic relations just as the illusive search to arrive at a mathematical 'tipping point' in residential and educational segregation studies has proved.

In general, the smaller the size of a minority the less resources are needed to bring about an acceptable degree of racial and ethnic equality. But this is only valid if economic growth rates are held constant; it says nothing about the levels of concentration and dispersal which create the reality in the local situation; it ignores the articulation of minority voting power and political mobilisation with different political systems and the ability of immigrants and minorities to pressure government, parties and the courts for a fairer share of resources; and it fails to account for the degree of ignorance and misperception which so often renders objective figures on the relative numbers of immigrants or racial minorities largely irrelevant in racist rhetoric or nationalist propaganda.[11] A decade after Pettigrew's perceptive assessment, a joint Conference of British and US academics, convened in May 1982, largely confirmed the converging trends of race relations and policies between the two societies. As Nathan Glazer wrote in his introduction to the report published under the title, *Ethnic Pluralism and Public Policy: Achieving Equality in the United States and Britain*:

> If Gunnar Myrdal could describe, in the 1940s, an American dilemma in which constitutional commitment to individual equality struggled with the reality of prejudice and discrimination against blacks and in lesser degree those of other non-white races, we can, in the 1980s, in the aftermath of Empire and the emergence of a substantial non-white population in Britain, speak of a similar British dilemma.
>
> (Glazer and Young, 1983: 3)

To be sure, significant differences did remain and this applied to the realm of policy: while Americans started with an assumption of diversity, the British tended to regard diversity as a departure from attempts to establish national norms and standards. This is yet another reflection of Connor's distinction between immigrant and homeland states. Nevertheless, despite somewhat different patterns of residential segregation, British society clearly exhibited similar types of urban ethnic violence and systematic forms of educational disadvantage for racial minorities that had long been the norm in the United States.

THE BACKLASH AGAINST AFFIRMATIVE ACTION

One persistent difference between the two societies was the reluctance of the British, including most of the leaders of the minority communities, to advocate policies of affirmative action with any real conviction. In America, a wide range of measures – from university scholarships reserved exclusively for blacks to government contracts awarded preferentially to minority-owned businesses – were slowly added to the arsenal of weapons designed to redress the enormous inequalities in racial outcomes. While it has always been a controversial issue, the notion that extraordinary tactics might be unavoidable, and indeed justified, in an effort to 'level the playing field' before reaching the desired goal of open, individual competition in a colour-blind society, figured prominently in debates over civil rights. In Britain it received very little attention and, of those who were aware of the measures being adopted on the other side of the Atlantic, few considered them appropriate to the local situation. Why this was so is probably related to several of the differences already noted between the two societies. The strength of African-American claims rest on a combination of factors, most notably being an 'immigrant', albeit an involuntary one, in an immigrant society, combined with the tragic history of slavery and segregation that took place on US soil. Despite Britain's role in the slave trade and the exploitative nature of colonialism, little of this moral legacy has been translated into a perceived need to compensate colonial immigrants, or their children, for past injustices. 'We are over here, because you were over there' represented a plea for equal immigration and legal status, rather than the restitutive claims that comprise the core justification of much affirmative action.

As the more conservative period of the 1980s took shape, the political drive for racial equality diminished and the overall impact of economic policies that tended to generate greater social inequality had a disproportionate effect on those immigrant groups and ethnic minorities who were already disadvantaged. The entrepreneurial philosophy of the New Right allowed certain segments of the immigrant and minority communities to prosper, particularly those who had specialised business skills and who also possessed significant stocks of human and financial capital. Groups like the Cubans in Miami (Portes and Stepick, 1993) or the Ugandan Asians in London were conspicuously successful, but for many immigrants and racial minorities the playing field appeared to be increasingly uneven. The gap between the African-American middle class and the urban underclass became, depending on one's political perspective, either an illustration of the fallacy of 'trickle down' economics, or the failure to break the stranglehold of welfare dependency. Much the same division could be found in Britain between those individuals of ethnic minority background who had clearly entered the middle class and those living in deprived areas such as the East End of London, Brixton or Moss Side.

Thus the ascendancy of Conservative and Republican administrations on either side of the Atlantic marked a profound change in political mood that was to have significant long-term consequences for the development of race relations and immigration policy in both societies. In America, the twelve-year Republican control over the White House was mirrored in a series of conservative appointments to the Supreme Court. This shifted the balance against an aggressive legal assault on racial inequalities towards a much more restrained interpretation of Civil Rights legislation. The issues were complicated and while the important 1978 *Bakke* decision upheld the use of race as a legitimate criterion in deciding university admissions (provided income and other relevant background factors were also used in assessing candidates), many were uncomfortable with Justice Harry Blackmun's argument that 'in order to get beyond racism, we must first take account of race'. Not only conservatives, but also some liberals were having reservations about what came to be called reversed racism or 'affirmative discrimination' (Glazer, 1975).

The fear was that using racial categories as a mechanism of social policy would simply entrench racial separation. Such actions, however well-intentioned, violated one of the cardinal ideological principles of American society – the core value of individualism. The reality that African-Americans had been outside the pale of individualistic inclusion for more than three centuries was quickly forgotten when cases of individual inequity started to arise. Justice William Douglas had raised this matter, in his dissenting opinion in the 1974 *DeFunis* case, when he pointed to the need to give serious consideration to the plight of poor Appalachian whites, as much as black applicants who had pulled themselves out of the ghetto, if the equity issue was to be addressed consistently. The demands of racial justice and class inequalities were becoming intertwined in ways that provided plenty of political ammunition to the opponents of affirmative action.

Attempts to formulate the issue in terms of mutually exclusive altern-atives served the political positions of different parties but hardly addressed the complex reality of black–white relationships in American society. As Massey and Denton stressed, the roots of US apartheid lay in the stubborn persistence of segregation which created a chain reaction of disadvantage, virtually ensuring the perpetuation of an urban underclass. Thus:

> The issue is not whether race *or* class perpetuates the urban underclass, but how race *and* class *interact* to undermine the social and economic

well-being of black Americans. We argue that race operates powerfully through urban housing markets, and that racial segregation interacts with black class structure to produce a uniquely disadvantaged neighborhood environment for African-Americans.

(Massey and Denton, 1993: 220)

Some liberals responding to the backlash among working class whites – carefully orchestrated by right-wing political strategists to mobilise the so-called 'silent majority' in support of the Reagan revolution – recognised a need to re-target affirmative action towards the 'truly disadvantaged' (Wilson, 1987). By concentrating on the need to help the poor, such policies would disproportionately assist racial minorities and, so it was argued, avoid the accusation that they were simply a new form of racial preference. Instead of pursuing policies that would overwhelmingly benefit the black middle class, such as scholarship preferences given to minority applicants to Ivy League Law Schools, programmes needed to be designed specifically to assist the poor blacks of the urban underclass. Above all, attention should be focused on providing basic jobs and initial educational opportunities for those suffering from multiple deprivations (Wilson, 1996).

One strategy adopted by some city, state and federal agencies was to mandate a fixed percentage of work on government funded or tax-assisted projects to minority businesses. This type of affirmative action was attacked on the grounds that it simply helped 'minority entrepreneurs' (always assuming that an acceptable definition of this category could be agreed upon) and was not of much direct benefit to the poorer members of the black community. However, given the crucial role attributed to ethnic entrepreneurship among other groups in American society – most conspicuously Jews, Chinese, Japanese, Koreans and Cubans – most of these objections to minority 'set asides' were couched in the language of free market economics, rather than expressed as a concern about inequities that might be generated between rich and poor African-Americans.

Still others maintained that any action that was not based on individual criteria was profoundly dangerous and would lead to the 'disuniting of America' (Schlesinger, 1992). It was claimed that American society's capacity to absorb generations of immigrants had been achieved by breaking down discriminatory barriers and linguistic diversity and not by promoting ethnic distinctiveness. However, this interpretation, once again, seemed to overlook the glaring exceptions to the assimilation theory: that African and Native Americans had suffered a level of exclusion that had persisted despite the fact that no other groups had been in the country as long as they had.

Views opposed to affirmative action were not confined to former liberals who had become disenchanted by what they saw as a misguided mutation of the original Civil Rights strategy. Robust support for the assault on affirmative action came from conservative minority intellectuals, many of whom had, during their own careers, received considerable assistance from racial preference policies but, like Supreme Court Justice Clarence Thomas,[12] had subsequently become determined critics of the system (Sowell, 1994; D'Souza, 1995). What Barbara Lal has termed the 'identity entrepreneurs', profiting from an emphasis on ethnic difference, have their counterparts among those individuals who have managed to generate a good living by denouncing the very means of their own success (Lal, 1996).

The academic debate about affirmative action took place against a background of specific political attempts to abolish or severely curtail these practices. Governor Pete Wilson of California based his unsuccessful campaign to run for the Republican presidential nomination on a platform that stressed anti-immigrant measures and the repeal of affirmative action policies. He miscalculated that the same sentiments that had led the Californian electorate to pass Proposition 187 – a measure designed to cut off education and welfare rights to the children of illegal immigrants – would have a particular resonance with the conservative activists who have a disproportionate influence over the Republican primaries. Not only was Proposition 187 challenged in the courts and declared unconstitutional, but Wilson's sudden conversion to these views, after a political career consistently supporting preference policies, was judged to be opportunistic and unconvincing. Nevertheless, the momentum against affirmative action continued with the Regents of the University of California system forcing a reluctant administration and faculty to abandon the admissions policies that had helped to create some of the most racially diverse campuses in the nation. Such legal challenges were not confined to California: the University of Maryland had been ordered to rescind a scholarship programme designed exclusively for blacks and, in March 1996, a United States Appeal Court ruled that the University of Texas could not use an argument based on the benefits of diversity to justify preference policies designed to recruit black and Hispanic students to its Law School. This was seen as the first major decision against 'reverse discrimination' since the Supreme Court had narrowed the scope of affirmative action in June 1995. Whether the Texas decision will be upheld at a higher level remains to be seen, but the fact that the three Appeal Judges were appointed by Presidents Reagan and Bush shows the delayed impact of a long era of Republican control over the White House.

Another side of the conservative backlash could be seen on the political margins of society in the activities of a range of extremist organisations, such as the militias and a variety of hate groups.[13] The Oklahoma bombing finally focused public attention on these fringe groups whose armed and angry members constituted a threat not simply to minorities but to the peace and security of the whole society. Fomented by the bigoted chatter of the radio talk shows, and encouraged by a new permissive intolerance propagated by the Buchananite wing of the Republican party, elements of such groups passed a new threshold of destruction when they directed their violence beyond the traditional scapegoats to a target that resulted in the indiscriminate slaughter of government employees and their children.

It is not surprising that the neo-Nazi extremism of the Aryan Nations and the intolerance of the Michigan Militia found an echo in some of the rhetoric of black separatist groups like the Nation of Islam, under its charismatic leader Louis Farrakhan. Just as the verdict in the O. J. Simpson trial had exposed the polarisation of black and white world views, so too did the interpretation of the Million Man March on Washington DC in October 1995.[14] For most African-Americans the March symbolised a new dedication of black men to family commitment and community solidarity; for many whites it was an event tainted by Farrakhan's prominent participation and racist tirades.

On the same day as the march, President Clinton delivered a major address on race relations at the University of Texas in which he deplored the rift between blacks and whites that was, as he put it, 'tearing at the heart of America'. He dismissed the neo-conservative interpretation of the situation, pointing to the persistent economic disparities between the races, and argued:

> It is so fashionable to talk, today, about African-Americans, as if they had been some sort of protected class. Many whites think blacks are getting more than their fair share, in terms of jobs and promotions. That is not true.

Perhaps the most important statement in the speech was an emphatic rejection of the arguments against preference policies: 'I want to mend affirmative action, but I do not think America is at a place today where we can end it. The evidence of the last several weeks shows that.'[15]

The argument over affirmative action persisted throughout the November 1996 election and into its aftermath. Fifty-four per cent of California's voters approved a ballot initiative – Proposition 209 – outlawing preferences based on gender and race in state contracting, hiring and university admissions. Once again, it was immediately challenged as a violation of the equal protection clause of the fourteenth Amendment of the Constitution on the grounds that it placed women and minorities seeking redress from discrimination at a disadvantage. Governor Wilson attacked the Clinton administration's support for the legal challenge against Proposition 209 as 'absolutely Orwellian', while the Attorney General, Janet Reno, reiterated the opposing position in a speech marking Martin Luther King's birthday on 15 January 1997. While acknowledging some progress on matters of race, gender and other forms of discrimination, she argued that there were still considerable barriers impeding racial and gender equality.[16]

Whatever the differences over affirmative action – while always controversial, it had significantly greater acceptance among Americans than Britons – the two societies had contrasting approaches to basic law enforcement in the area of civil rights. The role of the Commission for Racial Equality in assisting individuals with the prosecution of their cases under the 1976 Race Relations Act has both strengths and weaknesses. Although the use of civil, rather than criminal, law had a distinct advantage in lessening the burden on the complainant in terms of evidence and proof, it lacked both the moral force of the latter and its ability to deter future discriminatory behaviour by the imposition of heavy sanctions.

The legalistic emphasis of the US Constitution provided a wide array of options for those fighting discrimination in the courts. These included individual appeals to the protections enshrined in the Constitution, and the effective use of class-action law suits that might be based on a single incident but had broad ramifications for all types of similar actions. If successful, such cases could produce substantial fines and punitive damages, bringing immediate pressure on employers, agencies and other vendors to discontinue discriminatory practices or face severe legal penalties. It is probably true that British anti-discrimination enforcement could be improved by borrowing some of these legal remedies, including the adoption of a 'Bill of Rights', possibly within a wider European context. But such measures need to consider the rather different legal cultures of the two societies and the critical factor of political leadership and commitment.

CONTINUING TRENDS IN TRANSATLANTIC RACE RELATIONS

While it is difficult to assess the long-term effects of recent global changes on both the United States and Great Britain, the immediate impact appears significant. The Maastricht Treaty of December 1991, and the completion of a single internal market for the European Union in January 1993 had broad implications for all its member states, not least the United Kingdom. Racial and ethnic discrimination remains a stubborn fact of the 'New Europe', racist immigration legislation persists, violence and even murders against ethnic minorities occur with depressing frequency (Baimbridge, Burkitt and Macey, 1994).

There is a wealth of evidence to document the extent of racial disadvantage in both Britain and America. Attempts to assess the relative openness to economic achievement of the two societies raise enormous methodological problems but some useful analyses exist. An interesting empirical study of occupational attainment of six groups of non-white immigrants in London and New York sheds some light on this issue (Modell and Ladipo, 1995). While it would appear that New York provides a somewhat more open environment for non-white, immigrant males, the results are less convincing for women and, as the authors stress, apply only to these particular immigrant groups in the two specific cities.

Despite the persistence of significant racial disadvantage in the United Kingdom, there are some signs that the trends may not be completely negative. In an analysis of the occupational profiles of black and Asian minority ethnic groups for the period 1966–91, Iganski and Payne (1996) noted a significant decline in racial disadvantage in the British labour market. Looking at the relative chances of access to the 'service' class of employers, managers and professionals of four groups – whites, Indian, Pakistani/Bangladeshi and West Indian – the authors conclude:

> In a time span equivalent to a single generation, the greater part of the original differentials has been removed. Although our data can only offer indirect evidence, it is not possible to see how they are compatible with the existence of a 'cycle of cumulative disadvantage'.
>
> (Iganski and Payne, 1996: 129)

However, in qualifying their findings Iganski and Payne note that gender differences remain substantial and in some cases are more significant than ethnic differences, so that 'it would make no sense to explore ethnicity without taking into account its interaction with gender'. None the less, they argue against the view that minority ethnic groups are more vulnerable to industrial restructuring, since their changing career patterns mirror those of the white population which implies a further narrowing of the occupational gap.

While such evidence suggests that the complex restructuring of the British economy as a result of global economic forces may not have had entirely negative consequences for ethnic minority employment, it should not disguise the fact of persistent tensions remaining in public life. Evidence from the British Crime Surveys in the 1990s reveal annual estimates in excess of 100,000 racially motivated incidents, a figure that may well underestimate the actual levels of violence. In the opinion of one expert:

> It would hardly be an exaggeration to say that one in every two Afro-Caribbean and Asian families directly or indirectly suffered from the effects of racial incidents in 1991. The amount of distress within these communities was quite considerable.
>
> (Parekh, 1994(b): 1)

A rather similar pattern of uneven progress can be found in the contemporary US scene. Some gains in minority educational attainment, though not necessarily translated into comparable improvements in occupational status, have to be set against increasing segregation in schools and only modest trends towards integration in housing (Farley and Frey, 1994; Massey and Denton, 1993; Orfield, 1994). As in Britain, the most glaring discrepancies can be found in the crime statistics. African-Americans in California, who make up only 7 per cent of the population, now constitute almost a third of the state's prison population, and while blacks are arrested at more than twice their representation in the general population, they are imprisoned at four and a half times their overall percentage (Center on Juvenile and Criminal Justice, San Francisco, 1996).

Similarly mixed signals come out of the political arena: on the one hand black leaders like Colin Powell and Alan Keyes have played an unusually prominent part in Republican politics, and the Clinton cabinet is considerably more diverse than its predecessors. On the other hand, immigration and affirmative action have been under sustained attack at both the state and national levels. A particularly important indicator of the uncertain political climate can be seen in the funding problems faced by the civil rights enforcement agency, the Equal Employment Opportunity Commission. Its caseload has increased some 42 per cent since 1990, mainly as a result of Congress adding disability discrimination cases to its responsibilities, but its funding has remained the same. As the election year of 1996 demonstrated, arguments ostensibly about balanced budgets, welfare reform and 'family values' have profound consequences for the lives of minorities and immigrants in American society.

That the Maastricht Treaty raised a new set of complex questions about citizenship, immigration and race relations in Britain is beyond dispute. In much the same way, the anticipated impact of the North American Free Trade Agreement on the United States has produced a renewed debate about the meaning of American identity and has also been associated with a major backlash against illegal immigration, a coordinated assault on affirmative action and new levels of openly expressed xenophobia. The initial reactions to the Oklahoma bombing; the persistent racial sub-text of the O. J. Simpson trial; and the first verdict and repercussions of the Rodney King beatings, illustrate these disturbing trends. In Britain, racial conflict has been revealed at both ends of the political spectrum: from crass ethnocentrism openly expressed by senior government ministers to the grassroots racism of the British National Party, whose success in a local council by-election in Tower Hamlets during the autumn of 1994 was followed by a dramatic increase in the number of racial attacks reported to the police (Cross and MacEwen, 1994: 368).

All these disturbing developments have to be set against some undeniable improvements in the economic, social and political status of important segments of the African-American community. While it would be wrong to suggest that there has only been an 'illusion of progress', it would be just as misleading to subscribe to a belief that a situation of genuine equality of opportunity has been achieved. Indeed, Pettigrew's warnings about the state of Anglo-American race relations need to be taken as seriously today as they should have been twenty-five years ago.

NOTES

1 Earlier versions of this chapter were presented at the section on International Migration: 'Global Migration in Comparative Perspective', ASA Meetings, Washington DC, August 1995; at the Mellon-Sawyer Faculty Seminar on Comparative Race and Ethnicity at Stanford University; at the sociology departments of the University of California, Los Angeles and the Flinders University of South Australia; and at CISME, University of Adelaide. We are grateful for the suggestions and critical comments made by the participants at these meetings, as well as for those provided by Barbara Lal, Bhikhu Parekh and Tom Pettigrew. The opinions expressed are solely those of the authors.

2 One such difference is related to the important distinction between language and culture. This is best illustrated by the quip attributed to George Bernard Shaw that Britain and America are 'two societies *divided* by a common language'.

3 For insightful discussions of the importance of these issues in the wider context of the post-cold war period, see Brubaker (1992); Martinelli (1995); Parekh (1994a); and Smith (1994).

4 There is a burgeoning literature on the inter-relationships between minority groups on either side of the Atlantic seen in the writings of, for example, Bhachu and Gibson (1991), Gilroy (1993) and the increasing emphasis on 'diaspora studies'.

5 Connor illustrates the distinction in the Latin American context by reference to the amusing, but insightful, popular claim that: 'The Mexicans are descended from the Aztecs; the Peruvians are descended from the Incas; and the Argentinians are descended from boats' in Stone (1995b: 7).

6 William Branigin, 'White House Favors Curbs on Foreign Workers', *Washington Post*, 13 March 1996. Attempts to measure the costs and benefits of immigration are notoriously difficult: while the economist Donald Huddle of Rice University estimated that costs exceeded taxes by $42 billion in 1992, Jeffrey Passel and Rebecca Clark of the Urban Institute argue that Huddle ignored social security taxes and overestimated immigrants' benefits. Passel and Clark claim that immigrant contributions to taxes exceeded their benefits by $25 billion. See Robert Samuelson, *Washington Post*, 7 December 1994.

7 For the broader context between Europe and the United States, see Thomas Faist (1995) and the earlier article by John Stone (1985).

8 In Powell's language: 'As I look ahead, I am filled with foreboding. Like the Roman, I seem to see "the river Tiber foaming with much blood". The tragic and intractable phenomenon which we watch with horror on the other side of the Atlantic, but which there is interwoven with the history and existence of the

States itself, is coming upon us here by our own volition and our own neglect.' *The Observer*, 21 April 1968. Also cited in Solomos (1995: 167).

9   *Hansard*, 721, 1965: cols. 378–85. See also Solomos (1995: 171).

10 For a more recent comparison of the legal situation, see the Special Issue on comparative anti-discrimination law edited by Cross and MacEwen in *New Community*, April 1994.

11 A survey of attitudes conducted during August and September 1995, sponsored by the Washington Post/Harvard University and the Kaiser Family Foundation, found that there was a systematic distortion of knowledge concerning the size of ethnic groups in America. White respondents who made up 74 per cent of the total population (according to 1992 Census data) believed that whites constituted barely one half of the population (49.9 per cent). The same respondents thought that blacks were almost twice as numerous (23.8 per cent) as they are in reality (11.8 per cent). Black respondents shared the same distorted figures of all minority groups including a four-fold exaggeration of the size of the 'Asian' category (12.2 per cent as opposed to the actual figure of 3.1 per cent).

12 In a rare meeting with an invited group of black journalists and other African-Americans, Thomas defended his views of a 'colorblind Constitution' and argued against 'the prevailing point of view of some black leaders that special treatment for blacks is acceptable'. *Washington Post*, 28 October 1994.

13 In America, skinheads began to replace the Ku Klux Klan as the most violent racist groups after their importation from Europe in the mid-1980s. At least forty murders have been attributed to racist skinheads since 1988, as well as thousands of assaults, firebombings and desecrations. See S. Kovaleski, 'Racist Skinheads Eclipsing Ku Klux Klan in Violence', *Washington Post*, 16 January 1996.

14 The march was organised by a broad coalition of African-American groups sharing a common concern about the difficulties facing young black men. It hoped to reaffirm a positive commitment by black males to family and community at a time when the media too often stereotyped a whole generation as mired in the pathologies of criminal sub-cultures and parental irresponsibility. Ironically, the media's spotlight on Farrakhan tended to obscure the strong support for the march from most sections of black society and the limited appeal to most of the marchers of the extreme separatist views of the Nation of Islam.

15 Clinton clearly viewed this speech as emulating President Johnson's famous address ('We Shall Overcome') to Howard University in 1965 at the height of the Civil Rights struggle. For the full text: *Washington Post*, 17 October 1995, A13.

16 In Reno's words: 'We have not completed our journey when the unemployment rate for black males is twice as high as it is for white males. . . . We have changed our laws, but we have not always changed our ways. Old habits die hard . . .', reported in *Washington Post*, 16 January 1997. For the challenge to Proposition 209, see articles by Pierre Thomas and William Claiborne, *Washington Post*, 28 November and 21 December 1996.

REFERENCES

Baimbridge, M., B. Burkitt, and M. Macey, 1994, 'The Maastricht Treaty: exacerbating racism in Europe?' *Ethnic and Racial Studies*, 17,3: 420–41.

Banton, M., 1955, *The Coloured Quarter*, London, Cape.

Bhachu, P. and M. Gibson, 1991, 'The dynamics of educational decision-making: a comparative study of South Asian parental strategies in Britain and the US' in Gibson, M. and J. Ogbu (eds), *Minority Status and Schooling: Immigrants versus Non-immigrants*, Philadelphia, Garland Press.

Brubaker, R., 1992, *Citizenship and Nationhood in France and Germany*, Cambridge, Mass, Harvard University Press.

Center on Juvenile and Criminal Justice in California, 1996, San Francisco, CA.

Connor, W., 1994, *Ethnonationalism: The Quest for Understanding*, Princeton, Princeton University Press.

Cross, M. and M. MacEwen (eds), 1994, 'Comparative approaches to anti-discrimination law' [Special Issue], *New Community*, 30,3 (April).

D'Souza, D., 1995, *The End of Racism*, New York, The Free Press.

Faist, T., 1995, *Social Citizenship for Whom?: Young Turks in Germany and Mexican Americans in the USA*, Aldershot, Avebury.

Farley, R. and W. H. Frey, 1994, 'Residential segregation trends 1980–1990' Report, University of Michigan, Population Studies Center.

Gilroy, P., 1993, *The Black Atlantic*, Cambridge, Mass, Harvard University Press.

Glazer, N., 1975, *Affirmative Discrimination: Ethnic Inequality and Public Policy*, New York, Basic Books.

Glazer, N. and K. Young, (eds) 1983, *Ethnic Pluralism and Public Policy: Achieving Equality in the United States and Britain*, London, Heinemann.

Iganski, P. and G. Payne, 1996, 'Declining racial disadvantage in the British labour market', *Ethnic and Racial Studies*, 19,1: 113–34.

Lal, B., 1996, 'Identity entrepreneurs: the profits of difference' (forthcoming).

Landes, R. 1952, 'Preliminary statement of a survey of Negro-white relationships in Britain', *Man*, vol. 52, September.

Martinelli, M., 1995, *Migration, Citizenship and Ethno-National Identities in the European Union*, Aldershot, Avebury.

Massey, D. and N. Denton, 1993, *American Apartheid: Segregation and the Making of the Underclass*, Cambridge, Mass, Harvard University Press.

Modell, S. and D. Lapido, 1995, 'Context and opportunity: minorities in London and New York', paper presented to the ASA section on Comparative Migration, Washington DC, 19 August.

Orfield, G., 1994, *Turning Back the Clock: The Reagan–Bush Retreat from Civil Rights in Higher Education*, Joint Center for Political and Economic Studies Press.

Parekh, B., 1994(a), 'National identity and the ontological regeneration of Britain' in Gilbert, P. and P. Gregory (eds) *Nations, Cultures and Markets*, London, Avebury.

—— 1994(b), *Racial Violence: A Separate Offence?*, London, Charta Mede Associate Company.

Patterson, S., 1963, *Dark Strangers*, London, Tavistock.

—— 1968, *Immigrants in Industry*, London, Oxford University Press.

Pettigrew, T., 1970, 'Review article on *Colour and Citizenship*', *Race*, 12,2: 345–48.

Portes, A. and A. Stepick, 1993, *City on the Edge: The Transformation of Miami*, Berkeley, University of California Press.

Rose, E. *et al.*, 1969, *Colour and Citizenship: A Report on British Race Relations*, London, Oxford University Press.

Schlesinger, A., 1992, *The Disuniting of America*, New York, Norton.

Solomos, J., 1995, 'Racism and anti-racism in Great Britain: historical trends and contemporary issues' in Bowser, B. (ed.), *Racism and Anti-Racism in World Perspective*, Thousand Oaks, Sage.

Sowell, T., 1994, *Race and Culture: A World View*, New York, Basic Books.

Smith, A., 1994, 'The problem of national identity: ancient, medieval and modern?', *Ethnic and Racial Studies*, 17,3: 375–99.

Stone, J., 1985, 'Ethnicity and stratification: Mexican Americans and European Gastarbeiter in comparative perspective' in Walker Connor (ed.) *Mexican Americans in Comparative Perspective*, Washington DC, The Urban Institute Press.

—— 1995, 'Ethnic conflicts in the post-cold war era: problems in advanced industrial societies', Washington DC, Woodrow Wilson Center Report.

Wilson, W., 1987, *The Truly Disadvantaged: The Inner City, the Underclass, and Public Policy*, Chicago, University of Chicago Press.

—— 1996, *When Work Disappears: The World of the New Urban Poor*, New York, Knopf.

13 Conclusion

Peter Newsam

Each of the contributors to this volume has had a specific contribution to make. Between them, they have analysed, commented upon and further developed the main themes which have exercised the minds and engaged the efforts of all those who, like myself, have been and remain personally or professionally concerned with race relations in the United Kingdom. I am most grateful for their work and to Bhikhu Parekh, Peter Sanders and Tessa Blackstone for editing the whole work and providing chapters of their own; and I am particularly honoured to be invited to contribute a final chapter. Attempting to summarise what has already been so clearly set out would be unhelpful.

My aim in this chapter is different. Now that twenty years have elapsed since the Race Relations Act (RRA) of 1976, it is beginning to be possible to place what has happened since into historical perspective. That is for historians to do with a proper degree of objectivity. My more limited contribution in this chapter will be first, to describe the years between 1976 and 1982, principally from a personal point of view. My justification for doing so is that I believe that my views then were similar to those of others who, like myself, were working within this country's national and local administrative structures; in my case as Deputy Education Officer to the Inner London Education Authority (ILEA). Second, I shall describe some of the issues which affected the Commission for Racial Equality (CRE) between 1982 and 1987, during which period I was its Chairman and, for most of that time, also its Chief Executive. The issues I have chosen illustrate some of the problems the CRE then faced and the degree to which it was or was not successful in dealing with them. Finally, as someone who has been otherwise engaged since 1987, I offer an outsider's view of what has happened in the last decade and how the future for race relations now looks.

When the 1976 Act was passed, ILEA was the largest local education authority in England and certainly the most diverse in the United Kingdom in terms of its population. Some 40 per cent of children were born to mothers who themselves had been born outside the United Kingdom and the spread of languages spoken in the home and the different cultures these reflected were greater than those of New York. Yet the passing of the 1976 Act went almost unnoticed.

There were two reasons for this lack of interest. The first was that ILEA was preoccupied with a heavy weight of other problems. Selection to secondary schools was to end, after a contentious series of discussions and legal wrangles, in September 1977. A sharp fall in the secondary school population was predicted, from a high point of 179,000 in that year to 110,000 ten years later. This would involve further trouble with school closures and amalgamations and all the unrest that accompanies change on this scale. There had been a steady decline in reading standards in the primary schools which was only just being successfully reversed. Attacks on ILEA, from various powerful sources, were mounting. And so it went on. So the immediate reaction to the 1976 legislation was that it constituted a diversion from far more pressing problems.

The second reason concerned the legislation itself. The prevailing view within education, nationally as well as in London, was that the law and race relations, so far as education was concerned, had little to do with each other. Provided the schools did the best they could for all children, they could not reasonably be said to be contravening anything the law might be requiring. That was the general view and, though I recall hearing David Lane, the CRE's first Chairman, talk of the plans he had for the new Commission with its new powers, I also recall my colleagues and myself concluding that investigations, complaints and the whole notion of unlawful discrimination had little to do with us. We meant well and were trying hard. It followed that, as ILEA was already heavily involved in legal issues, the less legislation on race had to do with education the better.

So far as the performance of ethnic minorities in London's schools and colleges were concerned, it was already recognised that there were serious issues to be dealt with. ILEA's Research Branch, at that time led by Professor Alan Little, had produced during the early 1970s a series of disconcerting reports. It was evident from these that too many of the children of first generation immigrants were not doing well in school. It was also evident that many parents, notably those whose own education had been in the West Indies, were becoming increasingly angry about this. The prevailing view, among inspectors, administrators, heads, teachers and politicians alike, was that the problem was a transitional one. New populations required time to settle in but, once they had done so and schools had, in ways never clearly specified, got used to them, their performance would improve. Indeed, the general view was that this was already happening. But it was not. The research evidence was clear. Differences in performance that were evident in the early years of school were tending to widen over the period of compulsory schooling. So there was, it had become apparent, a straight-forward educational problem to be dealt with.

Individual inspectors within ILEA had worked hard to find ways of resolving these problems of performance within the school system. Efforts were made to find more teachers, to act as role models, from within minority populations; new and more acceptable materials and books were being introduced into schools; language skills were developed for those for whom English was not a first language, and so on. Well resourced multicultural education was, it was thought, the best way to improve the educational performance of minorities. Preserving, even celebrating, cultural identity would enable integration into this country's social and education system to take place with increasing success.

It was with piecemeal developments of this kind in the background, as part of the general setting of education in a large conurbation, that in the early autumn of 1976 a visit to New York took place. The small group consisted of several wardens of ILEA Teachers' Centres, an inspector, a member of ILEA, who years later became the Chief Education Officer of Tower Hamlets and, at the last moment, myself.

Of the many aspects of the visit that had relevance to London, three were particularly important. For the first, I am quoting from a report written for ILEA's Policy Committee on my return.

> In 1960, about two thirds of the [New York] school population was white and one third black or hispanic. The proportions now [1976] are reversed and the trend continues. On the other hand, two thirds of those who vote and pay taxes are white and only about one third black or hispanic. As the City itself finances all services, including welfare payments to the elderly, the police and fire services, the dominant interests of the majority of voters and tax payers do not necessarily include that of educating the children of the minority.

This may read naively now, but at the time it was a new thought that substantial numbers of influential people might be prepared to turn their backs on problems which, collectively, they were in a position to relieve. At the time, of course, the City of London, which has few children of its own, largely contributed to the education of children throughout inner London. This is a function of which it has since been relieved.

The second effect of the visit was to initiate a re-thinking of London's approach to multi-ethnic education. That re-thinking began abruptly. I had been describing the way London was trying to deal with its recently-diverse school population when the Deputy Chancellor (Deputy Chief Education Officer) of New York, Bernie Gifford, intervened. Gifford's own upbringing had been in Harlem. He had thereafter achieved impressive academic success before becoming an influential educational administrator. Gifford asked if he could continue my talk. He then did so in much the same way as I had intended. When asked how he had managed this he remarked that this was the way he and others had talked before learning the lessons of 1968.

The year 1968 was the one in which there were violent disturbances in a number of New York schools. Parents, mostly black or hispanic, drove teachers, mostly white, out of the schools and wanted to take them over. The compromise finally reached, after a turbulent few months, was a degree of decentralisation designed to increase local control. To this was added an emphasis on accountability, with schools publicly ranked from 1 to 800 in terms of the scores pupils achieved in writing and other tests. Whatever else this had done, it had evidently not prevented a continued fall in the level of results achieved by the school system. Gifford's point, emphatically expressed, was that if London continued to treat issues raised by ethnic diversity in the way we had been describing, it would be almost certain to encounter the same problems that had affected New York.

From this interchange followed the third consequence of that visit to New York. Soon after returning to London, I was appointed as ILEA's Education Officer and wrote to the Leader of the Authority to explain what I thought the main issues were that confronted us. Item three of five issues raised was 'Race relations and children of minority groups'. With New York in mind, the core of what was then said was that the various initiatives we had taken 'leave out the crucial point: the quality of what is happening in the schools themselves', and that we were at risk of trying to deal with a whole range of matters arising from London's ethnic diversity by adding little bits on to an existing school system rather than re-thinking the system itself.

My purpose in describing at some length a visit undertaken so long ago is to emphasise this last point. Responding to ethnic diversity is not, either then or now, simply a matter of deciding what to do about this or that group of people and any 'problems' they may have or present. It is first of all a matter of deciding what kind of society or system we are trying to create or, it may be, avoid. Only after having done so, can sensible policies be devised.

These are difficult issues for busy politicians and administrators to reflect and decide upon. Both, within ILEA, were initially nearly all opposed to taking any initiative with race as its centre; above all, they were opposed to any systematic extension of ethnic monitoring, which ILEA's research division already had partially in place. The strength of that opposition did not reflect hostility to ethnic minorities; it reflected deeply-held fears and beliefs. Politicians, particularly Jewish ones, with memories of the 1930s and the holocaust, thought attaching labels to ethnic groups both offensive and potentially dangerous. Others, though not Marxists, were still influenced by thinking which warned against attempts to split the working class the better to be able to control it. Singling out ethnic minorities, most of whom were among the poorest of London's citizens, for special treatment seemed to be doing just that. Others stuck firmly to the notion that, provided each child was treated on his or her own merits and his or her own needs were met so far as that child's teacher could contrive, as a matter of logic and educational principle there could be no other dimension to consider.

With the passage of years, attitudes to these issues have changed. So far as ethnic monitoring is concerned, the shift in thinking only really came when equal opportunity policies relating to employment, limited in scope though these were initially, began to be adopted. It then became possible to talk about monitoring or auditing an equal opportunity policy, which required information about what was happening to individuals, rather than simply monitoring the individuals for purposes which were often unclear.

The initiatives which, early in 1977, ILEA decided to take on educating a multi-ethnic society were not particularly impressive; but they were a start. They were announced at the only press conference, at least during the 1970s, at which the leaders of both political parties in ILEA shared a platform. This was an issue, their shared presence indicated, that was too sensitive and too important to be allowed to become contentious. Unfortunately, this approach was abandoned some years later.

One consequence of ILEA's developing approach to multi-ethnic education was the appointment of the first inspectors to come from within the minority communities themselves. The teachers and others so appointed had always been there, in the schools and colleges, and were fully competent to work at the level required, but they had never previously applied to join what had appeared to them an all-white establishment that would be bound to exclude them.

A second consequence was the creation of a number of access courses for ethnic minorities wanting to enter higher education institutions. These were designed to enable students, many of them mature students with family responsibilities, to spend a year raising their educational standards so that they could enter forms of professional training on equal terms with other students. The ILEA's were the first such courses to be created and they have since been widely adopted elsewhere and proved remarkably successful.

Other lessons had to be learnt in the late 1970s. Jobs for school leavers began to be scarce and the level of discrimination against black youngsters became particularly worrying. With the same qualifications as white school leavers, black youngsters were having to attend many more interviews with far less success; and they knew it. The effect on those young people and their relationship with those around them was both understandable and marked. They saw a white community in control. It was a community that knew what was happening to black youngsters and could, they believed, put matters right but refused to do so. By refusing to do so, those in authority were, in effect, intending the discrimination that those black youngsters were encountering. Hence, to many of those black youngsters, it was a white-dominated system that was directly to blame for the way they were being treated.

In practice, of course, people in the education system were not able to influence to any real extent the way employers behaved. But the young people discriminated against were not to know this. Resentments grew. Relations with the police and others in authority deteriorated and, in 1981, the violent disturbances that Bernie Gifford had predicted in 1976 forced themselves on the public's attention. The lesson to be learned and re-learned, eloquently presented in Lord Scarman's Report, was that it is impossible to develop good race relations where there is a deeply felt sense of injustice.

The connection between education and the state of race relations had already begun to be explored nationally. In March 1979, Tony Rampton had been asked to chair an inquiry into the education of ethnic minorities. Shortly after providing an interim report, ill-received by ministers, on 'West Indian Children in Our Schools' he was succeeded by Michael Swann. The 'Swann' report finally came out in 1983.

One feature of the Swann Committee's meetings, which I attended until 1982 on joining the Commission for Racial Equality, was the repeated and sometimes contentious debate on 'racism'. On the one hand, racism was perceived as the underlying cause of discrimination and a wide range of other disadvantages from which all minority groups were, it was argued, bound to suffer. On the other hand the view was that, observably, what different ethnic groups were experiencing in the education system and elsewhere was by no means uniform and the term 'racism' was obscuring rather than shedding light on why this was so. What was at issue here, some members of the Committee concluded, was the importance some felt of refusing to allow the united force of the different minority groups, all to be described as 'black' whatever their skin colour might actually be, to be diminished by being separately considered as discrete groups with different needs, opportunities and experience. As a colonial power, Britain had been adept at dealing with majorities in this way and a number of ethnic minority members of the Rampton/Swann Committee, reflecting strongly-held views outside it, did not want history to repeat itself.

It was in the midst of this ultimately unsatisfactory and unresolved debate that I was asked by the then Home Secretary, William Whitelaw, to succeed

David Lane, whose five-year term of office as Chairman of the Commission for Racial Equality was coming to an end.

I accepted for two reasons. The first was that I had become convinced that, though education could do much to advance the cause of the country's ethnic minorities, most of the problems they faced lay elsewhere; above all in employment and housing. Second, that those problems, if they could be solved at all, were in the hands of the majority, the white community of which I was a member and with whose ways of working, certainly in its official structures, I was familiar. It is a sign of progress that reasoning of that kind has for some time been increasingly out of place. Dealing with the majority and its institutions is no longer, as the leadership of the CRE itself has since successfully demonstrated, the preserve of members of that majority.

The work of the Commission and the tightly drawn parameters within which it has had to operate has been described in chapter 3. For my part, five features of the years between 1982 and 1987 seemed to me at the time particularly significant.

The first concerned the role of the Home Secretary, formally responsible for race relations and the work, as part of that responsibility, of the CRE. Successive Home Secretaries found it almost impossible to say anything positive about the presence of ethnic minorities in the United Kingdom. When they did, as Leon Brittan did shortly after becoming Home Secretary in 1983, their remarks were followed by a silence, rather as though their voices had been suddenly switched off. The political problem was obvious. It was hard to sound genuinely welcoming to minorities without under-mining an immigration policy (see chapter 5) which increasingly was not. But the lack of public endorsement of the Commission's work was unhelpful. If mistakes were made, the CRE was not going to be defended, even its existence could come to be questioned; so it had to be careful as well as forceful. Above all, it had to be in the right.

A second feature of those years was the need to find ways of using the 1976 Act to the best advantage. One way was to ensure that Parliament approved a Code of Practice for Employers. A Code of this kind provides a degree of formal backing to anyone seeking to persuade employers to adopt fair employment practices. The Code itself has no statutory force but neglect of its recommendations can be taken into account, and sometimes has been, in hearings before industrial tribunals.

The Code that finally emerged in 1983 was not to everyone's liking. The wording relating to the responsibilities of small employers caused the two formidable Trade Union members of the Commission, Bill Morris of the Transport and General Workers Union and Ken Gill of the Amalgamated Union of Engineering Workers, to walk out of the meeting at which the

Code was approved by the Commission. That that approval had to depend on the Chairman's casting vote did not help matters. A problem of a rather different kind arose when the Code, before being laid before both Houses of Parliament, had to be approved by Norman Tebbit, the then Secretary of State for Employment. Despite the unanimous view of an all-party Select Committee that small firms, employing under 200 people, should be excluded from the provisions of the Code, Norman Tebbit was sufficiently open to argument to accept the Commission's view that this was absurd: few employers in inner-city areas employed as many as 200 people. Accordingly the Code, subsequently amended, was approved and has been valuable in promoting improved employment practices.

The 1976 Act itself, and the CRE's efforts to amend it, was a third feature of my years as CREs Chairman. No legislation is proof against the ability of the courts so to interpret it that Parliament's intentions are frustrated. For all its good intentions and, in the main, skilful drafting, the 1976 Act has proved no exception to this. So amendments were and still are needed. There appeared to be two reasons why no Home Secretary took the matter forward. The first and obvious one was that there was little political support for providing more effective ways of ending discrimination on racial grounds. The second was less obvious. It was that, even if helpful amendments to the legislation were proposed in the first instance, there could be no guarantee that, on the floor of the House, they would not be countered by others which would undermine elements in the existing legislation which were working effectively. It was for this second reason, I believe, that Home Office officials, as well as ministers, were unenthusiastic about pressing for changes which, they well understood, were needed to give effect to Parliament's original intentions.

A fourth feature of the years I am describing concerns these same officials. Almost without exception they did what they could, perhaps to the disadvantage of their own careers, to enable the Commission to function effectively. Obstruction would always have been easy but only once became serious. This was when the Commission's investigation into immigration procedures required the use of notes from official files, notes unflattering to the officials concerned, that had been made at interviews in Bangladesh. But even then, after some delay, the Commission was able to proceed.

Apart from the failure to persuade government to amend the legislation, for example, to enable the Commission to accept binding agreements with employers rather than have to go through the whole expensive and time-consuming non-discrimination procedures, a strongly-argued move towards contract compliance was similarly frustrated. What was being asked for here, in vain, was that government, in placing its own substantial contracts, should enquire into the equal opportunities performance of companies seeking to win those contracts. Other things being equal, it would be made known that effective equal opportunity policies would be an advantage, a factor to be considered when the decision to award a contract had to be made.

A final feature of the Commission's work was that many of its successes had to go unrecognised. I recall a young black milkman, some time in 1984, being asked a question in a television programme about the CRE. He then expressed the view that it was a useless organisation without teeth. What that young man did not know was that, only a few years earlier, there had been no black milkmen in his firm, one of the largest in London. All recruitment had been by word of mouth, with one white milkman recommending an always white friend or relative. Private persuasion rather than public law enforcement had caused the change to take place. To this example, from Building Societies to broadcasters, many others could be added. In race relations, failures are usually well-publicised, successes routinely ignored.

Despite the frustrations and occasional setbacks of those years 1982–87, my abiding recollection is of the commitment of the Commissioners themselves and of the patient negotiation and sheer refusal to be discouraged displayed by many members of the Commission's staff; and of course there were hard-won successes to record and celebrate.

Since leaving the CRE in 1987, I have been engaged in activities which do not have race relations at their centre; though the nature of our society in the United Kingdom means that the prevalence of persistent and unlawful discrimination on grounds of race, in almost every aspect of the way institutions function, can never be ignored.

Most of the problems that troubled the early 1980s are still with us. The political climate has, in a number of ways, remained unhelpful. Government unwillingness to amend the Race Relations Act, to give effect to the full investigative powers Parliament plainly intended the Commission to have, may have led the Commission to rely more heavily on promotional work than it would otherwise have thought desirable. To set against this, there have been a number of complaints of unlawful discrimination, supported by the Commission, upheld by the courts and in the process establishing higher and more appropriate levels of compensation for those affected.

In general, such improvements in the position of disadvantaged groups as there have been have been marginal, but none the less welcome for that. For example, educational performance is in some instances improving. Ten years ago, a combination of factors seemed to be keeping children of Bangladeshi origin, with rare exceptions, consistently among the lowest performers within the school system. The degree to which the problem lay with the children and their families rather than with the school system remained unresolved. In one education authority at least, Tower Hamlets in London, a determined effort, sustained over several years, has lifted the performance of Bangladeshi children to levels seldom found elsewhere. So improvement has been shown to be possible and schools everywhere now have something to aim at. Perhaps the essential point, articulated by Professor Parekh (TES, March 1985) in a critical commentary of the treatment of the issue in the Swann Report, and further developed in chapter 6, is that stereotypical assumptions about individual minority groups or such groups collectively are increasingly inappropriate. All can achieve. How to ensure this, rather than whether it is possible, is now the question to be answered.

To set against improvements of this kind, other issues, such as the differential exclusion of black pupils from school, keep looking as though they are likely to be dealt with but then other factors, such as reduced funds for special measures of any kind, cause the problem, long-diagnosed and regularly reported on, to remain untreated.

Behind issues of school performance and the differential treatment or experience of some groups within the school system, since the mid-1980s moves towards improved race relations have been affected by two developments, both adverse.

The first has been the planned diminution of the over-arching influence of local authorities. During the early 1980s, an increasing number of local authorities were taking a lead in promoting soundly-based measures to ensure equal, non-discriminatory access to the services they offered. A succession of measures, from the re-organisation of local authorities to the outright abolition of some of those, such as the Greater London Council, which had taken a lead in devising such policies, has left a vacuum which central government departments have proved quite unwilling or unable to fill.

A second adverse factor, within education, has been the National Curriculum itself. Whatever the merits of a curriculum in the form that has developed since the Education Reform Act 1988, one disadvantage is that it has led to a serious degree of over-loading. In turn this has led to the neglect of areas of personal and social education that do not sit easily within the prescribed curriculum framework. Relationships and the whole area of information and discussion that relates to these require time and intellectual space if they are to be treated adequately. Both now tend to be lacking.

It is difficult and probably unhelpful to attempt to summarise the gains and losses, so far as race relations are concerned, over these last few years. Some things have definitely got worse; notably the official attitudes implicit in ever more restrictive behaviour towards immigration, asylum seekers or anyone not immediately seen as an acceptable addition to the UK population.

On the other hand, some things have got better. Public attitudes in the 1990s in some ways seem less raw, though instances to the contrary keep occurring to puncture any premature optimism. But at least the notion of 'swamping' seems less prevalent than it used to be. That some 5.5 per cent of the UK population can be defined as indentifiably different – 'non-white' as the statistics sometimes negatively put it – puts the issue of diversity into perspective. A culture supposedly reposing in over 94 per cent of a population cannot plausibly, if it has any vitality at all, be swamped by the remaining 5 to 6 per cent. This seems increasingly to be recognised and is a factor that should, before long, influence an immigration policy grounded in the opposite assumption.

What, then, of the future? The prospect of revised legislation on race relations seems remote so, inevitably, the question whether there are other ways forward arises. Evidently there are some principles which underlie the way people – male, female, young, old or from any ethnic group – should behave towards each other in any society which has justice as one of its central tenets. To discriminate against anyone, unless the grounds for doing so can be objectively justified, must be unjust, though it may sometimes be convenient. And it is these underlying principles which have, over the years, become increasingly laid down in international law or in conventions to which this country is a signatory. It may be, therefore, that if the way to the necessary amendments to the present Race Relations Act remains blocked, strengthened rights for all will bring with them strengthened rights for the most disadvantaged; rights enforceable in our own courts and, in some circumstances, in international courts of law also.

There are distinct issues relating to race relations and to unlawful forms of discrimination on racial grounds. But, without losing or diminishing the importance of what sharply focused legislation on race has already achieved, there is room for a wider debate. Such a debate could have two elements. The first would explore and seek to reach agreement on the issues explored by Bhikhu Parekh (see chapter 1). We need to find new ways of perceiving and responding to the racial diversity which is a distinguishing feature of the United Kingdom today. The second and related element of the debate would proceed from the recognition that we are now living in a society increasingly divided into social and economic winners and losers. Thus, the importance of avoiding 'approaches which lead to polarisation around racial identity', an issue developed by Tessa Blackstone in chapter 6, is itself growing. In these circumstances how human rights can universally be assured is one of the most difficult questions which this country faces as it enters the third millennium. Race relations is an important part, but only one part, of that fundamental question: how society now sees itself, and how the legislative principles which support human rights, in all their aspects, can best be used to secure fair treatment for all.

One final comment in retrospect: this country owes more than it has yet acknowledged to the people who created the 1976 Race Relations Act and to the then Home Secretary, Roy Jenkins, who put his own stamp upon it. The country owes rather less to the courts who have so narrowly interpreted the Act's provisions and rendered some of its intentions ineffective. It owes still less to a succession of politicians who have declined to do other than tinker with the legislation and remain, on all sides, seemingly uncommitted to doing more. On the other hand, majority and minorities alike owe a great deal to the many people, in voluntary organisations or as individuals, who have tried to enforce the letter and promote the spirit of the Race Relations Act. This remains one of the most comprehensive legislative efforts to promote good race relations to be found anywhere in the world.

Index